Diller + Scofidio (+ Renfro). The Ciliary Function

Guido Incerti
Daria Ricchi
Deane Simpson

Diller + Scofidio (+ Renfro)
The Ciliary Function

Works and Projects 1979–2007

Preface by Reinhold Martin

Cover
ICA, exterior view from North-East
Boston, 2006
Photo by Iwan Baan

Back cover
Elizabeth Diller and Ricardo Scofidio
in their New York City studio

Editor
Luca Molinari

Design
Marcello Francone

Editing
Laura Guidetti

Layout
Paola Ranzini

Translation
Language Consulting Congressi S.r.l., Milan
Robert Burns (from Italian into English)

First published in Italy in 2007 by
Skira Editore S.p.A.
Palazzo Casati Stampa
via Torino 61
20123 Milano
Italy
www.skira.net

Printed and bound in Italy. First edition

ISBN: 978-88-6130-067-5

Distributed in North America by Rizzoli International
Publications, Inc., 300 Park Avenue South,
New York, NY 10010
Distributed elsewhere in the world by Thames
and Hudson Ltd., 181a High Holborn,
London WC1V 7QX, United Kingdom

Contents

Reinhold Martin

Preface
Moving Targets (Benchmark)

There is a small marker that recurs with astonishing regularity in the work of Diller + Scofidio (+ Renfro), sometimes explicitly, sometimes implicitly. Call it a crosshairs, an "x"—or really, a "+"—marking any number of spots, whether they are occupied by buildings and/or parts of buildings, or by viewers and/or users. To the extent that this sign also marks the collaborative space between partners, and thus the space of the architectural firm itself, it could well have been included in either of the two "Iconography" sections that follow below. Or, to put it more grandly, this "+" could be understood as something like a meta-sign, a self-effacing signature that nevertheless marks a particular aesthetic, or even a style.

It would not be an exaggeration to say that this mark has been there from the beginning, or at least as early as the drawings for *The Rotary Notary* (1987). It can be found, for example, in the form of "benchmarks" and other locating devices on reconstructions of the perspectival space in Duchamp's large glass associated with that project. It is on the cover and throughout *Back to the Front: Tourisms of War*, the anthology for which Elizabeth Diller and Ricardo Scofidio acted as editors, contributors, and co-designers. It is to be found marking the center of each suitcase in the *Tourisms: suitCase Studies* (1991), and jet-lagged travelers arriving at JFK's Terminal Four will find it performing a similar function behind the lenticular screen of certain panels that comprise *Travelogues*. It locates the video cameras in a cross-sectional drawing of *Facsimile* (2004). And in different forms and in different ways, this same mark can be found organizing the architecture of the Slow House, Blur, the ICA, the Lincoln Center renovations, the High Line, Tivoli...

The mark in question bears a family resemblance to another, rather habitual crossing of lines that arguably only architects really understand. This habit is what used to be called "crossing the corners," a technique found in abundance on D+S(+R) drawings that was commonly used in hand-drawn construction documents to emphasize the (normally perpendicular) intersection of walls or other elements. More than just a signature drawing style, in the work of D+S(+R) the crossing of lines graphically locates and secures objects in three-dimensional space. In the drawings—but also in the architecture—it works to hold things down in order (paradoxically) to set them in motion, a function duly acknowledged by the preponderance of dashed and dotted lines on many of the same drawings. Together, these two sets of lines describe fixity *and* movement, anchors *and* vectors.

Moving Target is the title of a collaborative dance work performed in 1996, in which Diller + Scofidio sliced the mathematical "normal" (ninety degrees) in half, with a large mirror/screen tilted at forty-five degrees (an "interscenium") bisecting the right angle formed by the intersection of stage and backdrop (proscenium), and reflecting the actions of dancers in plan, below. By now it has become commonplace to note that the work of D+S(+R) can be characterized by a certain interruption of the normal. What might be less evident is the relation between the social and aesthetic norms they have so consistently probed, and the mathematical normal marked by the intersection of vertical and horizontal that is inscribed into the "+" sign and the crosshairs. In *Moving Target* as in so many of the works, the "+"—the (now bisected) intersection of vertical and horizontal—sets the stage, so to speak, for the dissection of those other norms in the exaggerated performances of everyday life.

To appreciate this "+" as a more general organizational diagram with architectural consequences, it is necessary to observe that, understood as a crosshairs marking a target, our two-dimensional mark aligns itself along a third axis that we can call the axis of projection. In the construction of linear perspective, this axis runs normal to the picture plane and is defined by the coincidence of vanishing point and standpoint (or point of view). The vanishing point, in turn, marks the intersection of an absolute vertical (the height of an infinitely distant object) and an absolute horizontal (its width, along an infinitely wide horizon). While together, the vanishing point and the standpoint orchestrate the projection of height and width (measurable in plan and section) into the depths of the X-Y-Z coordinate system that defines perspectival space and locates subjects and objects within it. It is this coordinate system that is ultimately condensed into the graphic mark we have been following, which can now be understood as a benchmark in another sense: a degree-zero against which to measure architectural space, if not a degree-zero against which to measure architecture as such, appearing and disappearing between its poles.

It may seem entirely appropriate to open a consideration of the work of architects so sensitive to the construction of drawings, and to the rhetoric of construction contained therein, with such graphic observations. But what happens when graphic rhetoric meets so-called reality, and D+S(+R)'s "constructed" drawings become drawings that guide the construction of actual buildings? Unfortunately, such a question is blatantly misplaced. For what has this firm been doing for the last twenty-plus years other than building? That is, what have they been doing other than translating between constructed drawings and construction drawings, again and again, by way of specifically architectural techniques? It might be more accurate, instead, to look for the evidence of such a translation. Evidence, that is, of the movement of the "+" sign that marks the drawings (and all that it entails) into the various constructed objects that have during the course of the firm's robust history, come more and more to resemble pathologically normal buildings.

From the frame with nothing in it called the Slow House, to the anti-object of Blur, to the extruded cross-section of Eyebeam, to the softening of the surround in which the proscenium sits at Lincoln Center, to the mediatheque/window opening onto an unfocussed view of water without horizon at the ICA/Boston, by working with (and against) the graphic, mechanical, and conceptual conventions of orthographic projection and linear perspective, Diller + Scofidio (+ Renfro) have embarked on a new kind of architectural project: the invention of an a-perspectival space. In such a space, the ubiquitous "x" (or "+") marks the spot where subject and object used to stand but are no longer to be found. Instead, they have been displaced, set in motion, translated. Not only because subject and object exchange places in various works (viewer becomes viewed, user used), but also because they are held in place so firmly, and are so completely in the crosshairs of this work, that they cease to be an overriding concern. In effect, they vanish. In their place—the real target of this work, one might say—is the invisible axis that runs "normal" to the picture plane, the axis of projection itself, which now, in the a-perspectival space constructed in D+S(+R)'s many buildings at so many scales, no longer connects standpoint to vanishing point but rather, hangs suspended in a space of its own.

All of this is a way of saying that the work of D+S(+R) is nothing but pure projection. In other words, it is a *project*, plain and simple. A project that builds a new kind of space, embedded within the everyday space of objects and buildings. It may even be called a meta-project, since it works on the mode of projection itself, gently easing our imaginations out of the perspectival and into the a-perspectival, with a healthy dose of humor along the way. But what future does it conjure, what object of desire (or what world-historical necessity) does it project?

Imagine a future to which you—your presence, your point of view—are irrelevant, a future that is in some sense not your own. Can you do it? Can you really take yourself out of the position of the omniscient observer, the reader of the book of history and dreamer of things to come, standing in one place and putting it all in perspective? This is something like the future projected in this work. On the surface, it is increasingly populated with objects more or less recognizable as buildings and landscapes, with a few twists—a hyperbolic paraboloid-as-restaurant here, a floor-becomes-wall-becomes-ceiling there—all of which seem designed to resist capture in the perspectival space of the photograph or the digital rendering. This work is even peopled with "users," addicts of a sort who cannot resist its irreducibly architectural allure. But do not be deceived. It has you in its sights, even as you follow its pathways. Because the moving target is also you—your narcissistic desires as well as your utopian dreams.

In suggesting this, I am also suggesting that the function of the graphic mark, this "x" or "+" whose movements we have been following, is more than strictly *iconographic*. Its function is, to use a term favored by the great historian of perspective, Erwin Panofsky, *iconological*, in that it effects a non-literal translation between architecture and the world. In standing in for both the vanishing subject and the vanishing object, it claims for the act (and axis) of projection a certain autonomy as a properly architectural act bound to its own irreducible techniques and conventions. This act, repeated throughout the work of D+S(+R), is nevertheless capable of staging something like a "world view," not in the sense of an overview or total picture, but in the sense of a view of the world seen from *within* architecture. There is *nothing but* architecture in the work of D+S(+R), architecture that refuses to hold steady. And so this moving target, this moving "x" or "+", projects a future by bringing into view a possible world that cannot be put in perspective. Such a world is either so infinitely distant and unfamiliar, or so infinitely near and familiar, that you cannot see it from where you are standing. Nor can it see you, vanishing.

Introduction
The Ciliary Function

Walter Benjamin has described architecture as the emblematic form of art perceived "in a state of distraction."[1] Within this schema, architecture occupies the blurred background of our perception through what Benjamin refers to as the processes of tactile and optical appropriation. For Diller + Scofidio (Diller Scofidio + Renfro since 2004), architecture's typical role as backdrop is aligned also to its complicity in supporting the conventions of the everyday, making the materiality of the city indistinct through habitual use and incidental perception. It is through their varied body of work produced since 1979—ranging from installations, media work, dance and theater pieces, to buildings and urban interventions—that Diller + Scofidio (+ Renfro) have explored various modes of practice with which to interrogate architecture, placing it into focus, and at times out of focus. In this context, their practice may be compared to the functioning of the eye's ciliary muscle, responsible for distorting the lens of the eye to focus light on the retina. Contracting, to allow the eye to focus on closer objects, or relaxing to improve focus on those further away, the ciliary function aligns to D+S(+R)'s nomadic practice, one that oscillates in focal length between: the conventions of our architectural "background"; the actual events it supports in the "foreground"; and the social, cultural, economic and political codes that operate from further beyond the plane of the architectural "background."

While predominantly concerned with placing that which is in the background into focus, such as the spatial conventions of the everyday, their practice also explores placing out of focus that which is typically in focus. The exception to the distracted perception of everyday architecture that Benjamin defines is the case of the attentive gaze of the tourist in front of the iconic building or monument. D+S(+R)'s reaction to a program for just such a touristic icon for the Swiss Expo in 2002 was an indistinct building constructed of vaporized water. In literally building Blur, the architects were able to shift the focus of the project toward problematizing: vision; the perception of architecture; and the status of architectural itself. In a broad sense then, the ciliary function stands for the critical act of creative recalibration in response to the multitude of forces that produce our contemporary world.

This volume is directed toward presenting the broad range of attentions of D+S(+R). Rather than a monography only presenting the projects of the studio, it is conceived more as an interlaced "heterography," bringing together various registers of information. These range from interviews, an assembled "iconography" of the studio, floor plans charting the studio space over time, projects in printed and in animated form, and a chronology of projects and events. The three essays address different aspects of the discourse around the architects: the first, entitled *New York Stories* describes the specific cultural context from which the studio emerged; the second, *Some Notes on the Disciplinary Practices of Diller + Scofidio (+ Renfro)* outlines D+S(+R)'s particular position in relation to the discipline of architecture; and the third, *Transgendered Media* addresses the work of their practice through the lens of media. The DVD that accompanies this publication collects various projects that address the factor of time that is so important in their work.

Guido Incerti, Daria Ricchi, Deane Simpson

[1] W. Benjamin, *The Work of Art in the Age of Mechanical Production* (1936), in *Illuminations: Essays and Reflections*, Schocken Books, New York 1969, p. 239.

Edo Bertoglio, *Downtown 81*, 1981

In his famous interview with Hitchcock, François Truffaut asked about the difference between surprise and suspense. Hitchcock responded: *There is a distinct difference [...] We are now having a very innocent little chat. Let us suppose that there is a bomb underneath this table between us. Nothing happens, and then all of a sudden,* Boom! *There is an explosion. The public is surprised, but prior to this surprise, it has seen an absolutely ordinary scene, of no special consequence. Now, let us take a suspense situation. The bomb is underneath the table, and the public knows it, probably because they have seen the anarchist place it there. The public is aware that the bomb is going to explode at one o'clock and there is a clock in the décor. The public can see that it is a quarter to one. In these conditions this same innocuous conversation becomes fascinating because the public is participating in the scene. The audience is longing to warn the characters on the screen: "You shouldn't be talking about such trivial matters. There's a bomb underneath you and it's about to explode!" In the first case we have given the public fifteen seconds of* surprise *at the moment of the explosion. In the second case we have provided them with fifteen minutes of* suspense.
(François Truffaut, *Hitchcock*, Paladin - Granada Publishing, London 1978, p. 402)

Wikipedia, the most extensive online encyclopedia, describes Elizabeth Diller and Ricardo Scofidio's contributions to installation, video, and electronic art. Wikipedia is a learning tool that perfectly mirrors the professional concept that has characterized the work of the New York studio of Diller + Scofidio. Their practice involves interaction with users, who enter and move within the work, becoming part of it and therefore being able to modify it. Theirs is a creative culture produced by anyone desiring to engage in debate.

Elizabeth Diller graduated from Cooper Union in 1979, where Ricardo Scofidio had been teaching since 1967. The two immediately began working together, founding the studio Diller + Scofidio, which would also be their home for many years. Diller and Scofidio began their professional activity immersed in the ferment of 1970s New York and their work is a product of their time politically, culturally and economically.

NYC – The City and Its Economy
Between 1977 and the early 1980s, the US economy was characterized by sluggishness and recession. The oil crisis of the 1970s diminished access to resources, and the specter of bankruptcy loomed over New York. Tensions ran high in the city due to burgeoning poverty, homelessness and crime, leading to frequent clashes and demonstrations. Symptomatic of the times was the deliberate torching of buildings for insurance money. More extreme episodes of urban warfare and revolt such as the Tompkins Square Park police riot in 1988 culminated in an attempt by the city to evict the homeless and other "undesirables" who had staked out the park as their territory. A general increase in urban crime and the fear of violence drove many middle-class New Yorkers out of the downtown into the suburbs in the phenomenon dubbed "white flight."

These manifestations of urban duress were accompanied by the emergence and proliferation of underground cultures and artistic subcultures. Forms of expression developed out of the proletarian and black experience and differentiated themselves from the more elitist Pop Art.

NYC – Art
The center of gravity of the art world shifted from Paris to New York already in the 1950s. After decades as the crucible of avant-garde art, the French capital, depleted by two world wars, could no longer match New York, which had become a symbol of political and cultural renewal and economic boom. New York took in deserters from the old world such as the father of Dada and Surrealism, Marcel Duchamp.

The 1950s were the years of Action Painting, Abstract Expressionism, and biomorphic Surrealism. The work of De Kooning and Rothko, as well as Jackson Pollock, focused on the creative act of making rather than the final object. What became important in these practices was the physical act of making, thus fore-

Robert MacFarland, *Tompinks Square Park,*
1988

grounding action in the artistic disciplines. A few years later, Andy Warhol and Claes Oldenburg used art as a means to reflect the condition and contradictions of contemporary society. This was the beginning of Pop Art and a specific form of social criticism. Through an ironic, demystifying celebration of consumerism, Pop Art acted as a sort of social exorcist. By choosing advertising and the media as its dominant subject, it attempted to reject the commodification of art.

These themes, related to an open confrontation with society, were at the center of the performing arts and visual arts in the 1970s. Artistic production found its most supportive platform in SoHo and later in the East Village, where there was a proliferation of creative expression in the form of events. Visual art decreasingly consisted only of material works; the tendency was towards happenings where the artists themselves were involved in the production and the audience was also expected to interact.

The theatricization of art was certainly one of the most dominant singular phenomena of the second half of the century, giving birth to performance art and "happenings." Initially the performances were confined to private galleries or small theaters, but later spilled out into the city in bona fide street events. There were numerous examples of "guerilla theater," involving the dramatic staging of political and social actions in the parks and on the streets. Performance art also succeeded in bringing together different disciplines such as art and architecture, theater and cinema, or music and dance,[1] despite each being based upon very different media and modes of expression. The early works of Vito Acconci and Laurie Anderson are particularly relevant in this regard. They united art, performance, and political activism, as did Gordon Matta-Clark in "building cuts," where the act of making the piece became an integral part of the architectural work.

The technological aspect also increasingly be-

came foregrounded in the work of art—albeit slightly later. Technology began to exert a sort of fascination, in which artists were drawn to the possibilities offered by the forms of new media and tools. New technologies attracted many artists who used them as a means for exploring new languages in a variety of different fields and disciplines.

Also in cinema an overturning of the classic principles of the discipline occurred. Jean-Luc Godard, for example, introduced semantic innovations by transgressing traditional narrative models: through disjointed montage and the device of actors looking into the camera and directly addressing the viewer. He was one of the agents of a narrative revolution. Through disturbing the linearity of narrative and creating an altered sense of awareness and lucidity in the viewer.

Like many works of performance art, there was also a tendency in video art towards involving the viewer, making him or her part of the work, and an accomplice to the action. In all forms of art during this period, the boundaries between representation and viewer were increasingly blurred.

NYC – Architecture
The 1960s marked an epochal shift in the field of architecture as much as in the field of art. Frank Lloyd Wright died in 1959, Le Corbusier in 1965, and Mies van der Rohe in 1969. The decade sealed the collapse of the modernist paradigm, throwing into crisis all disciplines that had sought to fulfill the "modern" demands of order and clarity promulgated at the beginning of the twentieth century. First and foremost among these was architecture.

In 1966 the Museum of Modern Art published Robert Venturi's book *Complexity and Contradiction in Architecture*, which laid out the theoretical basis for post-modernism and populism in architecture. It shattered an atmosphere of unity to promote a rich-

Michael Graves, *Fargo-Moorhead Bridge*, 1978

Zaha Hadid, *The Peak, Hong Kong*, 1983

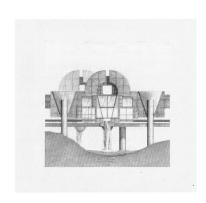

Daniel Libeskind, *Micromega 6*, 1979

Diller + Scofidio, *Traffic*, 1981

er and more ambiguous architecture, one that could merge into the complexity of the city, that could harmonize with the context that produced it.

If the modernists built static monuments to celebrate a single ideology or a universal style of life; the architecture of the 1970s exploded with contradictions. Architecture developed along two dominant opposing lines in this period. On the one hand a self-referential architecture emerged, which reinforced forms and languages that were already known and thus "safe" (later to be branded post-modern). On the other there were practices that seemed to dissolve the discipline, spread it out, and mix it with other disciplines. While in the 1920s and 1930s architecture may have experienced some interdisciplinary exchange with painting, and in the 1950s and 1960s with sociological and cultural critiques, in the 1970s and 1980s, architecture engaged with theory, veering into the territory of "paper architecture."

The emergence of a paper architecture and the growth of the debate "about architecture" was partly related to the lack of work for architects during those economically difficult times. And it was partly because of the theoretical debate and the attention it aroused that some of the architects were later awarded full-scale jobs in the 1980s and 1990s, after the economy had recovered.

Zaha Hadid's architectural drawings are idealistic manifestos. The work of Daniel Libeskind was judged more on the basis of his writings and drawings that on his built projects, to the point where the interpretation of his work was confined by critics to an artistic practice rather than an architectural one. Michael Graves began displaying the outcomes of his graphic experimentation in drawings of great delicacy. The first works of Peter Eisenman went so far as to conceive of architecture as a text where the site is seen as an active presence that affects and modifies the structure of the language.

While on the one hand the lack of built architecture was a result of the impoverishment of the construction market, on the other it was associated with neo-Marxist theories in circulation in the late 1960s according to which the built object became understood as a pawn to the dynamics of the market whose oppression must be escaped, thus rendering built architecture corrupt. The theories of Manfredo Tafuri, according to whom "the ubiquity of capitalism and the inevitable complicity with its power structures exhaust the architect's capacity for resistance," provided the theoretical basis for the work of many. Tafuri continues: "Precisely in the city that had experienced a collective architectural adventure in the 1920s and 1930s, in direct rapport with the public and with an aggressive clientele who clear-sightedly pursued their expansionist designs, there is an intellectual elite who seek to separate their own work from all structural conditioning, giving birth to polemics confined within the limbo to which they relegate themselves. If this happens it means that, once a high level of integration has been achieved in the pertinent fields, clear-cut spaces for culture can be cultivated, entrusting to them the task of pleasantly entertaining a select audience."[2]

Architectural discourse and the paper architecture of this period assembled in journals, books, and museums represent an abundance of thinking about architecture that explains the relationship between architectural thought through history and the development of architectural practice, and provides the architect with tools for exhibiting theories and images. However, at the same time, the gap between theory and practice widened and became quite controversial in those years.

Also in the academic realm, at Cooper Union for example, architecture was considered an autonomous discipline, independent of its professional implications. John Hejduk became Dean of the School of Architec-

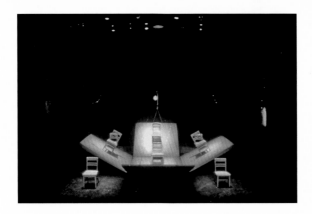

Diller + Scofidio, *The American Mysteries*, 1984

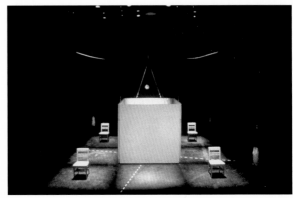

Diller + Scofidio, *The Rotary Notary and His Hot Plate (A Delay in Glass)*, 1987

ture in 1975 and emphasized architectural studies and research as something separate and distinct from the professional practice of architecture, which was viewed as something tainted and corrupt. He prompted a discourse on the role of architecture in society.

Architects in these years enriched the intellectual scene with discussions about philosophy, criticism, and social thought. While architecture in academia remained isolated from the real world, it is also true that it became a crucible for interdisciplinary debate and interchange.

At Cooper Union the subjects of study included Le Corbusier and Wright, defined as "modern classics," with more recent theories remaining outside of the ivied walls. While Proust and Gide were items to be found in the architecture school library, one had to go off on one's own to read the contemporary Robert Venturi.[3]

However, opposing the canonical approach to teaching, in 1967 a group of young architects, including Emilio Ambasz and Peter Eisenman, founded the Institute of Architecture and Urban Studies as an independent body for the research and development of architecture and urban design. The Institute closed its doors in 1985, but its magazine, *Oppositions*, published from 1973 to 1984, was an important sounding board for architectural ideas and criticism and a vital forum for architectural theory. This was another of the significant influences on Diller and Scofidio's development.

It was not until the late 1980s that the concrete practice of architecture would be redeemed and once again achieved legitimacy.[4]

Intermedia

Elizabeth Diller and Ricardo Scofidio's interests developed tangentially to the architectural discipline both because of their personal predilection and because of the context in which they developed. Elizabeth Diller stud-

ied at the Cooper Union School of Art and Architecture, where she later taught from 1981 to 1990. In 1990 she took a post as assistant professor at the Princeton University School of Architecture. She began her studies taking mostly art courses and a few architecture courses. For her the latter generated the most interesting debates,[5] especially those touching on the more general issues of space and culture, issues that would remain central in her research, design, and teaching. She cultivated her interest in the theater arts, especially experimental theater, as well as site-specific art, and all forms of environmental experimentation.

Ricardo Scofidio received degrees from Cooper Union, where he still teaches, and from Columbia University. By nature he was more disposed to heading in technological directions such as photography and video installations, but he never abandoned or missed a chance to follow impulses from science fiction and his other literary interests, and he maintained an interest in mechanical experimentation.

The decision to begin to work outside of the classical canons of architecture developed out of a series of external circumstances as well as from personal preferences. Scofidio had only recently stopped working with two other partners[6] when he and Elizabeth Diller began working as a couple. Although, in the early 1980s, Diller and Scofidio were interested in building, the only ones who could hope for actual building contracts in those years were the more conventional architects, figures more strongly associated with the establishment. Art, on the contrary, was considered a "non-field," an open field that posed no particular restrictions but rather embraced influences from sociology, history, psychology, and, naturally, from architecture.

With their interest in theater performance and their relationships with groups for whom the theme of the exhibition was central, they moved closer to the world of art, where they met up with Creative Time[7] and began to collaborate.

Diller + Scofidio, Blur Building, 2002

Diller + Scofidio, Blur Building, 2002

Intermedia: Site-Specific, Media and Theater
Diller and Scofidio's first work dates back to 1981. It was a temporary (and brief) installation entitled *Traffic*: 2500 red traffic cones placed in downtown New York. *Traffic* operates as a work at the borderline between public art[8] and conceptual urban design, a site-specific work of art. Site-specific art may be considered the source (and at the same time a derivative) of performing art. *Traffic* introduces a theme that would become a constant in Diller and Scofidio's work. An intervention is never thought of as being universal but always conceived and developed for a specific context and a precise location, a site specific work. In 1984 they produced *The American Mysteries* with Creation Production Company. It is a theatrical work that brings together the genres of the American thriller and Greek tragedy to explore and critique the explosion of violence in American culture. Diller and Scofidio designed nine different sets adapted to a theatrical work in nine acts. The nine scenes derive from the variation of a cube, the modulation of a minimal space. *The Memory Theatre of Giulio Camillo* is another work they did with Creation Production Company in 1986, a performance based on the work of Frances Yates on the life of the 16th-century architect and philosopher Giulio Camillo. Diller and Scofidio designed a suspension bridge that dangerously opened at half span, a *memory gap*. While both works express a deviation from the conventional architecture of building, the desire and capacity remain clear for an interdisciplinary work, where architecture plays a role in their artistic and theatrical expression.

Diller and Scofidio do not consider themselves as artists, nor do they fit easily into the architectural discipline. However, they construct their ideas as three-dimensional inhabitable space. From their first works, such as *The American Mysteries*, one can sense the desire to give a spatial aspect to their ideas.

In 1987, the theatrical work *The Rotary Notary and His Hot Plate (A Delay in Glass)* introduced an aspect of their work that was innovative with respect to that of many of their contemporaries. A rotating suspended mirror reflects the actors on the ground, whose movements are thus choreographed to be viewed both from the side and from above. *Delay in Glass* represents a project that marked a change in course, a turning point in their work. It marked the introduction of video technology as an instrument for artistic expression, and the media as a new syntactical method into their work.

Unlike many architects and intellectuals who found themselves involved in paper architecture projects, such as John Hejduk who articulated a technophobic position toward technology, Diller and Scofidio readily incorporate various forms of technology and media into their works. While the general tendency in their work has been to propose relatively formal pieces, they began to explore the nuances possible through the implementation of new technologies.[9] Video, monitors, and other forms of electronics have become integral components in their work. Despite the association of these technologies with the artificial/virtual experience of the surface of the screen, Diller and Scofidio's work is spatial, sensory and interactive. Viewers enter the work, looking at it, touching it, they become the subject and sense its texture, while in conventional architecture the viewer is a passive visitor.

Diller and Scofidio became the precursors of a period—the 1990s—in which, along with renewed economic prosperity, there was a paradoxical shift in discourse from paper architecture to digital architecture. A discourse on digital space opened up, and with it all the technologies of the virtual world. In contrast to much of the work of digital architecture, projects like Blur nevertheless succeed in mediating the tactile component with its virtu-

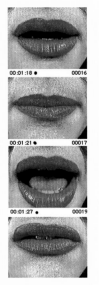

Diller + Scofidio, *Soft Sell*, 1993

al counterpart and presenting a tangible and concrete space even though the technological and partly virtual component is what dominates its production.

Diller and Scofidio expanded from the theaters and galleries to include the outer space around the buildings in their work. No longer exhibiting in closed and predetermined spaces, but rather in open spaces around the city, their works became true urban design projects. Their works live in the city, they become an expansion of visual art and enter into the everyday lives of city dwellers.

In *Soft Sell* (1993), sensual animated lips propositioned passersby from the walls of an abandoned adult cinema whispering, "Hey, you wanna buy…?". In 1994, *Overexposed* presented a video shot through the glass curtain wall of the former Pepsi-Cola Building on Park Avenue. It showed an uninterrupted sequence of twenty-eight minutes of everyday activities inside an office. The passersby viewing the video could thus pry into the lives of anonymous strangers with a voyeuristic thrill. With *Facsimile* in 2004, the intention was to reach the apex of this form of reality show when a screen mounted on the walls of the San Francisco Convention Center would show the activities going on inside the building around the clock in an indefinable hyper-reality. At the request of the client this ambition was altered to incorporate only pre-recorded "live" footage. Their first large-scale erected building dates to 2000: the Slither Building, a residential complex composed of 105 units. Each unit is slipped past its neighbor in plan, and staggered vertically to form individual entrances at unique elevations along a ramped circulation spine. Additionally, each unit is rotated to produce a slightly curved plan geometry in the building. In spite of its dimensions, the complex almost seems to move. While their projects

come closer and closer to the canonical conception of architecture, for Diller and Scofidio buildings and structures will never be something static in the Vitruvian sense of the term. They borrow Aldo Rossi's concept of the building as a shell, as nothing more than a sort of empty framework in which things are revealed.[10] The idea of architecture as the scaffolding for everything from dialogues to events was developed to the point where Diller and Scofidio succeed in combining the performative aspect of space with its static aspect. The building plays the role of protagonist and thus the city becomes a place that produces performances.

While a building like Blur dissolves and disappears in the rarefaction that it itself creates, where the visitor gains an understanding at the instant of entering the low resolution architecture, a building like the Brasserie draws visitors into the show almost against their will. Customers enter a restaurant and only once they are inside do they notice video screens presenting those entering the building. Hence, if at the beginning of Diller and Scofidio's career the users were spectators of performances, now the visitors and even the casual passersby become active participants in their constructions.

Diller and Scofidio adeptly exemplify the synthesis of three possible different ways of being architects, representing a union between professional practice, academic study, and artistic experimentation, just as they synthesize different ways of creating architecture and spectacles. In *Facsimile*, everything going on inside was thought to be constantly shown to the outside world with no secrets while in the Brasserie visitors do not become aware of the fact that arriving diners are in the camera's eye until they have already entered. The building's role as a player remains, in any case, protagonists and spectators still have their fifteen seconds of surprise or their fifteen minutes of suspense.

Diller + Scofidio, *Facsimile*, 2004

Diller + Scofidio, Slither Building, 2000

[1] The figure of Merce Cunningham is emblematic of his times. The dancer and choreographer worked with the avantgarde composer John Cage. Both of them rejected the formal methods of 20th-century art by using methods based on randomness and improvisation. Cunningham exemplifies this passage often using references taken from mass media to describe his ideas about dance. He was aware of the fact that technology can enrich the creative process, starting with dance choreography. He would have an influence on Diller and Scofidio's work and also the work of The Wooster Group.

[2] M. Tafuri, *La sfera e il labirinto. Avanguardie e architettura da Piranesi agli anni '70*, Einaudi, Turin 1980.

[3] Interview with Elizabeth Diller and Ricardo Scofidio, July 29, 2006.

[4] "In 1989 we were still working and talking about the critical practices of the 1980s actually to the point where we asked ourselves whether it was more appropriate for an architect with a certain amount of radical criticism behind him to actually build buildings or to completely give up on it. Attention was mainly addressed to theoretical work, to installations in art galleries and to virtual architecture. The change of course in the early 1990s derived from the emergence of a shared desire to do something about urban and technological issues (both construction and computer technology), the real problems of construction, and the performance of buildings." *Pedagogy* in B. Tschumi, M. Barman (eds.), *Index Architecture*, Postmedia Books, New York 2003, p. 143.

[5] Interview with Elizabeth Diller and Ricardo Scofidio, July 29, 2006.

[6] Edvin Stromsten and Felix Martorano.

[7] Creative Time is an arts-oriented organization that provides funding for public art ranging from street performances in Brooklyn to luminous installations in the New York sky. Each year they present five to seven projects that draw a large audience. Some of the projects are assigned by means of design competitions while others are commissioned. One of Creative Time's public initiatives is *Art on the Plaza*. Creative Time sponsors the independent work of interdisciplinary artists and creative minds representing a variety of approaches.

[8] Public Art Projects are an interesting phenomenon in America. The state finances architecture projects and a percentage of the total budget is earmarked for art projects in the space around the building which thus becomes an element of urban décor.

[9] Interview with Elizabeth Diller and Ricardo Scofidio, July 29, 2006.

[10] A. Rossi, *L'Architettura della città*, Marsilio, Padona 1966, p. 137.

Bibliography

G. Baird, "Criticality and its discontents," *Harvard Design Magazine*, Fall-Winter 2004–05.

J.G. Ballard, *La Mostra delle atrocità*, Feltrinelli, Milan 2001.

J. Baudrillard, *La société de consommation*, Folio essais, Saint-Amand 1986.

J. Baudrillard, *Il delitto perfetto*, Raffaello Cortina Editore, Milan 1996.

A. Betsky, M. Hays, *Scanning: The Aberrant Architectures of Diller + Scofidio*, Harry N. Abrams, New York 2003.

E. Diller, R. Scofidio, *Flesh. Architectural Probes*, Princeton Architectural Press, New York 1994.

E. Diller, R. Scofidio, *Blur: The Making of Nothing*, Harry N. Abrams, New York 2002.

G. Dorfles, *Ultime tendenze nell'arte d'oggi*, Feltrinelli, Milan 1961.

M. Hays, *Architectural Theory since 1968*, MIT Press, Cambridge (MA) 2000.

M. Tafuri, *La sfera e il labirinto. Avanguardie e architettura da Piranesi agli anni '70*, Einaudi, Turin 1980.

F. Truffaut, *Il cinema secondo Hitchcock*, Net Edizioni, Milan 2002.

B. Tschumi, M. Barman (eds.), *Index Architecture*, Postmedia Books, New York 2003.

P. Virilio, *Lo spazio critico*, Edizioni Dedalo, Bari 1998.

P. Zumthor, *Thinking Architecture*, Birkhäuser, Basel 1999.

Diller + Scofidio, *Overexposed*, 1994

Alfred Hitchcock, *Rear Window*, 1954

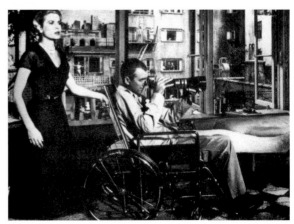

**Some Notes on the Disciplinary Practices
of Diller + Scofidio (+ Renfro)**

Detail, D+S(+R) studio, 2006

Marcel Duchamp, chess player

Introduction

The disciplinary status of architecture is a major theme in the work of Diller + Scofidio (Diller Scofidio + Renfro since 2004), which has often been described as installation art, set design, or new media art. The common perception of the architects as outsiders to the discipline can be tied to their continued exploration of an expanded *programmatic* and *organizational* approach to architecture. Diller + Scofidio (+ Renfro)'s approach to the first question, that of an altered *program*, is framed by their stated indifference to the disciplinary definitions, roles, subject matter, and output with which architecture is concerned. Their approach to the second question, that of how to create an alternate *organizational* model of disciplinary production, is driven by their reconfiguration of the organizational culture that is conventionally associated with the architectural studio. This reconfiguration is defined by an informal model of vertical and horizontal organization, which challenges the zrelationships between generalist and specialist, professional and amateur, virtual and material. Taken together, these approaches to program and organization offer possible reformulations of the broader disciplinary questions for architecture: the "what?," "how?," and by implication the "why?"[1]

In describing these tendencies, the practices of two figures inform the work of D+S(+R): the artist Marcel Duchamp, who influenced their indifference to disciplinary strictures; and the engineer Clarence "Kelly" Johnson of Skunkworks, the research and development division of Lockheed Martin, who inspires their reconfiguration of disciplinary organization.

Part 1. Program: the "What"?

D+S(+R)'s position developed in opposition to the "linguistic" model of formal representation that was prevalent in academic discourse during the early years of their practice. D+S(+R) define their role as investigators who examine the conventions of space found in contemporary "everyday" life, specifically those conventions which are tied to social, cultural, political, legal, and economic conditions.[2] For them, "space" is a different phenomenon to that addressed by a post-modern semiotic model. Instead of asking "what form represents," D+S(+R) ask "how do contemporary spatial conventions operate?" And "what alternate realities can be produced based on this awareness?" Space is understood in their practice in performative, rather than representative, terms. D+S(+R) ask these questions with a declared disinterest in the disciplinary regulated boundaries of architecture. "We're interested in a lot of things, from performance to construction," Diller has noted, "and it doesn't make a hell of a lot of difference what it's called."[3]

Role: Criticalities

Duchamp adopted a similar indifference toward the disciplinary boundaries of art, challenging the role, subject matter, and output of art after he abandoned what he described as "retinal art."[4] The artist for Duchamp was neither a painter nor a sculptor, but someone whose "experiments" placed "art back in the service of the mind." As the critic Nan Rosenthal rightly noted, Duchamp's most significant contribution was to sanction the artist's right to "question, admonish, critique, and playfully ridicule existing norms in order to transcend the status quo."[5] The genius of Duchamp's work continues to fascinate D+S(+R), who view him as "one of those figures that didn't exactly belong in any particular discipline or timeframe."[6] The indifference toward disciplinary conventions links the work of D+S(+R) and Duchamp. Diller and

Man Ray, *Marcel Duchamp as Rose Sélavy*, circa 1920–21

Scofidio's interest in the work of Duchamp is evident from the beginning of their partnership, most obviously in *The Rotary Notary and His Hot Plate* (1987), which was based on an analysis of the program, logic and spatial implications of Duchamp's *Large Glass*.

In questioning the normative conventions of architecture, D+S(+R) propose an alternate role in which "architecture can be used as a kind of surgical instrument to operate on itself (in small increments)."[7] According to D+S(+R), this form of critique, or more precisely "criticality," represents the red-line that runs through their work.[8] This term suggests a multiplicity of practices. It is necessary,

therefore, to differentiate D+S(+R)'s particular form of criticality from other forms that emerged within architecture from the 1980s onwards.

Two dominant strains of criticality may be defined within architectural discourse during this period: one textual, the other architectural. The textual approach emerged within the American academy under the broad influence of cultural studies and the writings of Manfredo Tafuri.[9] The second strain, labelled "critical architecture," has been associated primarily with the work of Peter Eisenman. The focus of critique in Eisenman's work is a negation of the internal assumptions of architecture, which is understood as an au-

Marcel Duchamp, *The Bride Stripped Bare by Her Bachelors, Even (Large Glass)*, 1915–23

Diller + Scofidio, *Analytical Drawing of Large Glass*, 1987

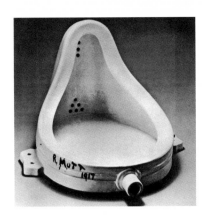

Marcel Duchamp, *Fountain*, 1917

Marcel Duchamp, *The Green Box*, 1934

Diller + Scofidio, *The Rotary Notary and His Hot Plate*, 1987

Diller + Scofidio, *Vice/Virtue* Glasses, 1997

tonomous discipline. While also operating architecturally, D+S(+R)'s mode of criticality differs from that of the "critical architecture" associated with Eisenman, and from that of the textual. Whereas Eisenman is focused on syntactically-based formal manipulation, employing complex geometry to destabilize conventional architectural form, such as in the Aronoff Center in Cincinnati for example, D+S(+R) are interested in challenging the less visible conventions of space, which are understood in the context of social, political, economic, cultural and technological conditions. Put another way: while Eisenman's focus of critique is formal and maintains the autonomy of architecture as a discipline, D+S(+R)'s critique is spatial and addresses aspects of the contemporary everyday that are commonly perceived as extra-disciplinary.

For D+S(+R), this criticality is defined by the specificity of the site, the program, and other phenomena that support the production of a specific space. In attempting to avoid re-enacting conventional architectural approaches, they challenge their existing "professional" knowledge by a process of "exteriorizing," which they define as "approaching an issue as a 'visitor'." Each assignment and program is viewed independently, with its own history and continuity. This approach is consistent across all projects, whether it is an urban plan, a building or a drinking glass. According to Diller: "If it's a water glass, we're interested in issues of hygiene and health. We're always rethinking conventions at different scales."[10]

Subject Matter: Roaming Concerns

For Duchamp, his disinterest in the disciplinarily defined role of the artist was tied to alternate forms of subject matter, in particular the banality of contemporary everyday life, rather than the beauty of the extraordinary. His fascination with the contemporary extended to technology, science, and the processes of industrial production. This wide-ranging interest is most obvious in the *readymades*, which reframe mundane mass-produced objects as works of art.[11] Representative of the highest aesthetic indifference according to Duchamp, these objects included a shovel, a urinal, a bottle rack. His preoccupation with contemporary science and technology also extended to the processes associated with developing his work. The preparatory studies for the *Large Glass*, for example, take the form of abstract, almost mathematical, pseudo-scientific diagrams and calculations that provide Duchamp a lens through which to interpret the world. His principal focus was to work with these non-conventional and non-figurative means to explore the realm of everyday life in all of its banality.[12]

In a similar manner, D+S(+R)'s fascination for the contemporary everyday and its varied manifestations also determines the subject matter of their work. Their roaming interests incorporate themes that include plastic surgery, reality television, crime, automobile racing, film-noir, jetlag, pornography, gastronomy, and magic tricks. These fascinations address broader problematics, beyond the conventional architectural practices of their contemporaries. These problematics are understood not in representational or formal terms, as with forms of autonomous architecture in the 1980's or digital architecture in the 1990s, but according to the performance of space in social, cultural, political, and economic terms. Broader categories applied to this expanded understanding of spatial subject matter could include: subjectivity, domesticity, gender, ritual, media and mediation, technology, globalization and the institution; all of which are related to contemporary human condi-

Marcel Duchamp, *11 rue Larrey*, 1927

tions in the late-capitalist world. The theme of subject matter in their work not only addresses personal fancy, and "matters of fact"—those assumptions that are the most easy to undermine— but more importantly: "matters of concern," those issues that are most at stake.

Output: Expanded Fields

In 1913, Duchamp asked: "Can one make works that are not works of art?" Instead of limiting himself to a single mode of expression, such as painting or sculpture, Duchamp moved toward a more open framework of experimentation, which includes such well-known works as the readymades, the *Large Glass*, and the *Étant donnés*, which destabilized the object of painting and sculpture respectively. The *Large Glass*, a two-dimensional painting on a glass window in a free-standing frame, can be viewed from multiple positions in space: from front, side and back, that extends the piece beyond the conventional framework of painting to a three-dimensional work. The *Étant donnés*, a three-dimensional sculpture enclosed in an inaccessible room, is designed to be viewed from the outside through peepholes, producing a monocular view that frustrates the conventions of sculpture, while also exposing the viewer in the act of viewing.

At the Venice Art Biennale in 1978, one of Duchamp's readymades, *11 rue Larrey*, the detached door that is supposed to lean up against the wall, was accidentally mounted in the corner of the room and painted over by workmen who mistook it for a door, rather than a work of art.[13] A similar mistake occurred during the period that D+S(+R)'s *Para-Site* was installed at MoMA in New York in 1989:

Overheard: (A guard reprimanding a woman applying her make-up in the convex mirror)

Guard: Please don't touch!

Woman: I didn't touch a thing. I was just looking.

Guard: You can look in the bathroom mirror down the hall. A woman like you doesn't need make-up anyway.[14]

Such a form of comic ambiguity was not a goal of D+S(+R)'s work, but a by-product of what occurs when a work goes beyond the conventional frame of the discipline.

During the 1980s, architectural activity typically consisted of either: producing buildings; or drawing buildings, termed "paper architecture." Although D+S(+R) only completed one and a half free-standing "buildings" in the first twenty years of their practice, it would be inaccurate to label their output as paper or theoretical architecture.[15] In fact, almost all of their projects have been realized to the finest detail. These projects were concerned with a variety of formats and mediums, such as: temporary site-specific installations, *Para-Site* (1989); permanent site-specific installations, *Travelogues* (2001); media projects, *Indigestion* (1995); dance collaborations, *Moving Target* (1996); theater collaborations, *Jetlag* (1998); products, *No Means Yes* perfume, *Vice/Virtue Glasses* (1997); events, *Traffic* (1981); print, *Case No. 00-17163, Flesh* (1994); interiors, the Brasserie (2000); buildings, Plywood (Kinney) House, Blur, ICA (1981, 2002, 2006), and urban projects, Lincoln Center, and the High Line (2003-). These works are all defined by an engagement in real space and a commitment to building and "testing" at full-scale.

This wide range of "built" work implies an expanded architectural materiality. In D+S(+R)'s terms, architectural materials are not only understood as conventional materials such as steel, glass and concrete, but are expanded to include various forms of media and technology. This is evident for example in the Brasserie, where elec-

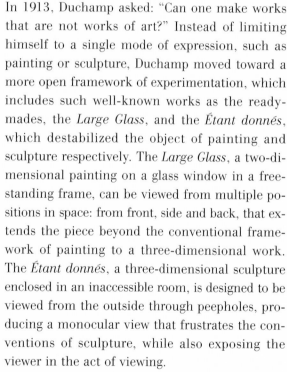

tronic "windows" capture both the blurred images of diners as they enter, and events on 53rd Street outside the solid basement wall. Other examples include the Blur Building, which incorporates water as its primary material, in vaporized, liquid, and commodified forms, and the Slow House, which juxtaposes the televisual window with the mediated "picture" window to which it is adjacent.

Part 2. Organization: the How?

D+S(+R)'s practice can be understood as an exploration of alternate forms of disciplinary organization. This is apparent in the culture of their studio, which celebrates the hands-on experimental garage culture of the amateur. As Ricardo Scofidio has noted, "I like to think of the place as kind of a Skunkworks."[16] Scofidio's reference to the legendary research and development division of Lockheed Martin, led by engineer Clarence "Kelly" Johnson, suggests an organizational model through which to consider the studio culture of D+S(+R).[17]

Since it was founded in 1943, Skunkworks has executed a series of highly challenging projects through small transdisciplinary teams of engineers and designers. The success of Skunkworks has been rightly credited to the organizational culture established by Johnson, which insisted "engineers get dirty on the shop floor."[18] This hands-on approach was incredibly productive, with Skunkworks inaugural project for the F-80, the first American jet-fighter of World War II, developed in 143 days.[19] As the garage bible, *Popular Mechanics*, noted of Johnson's approach, "Working a lot like guys building hot rods in their garages, engineers and production mechanics created the hottest planes ever to cut through the air. This informal process produced the most important planes of the 20th century."[20] This model

fostered a culture of innovators, chance takers and rule benders. Outlined in a set of organizational principles called "Kelly's 14 Rules," Johnson defined a flexible structure that celebrated experimentation and innovation, carried out in temporary and makeshift quarters like tents and unused hangers, and demonised unnecessary company bureaucracy. The allusion in *Popular Mechanics* to the amateur practice of the hot-rod enthusiast is equally relevant to the organizational culture of D+S(+R). In either context, the amateur does not suggest disciplinary incompetence, but rather a practice that is informal and openly experimental. "This is where amateurs have an advantage over pros," as one critic has noted. "A pro knows what he can deliver, and rarely goes beyond it. An amateur has no concept of his limitations and generally goes beyond them."[21] Examples of an amateurish disregard of limits are linked to the development of such everyday objects as the Hewlett Packard computer and printer, the Apple 1 computer, the Windows operating system, and Google, all of which were invented in home garages.[22]

In contrast to the sterile office interiors of many architectural practices, D+S(+R) work in the Manhattan equivalent of a home garage, an "artist's live-work loft" on Cooper Square. The former bird-seed store, in which Diller and Scofidio lived as well as worked until 2000, is an environment that is part-laboratory, part-workshop, and part-home factory. The informal nature of the studio supports a culture of testing, hotwiring, mocking-up, hacking and tinkering as well as more conventional architectural practices such as drawing, modelling, photographing, and living. The multiple roles, intellectual interrogation, and technical fascinations of the studio are closely related to Scofidio's personal obsessions, which range from

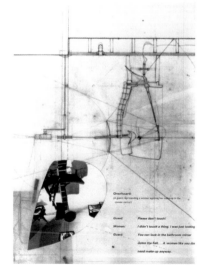

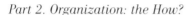

Diller + Scofidio, *Para-Site*, 1989

Aircraft designed at Skunkworks

car-racing and electronics to aviation and holography,[23] and Diller's and Scofidio's "day-jobs" as educators: Scofidio as a professor at The Cooper Union, and Diller at Princeton University (as well as at Cooper Union prior to 1991).[24]

Vertical Organization: Materialists
The organizational structure of Skunkworks dissolved the vertical distinctions between designers, fabricators, and testers. According to one former engineer, "All that mattered to [Johnson] was our proximity to the production floor [...] he wanted us only steps away from the shop workers, to make quick structural or parts changes or answer any of their questions."[25] This dissolution of roles even extended to testing aircraft, with the ninth of Kelly's Rules of Operation stating: "The designer must be delegated the authority to test his final product in flight. He can and must test it in the initial stages. If he doesn't, he rapidly loses his competency to design other vehicles." This rule emphasises the importance of feedback between the designer/engineer, fabricator, and tester, highlighting the need of responding to the performative requirements of a project.[26]

D+S(+R) suggest a similar break with the conventional vertical disciplinary borders in their own "built" projects. This is most obvious in the case of the self-initiated projects, such as *The withDrawing Room*, *Para-Site* and *suitCase Studies*; projects in which they operated as designers, fabricators and testers. According to Scofidio, "we would generate … the program, the concept, construct it, and step back and look at it."[27] D+S(+R) produce the majority of their projects in-house, dissolving the conventionally delineated roles of client, designer/architect, contractor, fabricator, and user. When in-house equipment or skills do not allow for a particular task to be car-

ried out, instead of working with anonymous sub-contractors, D+S(+R) work with a consistent group of specialized collaborators, with whom they have built longstanding relationships. These collaborations generate a form of extended "in-house" production. Collaborators include: wood craftsman Eric Rother; sports-car upholsterer Greg Georgi; Academy Award winning special effects technician Tom Brigham, who collaborated in the production of 3-D and animated lenticular images for the *Travelogues* installation at JFK; and the artist and steel fabricator Carroll Todd. Todd, for example, fabricated the steelwork for projects such as *Para-Site*, *The withDrawing Room*, the *American Lawn*, and *Master/Slave*. Over the years D+S(+R) and Todd developed an almost telepathic form of communication with one another to solve problems as they arose. The majority of the collaborators operate both as fabricators and artists, allowing a more empathetic and open communication and facilitating the extended in-house model.

D+S(+R)'s dissolution of vertical disciplinary boundaries suggests a form of expanded practice that allows for fast, cheap and flexible built experiments that might otherwise not be feasible. These blurred-task-organizations offer an immediacy of design to reality. In other words, they support the dissolution of the disciplinarily regulated border between: the virtual, the traditional domain of the architect; and the material, the domain of the builder or fabricator.

In the case of the more recent large-scale projects, these practices have continued through extensive prototyping. For example, prototypes, material tests and mock-ups have played a critical role in many recent projects including the development of the back-lit wall cladding system for the interior of Alice Tully Hall at the Lincoln Cen-

Diller + Scofidio, *Travelogues*, 2001.
Production detail, rotating suitcase, X-ray rig

D+S(+R) Studio, 2006

Skunkworks assembly floor

ter.[28] It is no coincidence that the design and manufacture of prototypes has also been the main venture of Skunkworks.

Horizontal Organization: Generalists

The organization of Skunkworks has also been directed toward reconfiguring the horizontal borders between the various specialized sub-disciplines of aircraft engineering, such as: avionics, hydraulics, radar and mechanical engineering. This involves a strategy to reduce bureaucracy and support the relationships between the various sub-disciplines.

According to Rich, Skunkworks is defined by highly challenging goals and "the freedom to take risks—and fail. That means hiring generalists who are more open to non-conventional approaches than narrow specialists."[29] For Rich, generalists are more likely to challenge the status quo than specialists. This shift from the "narrow specialist" toward informed generalists represents a significant shift away from the conventional models of modern organizational science, which have privileged specialization and the division of labour as key to productivity and innovation. It is interesting that the organizational model of Skunkworks has been seized by management and organizational consultants as one of the best models of practice for innovation.[30]

Within the architectural profession in America there has been a tendency toward larger firm sizes and increasing specialization, which first became evident following the economic recession of the 1970s and 1980s that forced many smaller studios to close. Specialization has emerged as the dominant culture within the organization of larger firms, with an increasing compartmentalization of tasks between management, designers, technical specialists, and so forth.[31]

In contrast to this trend toward specialization, D+S(+R) have maintained a position as generalists, with a declared indifference to disciplinarily defined programs. In a typical disciplinary scenario, the role of the architect is to manage the various specialized professional consultants, such as structural engineers or lighting designers, each of whom have an expertise and responsibility that is professionally defined. D+S(+R) reconfigure this conventional relationship by advocating an alternate working relationship with collaborators that challenges their own preconceptions. Project collaborations usually involve posing questions that lead to reconfigurations of commonly perceived professional solutions. This horizontal fusion of generalist and specialist is tied closely to the hacking and tinkering culture fostered by the studio. This model can be used to describe the development of a number of D+S(+R)'s works, such as the *Braincoat*, which involved a wide collaborative think-tank with individuals including sound and new media artist Ben Rubin, writer Doug Cooper, artist Natalie Jeremijenko, and industrial designers Ideo.

The informal vertical organization of an extended "in house" studio is also paralleled in the horizontal organization of projects, to the extent that the two often blur into diagonal relationships. Successful examples of this form of collaboration include: *Mural* with Mars-lander designers and fabricators Honeybee Robotics, the Brasserie *Bar Beam* with Ben Rubin and engineer Marty Chafkin; and *Moving Target* motion-tracking technologies with programmer and media-artist Kurt Woolford and the dance company Charleroi/Danses. The collaboration with cinema special effects artist Tom Brigham on *Travelogues*, for example, involved a D+S(+R) team working in Brigham's studio constructing various rigs and shooting

Diagrams, typical vs expanded disciplinary
organization

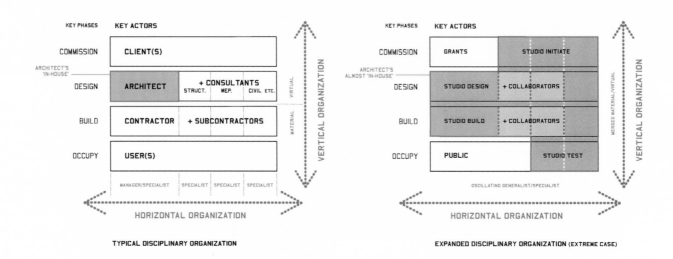

TYPICAL DISCIPLINARY ORGANIZATION

EXPANDED DISCIPLINARY ORGANIZATION (EXTREME CASE)

Diller + Scofidio, Organizational Diagram
for Blur, 2002

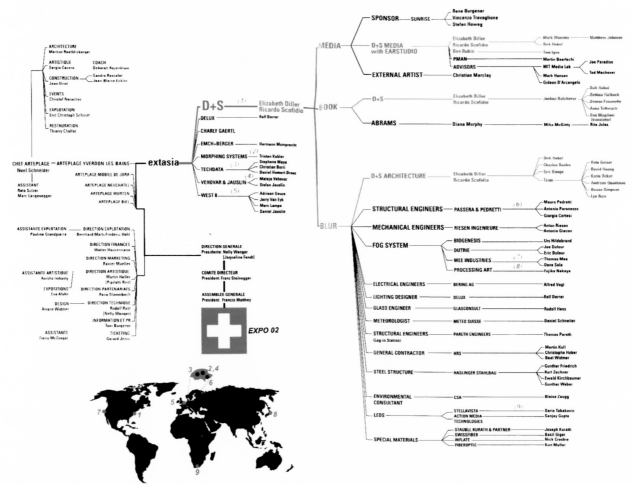

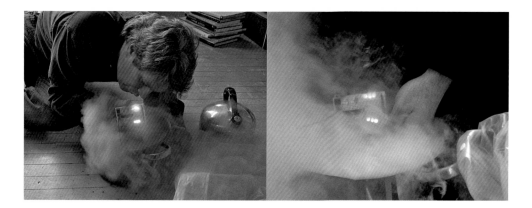

scenes with 35mm film camera that were then scanned and composited to produce 3-D animated lenticular screens.

Conclusion: Disciplinarities

D+S(+R)'s approach challenges the disciplinary conventions of architecture by questioning the relevance of those conventions. Organizationally, their studio is an alternate model of architectural practice, with a loose organizational structure that embraces the informal and the non-hierarchical, and allows a disciplinary flexibility in production.

While the practices of D+S(+R) challenge conventional programmatic and organizational approaches to architecture, it would be a mistake to classify their work as either non- or anti-disciplinary. The tools and methods they employ in the various works, whether it is a restaurant, a glass, a dance piece, or a museum, remain firmly grounded in the disciplinary rigor of architecture. This is reaffirmed in Diller's statement that they design architecture that is a tool to interrogate architecture.

In this context, D+S(+R)'s stated indifference to the architectural discipline can be understood as a feint that allows them to distance their work conceptually from the dictates of that discipline in order to critique it.[32] Such a critique is essential, as Mark Wigley has argued in his recent call for disciplinary agitation:

"Architectural agitators must be disloyal to their disciplinary norms. Architecture can only shake us when it takes the risk of not being called architecture. The challenge to architects is to challenge architecture, to shake us, and keep shaking. The concept of the architect must be expanded."[33]

Not only does D+S(+R)'s work suggest such a disloyalty, but it also suggests a disciplinary expansiveness and amateur-like practice that opens up the possibilities of architecture itself. Rather than interpreting their work as iconoclastic, which destroys the discipline, or dilettantish, which ignores disciplinarity altogether, it can be considered as an expansion of the disciplinary possibilities of the architect. The work is supported in this case by the perverse imagination of the individuals involved and fuelled by a desire to go beyond architecture as it is typically understood, but to go beyond it as architects.

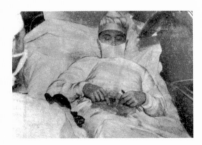

Soviet doctor Leonid Rogozov removes his own appendix, Antarctica 1961

Diller + Scofidio, Plywood (Kinney) House, 1981

[1] A disclaimer of sorts: the author was a collaborator in the studio of D+S from 1997 until 2003.

[2] D+S show some interest in language, but at a secondary level that extends to the naming of projects, an exercise that indulges in a form of Duchampian word play. The primary focus of the practice was, and remains, the question of space at a performative level.

[3] N. Princenthal, "Diller + Scofidio, Architecture's Iconoloclasts," *Sculpture*, vol. 8, No. 6, November–December, 1989, p. 23.

[4] Retinal art refers to art intended only to please the eye. Non-retinal art therefore would refer to: "Works of art that do not appeal primarily to the aesthetic delectation of the eye. The term was coined by Duchamp who professed an aversion to works that he considered 'retinal,' a tendency in the visual arts that he believed began in the mid-19th century. By contrast, he preferred an art that was non-retinal, that is to say, more cerebral—something that would appeal more to the mind than to the eye" (F. Naumann, *Marcel Duchamp: the art of making art in the age of mechanical production*, Abrams, New York 1999, p. 299).

[5] N. Rosenthal, *Marcel Duchamp (1887–1968)*, in *Timeline of Art History*, The Metropolitan Museum of Art, New York 2000, www.metmuseum.org.

[6] See Interview 1 with D+S in this volume, p. 57.

[7] Quote from D+S, *Keynote Address*, National Technology Conference, Phoenix (Ariz.), 29 January 1993; cited in G. Teyssot, *The Mutant Body of Architecture*, in E. Diller, S. Scofidio, *Flesh. Architectural Probes*, Princeton Architectural Press, New York 1994, p. 9. The notion of the architect as auto-surgeon finds a literal analogy in the case of the Soviet doctor Leonid Rogozov. In 1961, as a member of the 6th Soviet Antarctic Expedition, Rogozov diagnosed himself with an appendicitis. As the only qualified doctor in the remotely situated party of two, he removed his appendix through a twelve-centimeter incision in his abdomen. The operation was conducted with the support of an assistant (a trained mechanic) who held a mirror at forty-five degrees allowing Ro-gozov to see his internal organs during the operation. Rogozov's relationship to his own body—as both patient and surgeon—is defined by a particular distancing necessary during the operation. This distancing—achieved with local anaesthetic—is similar to the notion of criticality—employed by D+S in their work. Rogozov was able to find alternate constellations of subjectivity and objectivity in his role as surgeon and patient. http: //www.south-polestation.com/trivia/igy1/appendix.txt 2007.

[8] From original transcription of Interview 1 with D+S for this volume.

[9] The journals *Oppositions*, and later *Assemblage* played important roles in the dissemination of textual criticality.

[10] From original transcription of Interview 1 with D+S for this volume.

[11] Readymade (definition): works of art without artists to make them (F. Naumann, op. cit.).

[12] Particular subject-matter and themes in his work include, but are not limited to, the machinations of desire, chance, the erotic, mechanical reproduction, the copy, geometric precision, mathematics, and particularly language and language games.

[13] Described in F. Naumann, *Marcel Duchamp: the art of making art in the age of mechanical production*, Abrams, New York 1999, p. 294.

[14] E. Diller, S. Scofidio, op. cit., p. 190.

[15] The first is the Plywood (Kinney) House of 1981; the half refers to the completed first phase of the Gifu housing project "Slither" in Japan in 1999. The constructed foundations of the Slow House in 1991 have not been counted.

[16] From original transcription of Interview 2 with D+S(+R) for this volume.

[17] Another example is that of Jesse Scanlon writing for *Wired* magazine: "Their New York loft is less a drafting studio than a skunk works: a laboratory where they play with ideas about space and culture—and the materials that best capture these ideas, however briefly" (J. Scanlon, *J. Wired 8.02*, February 2000).

[18] "Kelly Johnson's Skunk Works Created The World's Most Amazing Planes," *Popular Mechanics*, September 1999, (from http://www.popularmechanics.com/science/air_space/1280596.html).

[19] Under Johnson, Skunkworks later designed, built and tested some of the most innovative aircraft of the cold-war including the F-104 *Starfighter*, the U-2 and SR-71 spy planes, and later under the leadership of Ben Rich, the F-117A stealth fighter.

[20] "Kelly Johnson's Skunk Works Created The World's Most Amazing Planes," cit.

[21] Cited in A. Zaero-Polo, *Roller Coaster Construction*, in *Verb Boogazine: Processing*, Actar, Barcelona 2001, p. 14.

[22] The emergence of this form of studio culture is tied closely to the particular period in which D+S(+R) have practiced —that of late-capitalism and the rapid advance of information and communication technologies. This has come about primarily due to the wide availability of inexpensive hardware—electronics such as personal computers, video cameras and so forth—and additionally, because of the accessibility of inexpensive software supporting multiple tasks such as desktop publishing, and video editing. The "democratization" of this technology, combined with the hands-on mentality of the studio has offered creative and critical possibilities to the amateur that was not previously available. This has allowed for alternate in-house and out-of-house scenarios with the use of tools such as home-video equipment, video editing and desktop publishing software. These technologies have been vital in the development of media projects particularly during the 1990s such as *Pageant*, *Moving Target*, and *Indigestion*.

[23] His passions also include Photoshop plug-ins, spy cameras and turbo chargers.

[24] The coexistence of various events with the everyday life of its two domestic inhabitants produced a rich spatial conflation of the worlds of hobby, fascination, love and work. These varied activities included: numerous photo shoots, ironing projects, perfume mixing and testing, sanding and spraying of plaster models, and the barium-latex spraying of objects for X-ray visibility. The pens and paper for the office were stored in the bedroom, and the living

room doubled as meeting room and model building area. For a number of years the toilet stood in the middle of the loft, separated from the rest of the space by a curtain. The project *Case No. 00-17163* was literally shot in the space, representing one of the more complete intersections of living and working. At times, these activities placed relations with neighbours under strain—concerning noise, fumes, and so forth. As the studio grew exponentially, maintaining this form of garage culture became increasingly challenging. Events in the last years at Cooper Square included a small laser cutter fire, and the stalking of D+S by a private detective employed by the building owner to prove that D+S were no longer living on the premises. After further reconfigurations of the space and the annexing of a similar sized space from the downstairs floor, the studio, with a staff of forty was forced to move to a new office space in the Chelsea neighbourhood of Manhattan in 2006.

[25] B. Rich, L. Janos, *Skunkworks: A Personal Memoir of My Years at Lockheed*, Back Bay Books, Boston (MA) 1996, pp. 115. With other aviation contractors, it was not uncommon to have a paper-heavy bureaucracy between aircraft designers and aircraft fabricators.

[26] Parallel to the erosion of the conventional division of labour, this practice is also based on a compression of the size of the workforce. The use of small teams of flexible individuals working long hours is not only designed to maintain secrecy but to tighten the communication and relations between the various members of the team. This is supported by rules 2 and 3: "3. The number of people having any connection with the project must be restricted in an almost vicious manner. 2. Strong but small project offices must be provided both by the military and industry. Use a small number of good people (10% to 25% compared to the so-called normal systems)."

[27] From original transcription of Interview 1 with D+S for this volume.

[28] The tendency toward dissolution of vertical organizational borders has also ex-

tended to more conventional "architectural" projects. D+S operated in the roles of designer, contractor and fabricator for a large number of items in the FFE (furniture, fittings and equipment) contract for the Brasserie. This aspect of the project extended to an extraordinary number of items that ranged from video beam to booth upholstery to lighting fixtures as well as to the bar. In this sense, the project was managed in a similar way to an installation project, involving design, and coordination of a series of collaborators—a theme that eventually generated some degree of tension with the "border police" of the division of labor—the unions that controlled the site.

[29] B. Rich, L. Janos, op. cit, p. 318.

[30] Examples of texts referring to the "Skunkworks" management concepts include: Charles W. Prather, Lisa K. Gundry, *Blueprints for Innovation* AMA, New York 1995; Clayton M. Christensen et al., *Harvard Business Review on Innovation*, Harvard Business School Press, Cambridge (MA) 2001; Tom Kelley, *The Art of Innovation*, Currency, Strawberry Hills (NSW, Australia) 2001.

[31] This division of labor within the architectural practice is mirrored in the increasing compartmentalization of architectural education into discreet roles that are deemed disciplinarily important, including: design, construction, structures, practice.

[32] Duchamp's stated indifference toward the disciplinary structures of art can be understood as a similar feint.

[33] M. Wigley, *Towards Turbulence*, in *Volume 10*, 2006, p. 9.

Bibliography

A. Betsky, M. Hays, (eds.), *Scanning: The Aberrant Architectures of Diller + Scofidio*, Harry N. Abrams, New York 2003.

E. Diller, R. Scofidio, *Flesh. Architectural Probes*, Princeton Architectural Press, New York 1994.

E. Diller, R. Scofidio, *Blur: The Making of Nothing*, Harry N. Abrams, New York 2002.

T. Gunn, *Road Diaries*, Project Two, Discipline Global Mobile, 1998.

J. Hulten, *Marcel Duchamp: Work and Life*, The MIT Press, Cambridge (MA) 1993.

C. (Kelly) Johnson, M. Smith, *Kelly: More Than My Share of It All*, Smithsonian Institute Press, Washington (DC) 1985.

"Kelly Johnson's Skunk Works Created The World's Most Amazing Planes," *Popular Mechanics*, September 1999 (from http://www.popularmechanics.com/science/air_space/1280596.html).

S. Kostof, *The Architect: Chapters in the History of the Profession*, University of California Press, Los Angeles 2000.

B. Latour, "Why Has Critique Run Out of Steam?," *Critical Enquiry*, Vol. 30, no. 2, 2003.

F. Naumann, *Marcel Duchamp: the art of making art in the age of mechanical production*, Harry N. Abrams, New York 1999.

N. Princenthal, "Diller + Scofidio: Architecture's Iconoclasts," *Sculpture*, Vol. 8, no. 6, November-December 1989, p. 23.

B. Rich, L. Janos, *Skunkworks: A Personal Memoir of My Years at Lockheed*, Back Bay Books, Boston (MA) 1996.

N. Rosenthal, *Marcel Duchamp (1887–1968)*, in *Timeline of Art History*, The Metropolitan Museum of Art, New York 2000, www.metmuseum.org.

J. Scanlon, "Making it Morph," *J. Wired 8.02*, February 2000.

B. Somol, S. Whiting, "Notes around the Doppler Effect and other Moods pf Modernism," *Perspecta*, no. 33, 2002, pp. 72–77.

G. Teyssot, *The Mutant Body of Architecture*, in E. Diller, S. Scofidio, *Flesh. Architectural Probes*, Princeton Architectural Press, New York 1994

M. Wigley, *Towards Turbolence*, in *Volume 10*, 2006.

A. Zaero-Polo, *Roller Coaster Construction*, in *Verb Boogazine: Processing*, Actar, Barcelona 2001.

A. Zaero-Polo, "Disciplines," in P. Dean (ed.), *Hunch: Disciplines*, no. 9, Episode Publishers, Rotterdam Summer 2005.

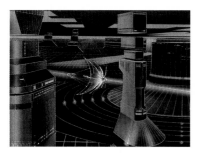

Steven Lisberger, *Tron*, 1982

Donna J. Haraway

Simians, Cyborgs, and Women
The Reinvention of Nature

Donna Haraway, *Simians, Cyborgs
and Women*, 1991

Introduction

There are only a few contemporary architecture studios that explore the impact of media in conceptual terms or incorporate this into the process of design. One of these was founded in New York in the late 1970s by Elizabeth Diller and Ricardo Scofidio, who were joined in 2004 by Charles Renfro. Few studios have investigated in such depth the impact that old and new media have had and continue to have on today's society, and the transformations they have wrought, not so much in architectural or formal terms, but in terms of new social codes and conventions. By applying the logic of the media, electronic and otherwise, Diller + Scofidio (+ Renfro) have altered the way we perceive the body in space, blurring its representation to allow projects to continually slide back and forth between different artistic fields in a sort of "transgendered" approach.

Gender and Virtual Cyborgs
Mutation and hybridization in corporeal space
The term gender[1] became a catchword in the early 1980s within the Lesbian, Gay, Bisexual, and Transgender (LGBT) movement to contest the mentality by which a person's sexual identity necessarily has to match his or her biological sex, and that a person's biological sex necessarily has to remain unvaried. The thought of bodily transformation still disturbs people who look, not without embarrassment, upon mutations brought about through plastic surgery.

Developing upon these issues of identity, in the early 1980s Donna Haraway introduced the figure of the Cyborg[2] into her political and social research. It represented a new form of subjectivity, a corporeal medium, created from the fusion of two terms, "cybernetic" and "organism." It would challenge assumptions about the nature of human

beings and the dualities man/woman, natural/artificial, body/mind, and even real/virtual.

The real/virtual basis of electronic media was explored in the 1960s by Myron Krueger,[3] among others, with his studies on spatial human-machine relations in works such as *Glowflow* (1969), *Metaplay* (1970), and *Videoplace* (1975). The spaces created by Krueger suggested a new artistic medium based on real-time human-machine interaction. His work in this artistic medium led him to coin the term "Artificial Reality". Artificial reality, a distorted reality or one counterposed to perceptual reality, would become a constant theme in D+S(+R)'s work. They have used not only electronic media (computers, monitors, video cameras) to achieve this, but also transmuted human bodies, mirrors, and everyday objects into media and messages.

D+S(+R)'s goal however, has not been to dissolve reality, to strip it of bodily substance as happens in cyberspace, where humans, in a consensual hallucination, enter into the space of the machine and lose touch with physical reality. In cyberspace, real and virtual no longer exist, but two "realities" interweave in an alien realm.[4] Instead, their projects use media to make different realities visible. They revisit the concepts of perception, the creation of meaning, perspective, reality, and form, associating them with movement, with the annulment of the physical dimension, and with illusion. These concepts are recognizable from D+S(+R)'s earliest projects, in which the transformation of space is accomplished via scenographic and architectural interventions. It was only later that they began incorporating the use of electronic devices in their work.

D+S(+R) set out to reveal contemporary changes in society, art, politics, and architecture by seeking to merge media with projects, moving

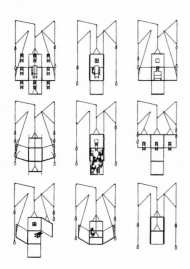

Diller + Scofidio, *The Americam Mysteries*, 1984

Diller + Scofidio, *The Rotary Notary and His Hot Plate (A Delay in Glass)*, 1987

along the unstable wave of change to explore spatial, material, bodily, perceptual, and even psychological transformations. The first idea for interaction with and transformation of architectural space was evident in 1984 with the theater piece *The American Mysteries*, for which the duo designed and personally constructed the stage set. The main architectural element is a cube that can be transformed, with a system of pulleys and counterweights. Its design is reminiscent of Duchamp's *Cemetery of Uniforms and Liveries no. 1*. The cube creates a room at the center of the stage that continually changes. It mutates from a writer's study to a detective's office, and then becomes the office of the mayor, thus creating a precise vocabulary through the spatial transformation process and the timeframe of the unfolding story.

The room opens to the outside world and to the audience. The volume is charged with force by virtue of its placement in the extremely powerful semantic space of the stage, a descendent of the Roman *scenae frons*, a fixed backdrop, and as such, a pure abstraction.[5] It is a space that has always represented the imaginary, *par excellence*. The box on the stage thus becomes both medium and message for a place located between reality and dreams, a synonym for truth and fiction. This dichotomy undermines any attempt to focus clearly and thus continuously challenges the meaning of the theater piece.

D+S amplified these investigations with *The Rotary Notary and His Hot Plate (A Delay in Glass)* (1987), a performance presented at the Painted Bride Art Center in Philadelphia on the 100th anniversary of Marcel Duchamp's birth. Here D+S enter into a relationship with the major work of the French artist, *The Bride Stripped Bare by Her Bachelors, Even* (better known as the *Large Glass*). This indirect encounter would open new conceptual territory

driven by the use of media. Media in this case also involves physical media, such as the rotating mirror above the stage and the distortions of perspective it allows. In the *Rotary Notary*, perspective is part of the project, but its meaning is different from the symbolic meaning explained by Panofsky.[6] In this piece, perspective constructs an intimate representation of the "real" and "virtual" spaces of the theater in a combined unitary view.

Inspired by the work of Duchamp, the architects used a rotating metal door that divides the "everyday" world in front from an illusionary world behind, and a reflecting mirror tilted at forty-five degrees that divides the space on the stage into two parts. The bride plays her part in one, and the bachelor in the other. Caught in a space fluctuating between "reality" and reflection, the two characters do not communicate with one another. A real space and a virtual one invert gravity and reframe the relationship between male and female. The mirror, like the *Large Glass* of Duchamp, is the medium that provides a view to different worlds and different times. It is a medium which tricks the viewer—paradoxically since it reflects the "truth"—and blurs their focus on "reality" itself.

Watchful Space

Electronic media was incorporated into the artistic realm thanks to the work of Wolf Vostell in the late 1950s.[7] It was developed further through the work of Bill Viola, Bruce Naumann, Dan Graham, and Nam June Paik. Paik was the inventor of "ready-made video," the first example of which (Pope Paul VI's visit to New York) was shown as *Café a Gogo* in 1965. Electronic art would subsequently focus on the "inner universe," entrusting performance to the electronic eye of the video camera. The concept of Body Art thus evolved and focused

Diller + Scofidio, *Para-Site*, 1989

attention on personal identity, the relationships between the individual and society, freedom and constraint, seeing and not-seeing, as well as themes such as surveillance and the relationship of the human to the machine.

D+S began using contemporary technologies to address some of these issues in 1989 with *Para-Site*, a site-specific installation at New York's MoMA. Here they picked up on the themes of Michel Serres's 1980 essay "The Parasite," seizing hold and clinging to the walls of the exhibition space with alien feet. Scanning and monitoring the entity into which it has penetrated, "Parasite" challenges the physical and social architecture of its surroundings—in this case, the museum and its authority as an institution. The scanning, decoding, and monitoring of the space is accomplished by video cameras focused on the revolving doors leading into the museum, the escalators inside the museum, and the outdoor garden. The monitors in the installation transmit fragmented images in which the real and the virtual are intermixed to create a complex interplay of perception.

Para-Site, a system of supplementary technological elements engaged in a symbiotic relationship with the architecture housing it, conjures images of the cyborg. It appears to exploit cybernetic imagery drawn from films such as James Cameron's 1984 *Terminator* in which a highly advanced cyborg is the memorable protagonist. Apart from the technological components, the installation also includes contemporary household objects such as tables and chairs. Their unusual positions, suspended from the ceiling or walls, and their nearness to and interaction with new technologies transforms their conventional meanings. As a result, they generate a disorienting space in which objects of everyday life mutate to take on sinister characteristics, encouraging visitors to take

a second look at and rethink that which had always been ordinary and familiar. The electronic eye enters domestic space, alluding to the disturbing element of Freudian memory.[8]

In installations and projects that followed, technology such as video cameras and monitors became increasingly important materials. In 1991, the studio received a commission to design a vacation house, later dubbed Slow House, which would never be completed. In this project, the house itself is a medium for exploring the themes of traveling and seeing, two concepts challenged by the new hot and cool media technologies.[9] Exploration no longer has only a corporeal meaning, as traveling via the television set (viewing from afar) or via the Internet,[10] but can be undertaken from a fixed position. A click of the mouse allows one to perform operations that a few years ago required a certain degree of dynamism.

In the Slow House, the incoming journey begins with a door, as in Duchamp's *Étant donnés* and ends with a window. The view to the outside world is doubled because a video camera placed outside shows the same view on a monitor mounted in the living room in front of the large window that provides the principal view of the house. The window, together with the windshield and the television screen, is one of the vehicles used by D+S to choreograph the spatial sequence of the Slow House. The space in the Slow House is thus a melting together of media, the automobile with its windshield for a moving view, the window for a view from within, and the monitor for the view from outside united by cinematic sequences that refer to the movement/duration blocks of Deleuze. The house becomes the point of contact between three different spatial modes accomplished via different media. It thus becomes the locus where those media realities converge and slow down,

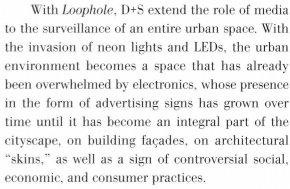

Diller + Scofidio, *Loophole*, 1992

until they stop. The curvilinear form of the Slow House was conceived in order to deform the reality of the views. They are electronic and non-electronic, frozen moments that might be unsettling for the occupants of the space, who find themselves to be observed observers. This evokes a phobia of the modern era which leads us to live in a self-monitoring mode: we keep an eye on ourselves as if we were someone else.[11] In Anthony Vidler's view, in a shift from the panoptic view to that of the cyborg, D+S's observers intersect in a complex manner. They shift their attention from registrations in the surveillance mode to a wide open network of glances and reflexes.[12]

Reflexes that were first tested in *Para-Site* would be developed later in *Loophole* (1992), a project at Chicago's Second Artillery Armory. The installation brings together the themes of transparency and surveillance. Closed-circuit video cameras placed at windows along a staircase focus through windows at the city, showing images on monitors along the flight of stairs. There are liquid-crystal screens in front of the monitors that can vary their state between translucency and transparency. They are thus able to reveal or obscure the image on the monitor behind them. D+S describe it as follows: "When the window panel becomes translucent the city view is exchanged for the fictional text. When it switches to transparent, the text blurs, revealing the view. A crosshair (the alignment of panel and window forming a gun sight) pinpoints the actual location of the object of fixation in the distant view—a person(s) in an apartment or office, window, at a street corner, etc., a precision target under surveillance by the video camera. Concurrently, the adjacent liquid crystal panel switches between transparent and translucent phases, either exposing a video still of that sighting, or obscuring it with the text."[13]

With *Loophole*, D+S extend the role of media to the surveillance of an entire urban space. With the invasion of neon lights and LEDs, the urban environment becomes a space that has already been overwhelmed by electronics, whose presence in the form of advertising signs has grown over time until it has become an integral part of the cityscape, on building façades, on architectural "skins," as well as a sign of controversial social, economic, and consumer practices.

Advertising, and the desire it is meant to arouse, is one of the psychological and media systems that the American government used in the middle of the 20th century to combat the threat of communist ideologies and their spread. Advertising is also a theme of sociological importance that played an important role in inspiring and stimulating the work of the two architects. In *Soft Sell* (1993), which they consider to be their most important early project, they enticed passers-by with seductive advertising messages. Using the entrance of the Rialto theater, a derelict adult movie theater on 42nd Street off Times Square, D+S reinterpreted the culture of advertising and the television screen by creating a parody of the messages addressed to each of us with the intention of sparking desires that can never be satisfied. Two enormous woman's lips, rear projected onto the doors of the movie theater, and a seductive and provocative voice from the ticket office, beckon to passers-by with words related to consumption but unrelated to sex, while a variety of adjectives are flashed on the four displays mounted on the doors such as "discreet," "virtuous," "innocent," and "genteel." These messages, addressed to people's voyeuristic and sexual instincts, appeal to desire through exclusively linguistic means, creating a sort of frustration and mental disconnect between the vocal message and the view of the full and

sensuous woman's lips. The project aroused very strong reactions and was highly successful. It operated on different perceptual levels such as: sight, hearing, and the mental associations constructed around the site. This approach would be further develped with the Blur Building, the most powerful semantic project of the studio.

Media Theater

The realm of technological media associated with entertainment, and the illusions it is capable of generating in our multimedia- and information-oriented society is an important inspiration for Diller and Scofidio in their scenography for the dance performances with Frédéric Flamand's Charleroi/Danses company: *Moving Target* and *EJM1 Man Walking at Ordinary Speed*. Diller + Scofidio collaborated with Flamand on the choreography and together they conceived of shows in which the main medium is the human body. The scenography was conceived to present the function of the body from all angles, whether "real", in the instant of the "aura" of the here-and-now described by Walter Benjamin,[14] or recorded at another moment in time. Video projections of dancers alternate with live action on the stage, thus making the performers as virtual as they are real within the space of the same performance.

The project *Moving Target* is loosely based on Nijinsky's diaries and addresses the dancer's schizophrenic universe. It develops intuitions from earlier performances, using once again the large mirror of *A Delay in Glass* hung at a forty-five degree angle above the stage. The highly reflective mylar mirror provides plan views of the dancers and their movements, providing a deeper and more complete bi-planar view of the body-machine. At the same time, video projections onto the mirror provide a continual cross-action be-

tween real and virtual, generating an "impossible" space between the stage and the screen, between "authentic" and mediated experience, revealing the reality of the fiction. Furthermore, via an optical tracking system (a product of military engineering), which follows the movements of the dancers, the computer, connected to the video projector, draws virtual cages that are reflected off the mirror to enclose the dancers on the stage below. The computer follows the movements of the dancers in real time and draws the geometry of the choreography. The machinery monitors the dancers, bringing to mind Oskar Schlemmer in the days of Bauhaus, when he designed costumes that transformed the human body into mechanical objects. He conceived dancers as marionettes controlled by strings.

Humans take back control from the machines in *Master/Slave* (1999), an installation at the Fondation Cartier in Paris. Here the electronic eye does not monitor humans, instead it is the human eye that watches and scans the machine. The toy robots in Vitra Chairman Rolf Fehlbaum's collection become surrogates for modern production robots designed by humans with the intention of replacing human labor in various production processes or demeaning jobs, so that we can dedicate ourselves more exclusively to intellectual and creative projects. But in our technophobic imagination, the robot is also the object that threatens to completely supplant us in the near future.

Master/Slave initially emphasizes the power of the human mind over that of the artificial one. The robots are forced to move along a labyrinthine conveyor belt in a glass and steel structure located at eye level that evokes images of 1960s office buildings. They are continuously watched, scanned, and judged by human eyes and by additional electronic eyes along the belt's path.

Diller + Scofidio, *Master/Slave*, 1999

Robotic technology would become an active protagonist in *Mural* (2003), an installation for the exhibition dedicated to D+S at the Whitney Museum of American Art. Here the medium, a robot designed by Honeybee Robotics (who also built *Spirit* and *Opportunity*, the vehicles that landed on Mars in 2004) moves along a rail mounted at the top of the partitions delimiting the exhibition space. The robot drills a continuous series of half-inch holes in the walls. As with the earlier *Para-Site*, the museum and its rules are challenged. The continuous movement along the rail, the obsessive whining of the drill, which keeps up its work incessantly for the entire duration of the exhibition, and the presence of an intelligent and mobile artificial intelligence, a robot, disturbs the visitors and violates the pristine white walls of the museum. The holes produce new spatial and perceptual openings, new cuts and vistas. The random placement of the holes offers some probability of holes being aligned between the various galleries and thus new views and clusters of holes can open broader sections of the wall. Thus the wall itself becomes a medium for providing a message. It becomes a more active representational component and not just a passive element supporting the image or the performance of the robot. With *Mural*, two instruments that are diametrically opposed in a technological sense become a media device to convey a single message.

Media Projects

After years in which their work almost exclusively took the form of temporary or permanent installations, in 2000 Diller and Scofidio had completed their first two building projects since the Plywood (Kinney) House of the early 1980s: the Slither Building in Gifu, Japan, a residential building they began designing in 1997, and the remodeling of the Brasserie in New York.

The designs for the Brasserie, one of the emblematic projects of the studio, afforded the chance to incorporate many concepts from the previous projects and performances into an interior architecture project. The space they would grapple with is no ordinary space. It is located in the basement of the Seagram Building, Mies van der Rohe's masterpiece and ultimate icon of modernist transparency, standardization, and efficiency, the medium and message *par excellence* of post-war modernism. Paradoxically, the interior shell of the Brasserie is the exact opposite of this. Originally built as a small commercial space, it had no street entrance. It was a completely dead, dark, insular space without any interesting features, and that is how the two architects found it when they were chosen to design the new Brasserie. It had no view toward or from the city, no contact with the city at all. And it was the first time that D+S had done work in the restaurant sphere.

The architects once again challenged the spatial design and the semantics of a specific location. They opted for electronic media as an element in the project to create and amplify a view of what would otherwise have been invisible. Firstly they provided the restaurant with a view of the city by installing a micro-video camera that captures scenes from the outside street and displays them on a monitor inside the restaurant. The second step involved a considered reaction to the entrance sequence of the restaurant. They converted the act of entering into an almost cinematic event by monitoring it with a video camera that, as in the Slow House, captures a space-time block. The diners' entrance produces a voyeuristic moment for those already inside the Brasserie via fifteen monitors mounted above the bar. The entrance into the scene also becomes a narcissistic and exhibitionist act prior to the activation of the senses of taste, smell, and touch in the restaurant experience. Dining in New York is an important social act verging on a media event, where one has to see and be seen.[15] This is especially the case with the Brasserie, which was a popular nighttime haunt of New Yorkers in the 1970s, and thus a social capacitor, a place for people-watching and a venue for the general excesses of the period.

In the Brasserie, Diller and Scofidio have sought total interaction between the user and the space. The space becomes a theater in which the diners perform. Once they cross the threshold, their role is blurred and they become an actor in a performance developed around them.

This blurring and altering of people's roles in space brings us to the project that synthesiszes D+S's many years of research into the use of new media technologies: the Blur Building. Built for Expo 2002 in Yverdon-les-Bains, Switzerland, Blur is an ellipsoidal, tensegrity structure perched above the lake. For the two architects, it represents a blurring of the distinction between art and architecture. The building/installation/performance becomes a *hybrid, transvergent* entity,[16] where the complete interaction of conventional building elements and electronic media, integrated both in the concept and in the design, almost overwhelms the senses of the visitor. The ability to control what is normally a chance meteorological event, and thus the form of Blur, generates a constantly changing skyline over the lake and in the surrounding landscape. This is achieved while limiting the obtrusiveness of the technology, seeking to produce the effect while minimizing what produces it.

The effect is an artificially created fog. It is a mist that prevents visitors to the building from

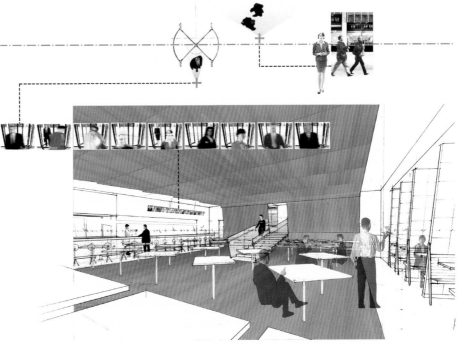

Diller + Scofidio, Brasserie, 2000

seeing what goes on beyond its "walls," and also prevents typical optical monitoring of the building interior. Its system of weather sensors and electronics, constantly monitored the environmental conditions of humidity, wind speed and direction, and temperature. The system balanced the telematic data and adjusted the 31,500 pressurized misting nozzles that used water drawn from Lake Neuchâtel below. The cloud mass enveloping the building was thus maintained, blurring the view of the underlying structure, or allowing it to dissipate, completely revealing it. The Blur Building responds to the environment, making adjustments, that affect the conditions and appearance of the surrounding environment, in so doing, creating new views for the visitors.

Visitors to the cloud were originally supposed to receive "braincoats" (which were not realized). These smart raincoats would track each visitor as they made their way through the pavilion. The braincoats were embedded with sensors and keyed to computer-coded information garnered from questionnaires filled out by each visitor when they entered the building. Compatible or incompati-

ble questionnaire responses would cause the LEDs in the braincoats to change color, indicating the visitor's attraction/repulsion responses to another visitor, better than any natural reaction of pleasure or discomfort.

Blur disorients its visitors while also thrilling them, demolishing the Cartesian assumption according to which perception brings certain knowledge. Through its architecture, Blur gives its visitors access to the center-less dimension of flight, of suspension in a space without edges, form and meaning. A gust of wind is all it takes to completely denude the Blur Building, exposing the visitors standing on the tensegrity platform instead of inside a cloud floating in the sky.

During the same period, the studio was also involved in the design of the Eyebeam Atelier's Museum of Art and Technology. They eventually won the design competition which included participants such as FOA, Greg Lynn, Reiser Umemoto, and MVRDV, all studios interested in the relationship between architecture and media.

D+S's design for Eyebeam is generated by an atypical Moebius strip.[17] The Eyebeam ribbon is an

Diller + Scofidio, Eyebeam Atelier's Museum
of Art and Technology, 2004

architectural transposition of wideband systems, symbols of accessibility and interconnectedness, used in contemporary communications. It recalls the thinking of Focillon, by which works of art become protagonists in the incessant flow of the creation and change of their own forms.[18]

The technological and functional components of the museum occupy the alternating surfaces of the ribbon. Each side of the ribbon contains the two principal functions of the museum: either the production or the presentation/exhibition space. The inner zone contains the engineering systems that provide the building's lifeblood. The ribbon, finite and self-enclosed, but unfinished, traces the sequence of spaces. In this case the media technology designs the space, in the full sense of the word "design." It is a space where once again the themes of vision and surveillance are pivotal, but are manifested with altered intentions from those of the previously described installations. The architecture created with the bending of the ribbon generates a fluid space in which the different functions on each of the floors are in visual contact with each other, but never in physical contact, cre-

ating a connection between all the building users and at the same time a barrier between their respective activities and temporal spheres. This has value as a factor in the creative process of the resident artists. It is a process dense with information that fluctuates between different scales and different realities, information that varies register and mutates, producing virtual images that become reality and vice versa. In a sense, it is information that is blurred, and this is what D+S(+R) have continuously explored throughout their careers, using media to distribute it by means of extradisciplinary works that create a blurred, subverted view of architectural space and of the messages generated by it and contained within it. This is a hybrid form of space born out of artistic and technological interference. It is a mode of space that is constantly mutating, incorporating new media technologies, challenging traditional architectural DNA, scanning the social processes that generated it.

[1] Regarding the emergence of the term and its social implications see E. Showalter, *Introduction: The rise of gender*, in *Speaking of gender*, Routledge, New York-London 1989, pp. 1–13; E. Ruspini, *Le identità di genere*, Carocci, Rome 2003.

[2] The term *cyborg* derives from the union of *cybernetic* and *organism*. The word *cybernetic* (Greek *Kybernetike*, the art of navigation) was coined by Norbert Wiener in 1947 and refers to the science that studies the interaction between humans and machines, and the development of machines that can reproduce the functions of the human brain. The word *cyborg* was coined in 1960 by Manfred Clynes and Nathan Kline, two doctors studying space travel and survival in extraterrestrial environments.

[3] Myron Krueger worked at the University of Wisconsin in the late 1960s and 1970s, and studied the interaction between humans and machines since 1960. He coined the term *artificial reality* associated with modern technologies and electronic media. Krueger's models, commercially developed in the Mandala System, do not require the use of stereoscopic glasses, gloves, or coveralls typical of virtual reality immersions. Instead the user enters a *room* where images are projected onto the walls by a computer which detects the occupant's *gestures* by means of a telecamera instead of sensors. The user thus *consciously* participates in an event that brings into play the basic mechanisms by which the user perceives physical reality. The user may participate with his or her body, have unusual experiences, engage in unusual behaviors, and *customize* the iconic environment in which a *simulacrum of his or her body* is incorporated.

[4] Cyberspace made its first appearance in William Gibson's book *Neuromancer*, Ace Books, New York 1984.

[5] A. Nicoll, *Lo spazio scenico*, Bulzoni, Rome 1971.

[6] E. Panofsky, in *Perspective as Symbolic Form*, 1927, studies perspective not as a mere technical expedient to make the image realistic, but as a product in which spatial organization represents a signifier of cultural, philosophical, and spiritual factors of various epochs, a worldview. Perspective is thus signified as symbolic form produced by a specific historical period. Panofsky gives a modern interpretation of a perspectival method used in ancient Greece and Rome in which space is considered to be discontinuous, as opposed to the homogeneous conception of space typical of the Renaissance and modern times.

[7] Wolf Vostell (Leverkusen 1932 - Berlin 1998). A pioneer in video-art, in 1958, in an attack on the misuse of television, he created his *Schwarzes Zimmer*, a "black room" of German memory, creating an analogy between Nazism and televised information and associating the death camps evoked in three installations connecting the Holocaust with the events of 1936, when the Nazi party used the Berlin Olympic Games and television as tools for propaganda.

[8] The uncanny in human psychology was studied by Freud in *Das Unheimliche (The Uncanny)* 1919.

[9] M. McLuhan, *Understanding Media: The extensions of Man*, 1st Ed. McGraw Hill, New York 1964; reissued by Gingko Press, Corte Madera (CA) 2003.

[10] In 1957 the United States government decided to create the Advanced Research Projects Agency (ARPA). Its ambitious mission was to seek a solution to security issues relating to the military communications network. The project was carried out in the middle of the Cold War with the collaboration of various American universities. ARPAnet continued to develop within the government and universities until the 1970s. In 1974, with the advent of the Transmission Control Protocol / Internet Protocol (TCP/IP), the name was changed to "Internet."

[11] A. Jardine, "Of bodies and technologies," *Discussion in Contemporary Culture*, no. 1, edited by H. Foster, The Bay Press for the Dia Art Foundation, Seattle 1987, p. 155.

[12] A. Vidler, *The Architectural Uncanny*: *Essays in the Modern Unhomely*, The MIT Press, Cambridge (MA) 1992.

[13] A. Betsky, M. Hays, (eds.), *Scanning: The Aberrant Architectures of Diller + Scofidio*, Harry N. Abrams, New York 2003, p. 75.

[14] The development of production methods, making the reproduction of works of art technically possible (by means of television, CDs, radios, computers, etc.), marked the end of the halo of uniqueness, originality, and non-reproducibility of the work of art, the *aura* that had been something sacred to the eyes of the bourgeois, who projected onto it their aristocratic dreams and ideals. The aura is thus this ideal halo that makes the unrepeatable uniqueness of the creative act sensible to the beholder. In mass society, where artworks can be reproduced at will, "technical reproduction can put the copy of the original into situations which would be out of reach for the original itself. Above all, it enables the original to meet the beholder halfway, be it in the form of a photograph or a phonograph record. The cathedral leaves its location to be received in the studio of a lover of art; the choral production, performed in an auditorium or in the open air, resounds in the drawing room. [...] One might subsume the eliminated element in the term 'aura' and go on to say: that which withers in the age of me-

Wolf Vostell, *Endogène Depression*, Smollin Gallery; New York City 1963

chanical reproduction is the aura of the work of art." (W. Benjamin "The Work of Art in the Age of Mechanical Reproduction," *Illuminations*, translated by Harry Zohn, edited by Hannah Arendt, Schocken Books, New York 1969, pp. 220–21.) Mechanical reproduction marks the triumph of the copy and the *always-the-same* for those stripped of wisdom. But in Benjamin's view, there is a revolutionary potential in all of this because it opens art to the masses, especially via cinema and photography, and thus provides them with access to its capacity to challenge the existing order.

[15] See the interview with D+S(+R) in this book.

[16] Regarding the term *transvergent*, see Markos Novak's essay, *Speciazione, trasvergenza, allogenesi: note sulla produzione dell'alien*, in *Architettura e cultura digitale*, edited by L. Sacchi, M. Unali, Skira, Milan 2003.

[17] The Moebius strip is one of the topological figures that has most strongly intrigued architects of recent generations (Van Berkel) and also those of earlier generations (Kiesler). Unilateral surfaces are surfaces that have only one side, as in the case of the Moebius strip. A continuous line can be drawn from one apparent "side" to the other without ever lifting the pencil from the surface. This surface also has only one edge. Because of this property, the Moebius strip has been assumed as a symbol of the infinite. It is a sort of alternative surface of three-dimensional space. One can follow the entire surface along the major axis and come back to the starting point without ever having crossed any edge. The strip has a single face. There is no inside and no outside.

[18] H. Focillon, *The Life of Forms in Art*, Yale University Press, New Haven 1942.

Bibliography

J. Abrams, "Il ristorante come spettacolo," *Domus*, no. 830, October 2000, pp. 118–25.

W. Benjamin *The Work of Art in the Age of Mechanical Reproduction*, in *Illuminations*, translated by Harry Zohn, edited by Hannah Arendt, Schocken Books, New York 1969.

A. Betsky, M. Hays, (eds.), *Scanning: The Aberrant Architectures of Diller + Scofidio*, Harry N. Abrams, New York 2003.

Dada. L'arte della negazione, De Luca edizioni, Rome 1994.

E. Diller, R. Scofidio, *Flesh. Architectural Probes*, Princeton Architectural Press, New York 1994.

E. Diller, R. Scofidio, *Blur: The Making of Nothing*, Harry N. Abrams, New York 2002.

E. Dimenberg, *L'architettura rovesciata: soglie urbane e immagine digitale*, in *Metamorph 9. Mostra Internazionale di Architettura*, Marsilio, Venice 2004, pp. 82–93.

D. de Kerckhove, *L'architettura dell'intelligenza*, Testo & Immagine, Turin 2001.

G. Deleuze, *Che cos'è l'atto di creazione*. Cronopio, Naples 2003.

N. de Oliveira, N. Oxley, M. Petry, *Installation Art in the New Millennium*, Thames & Hudson Ltd., London 2003.

R. Diodato, *Estetica del virtuale*, Bruno Mondadori, Milan 2005.

W. Gibson, *Neuromancer*, Ace Books, New York 1984.

W. Gibson, *Burning Chrome*, Omni 1982.

D. Haraway, *A Manifesto for Cyborgs: Science, Technology and Socialist Feminism in the late Twentieth century*, in *Simians, Cyborgs and Women. The Reinvention of Nature*, Routledge, New York-London 1991, pp. 149–81.

F. Kiesler, *Arte, Architettura, Ambiente*, Triennale di Milano-Electa, Milan 1995.

M. Krueger, *Responsive Environments*, The New Media Reader The MIT Press, Cambridge (MA) 1977.

M. Krueger, *Artificial Reality*, Addison Wesley, Boston (MA) 1992.

G. Orwell, *1984*, Oscar, Mondatori, Milan 1973.

T. Maldonado, *Reale e virtuale*, Feltrinelli, Milan 1992.

R. Manzotti, V. Tagliasco, *Coscienza e Realtà, una teoria della coscienza per costruttori e studiosi di menti e cervelli*, Il Mulino, Bologna 2001.

A. Marotta, *Diller+Scofidio, il teatro della dissolvenza*, Edilstampa, Rome 2005.

M. McLuhan, *Dall'occhio all'orecchio*, Armando editore, Rome 1982.

M. McLuhan, *Understanding Media: The extensions of Man*, 1st ed., McGraw Hill, New York 1964; reissued by Gingko Press, 2003.

M. Merleau-Ponty, *Fenomenologia della percezione*, Il saggiatore, Milan 1972.

W. Mitchell, *The City of Bits: Space, Place, and the Infobahn*, The MIT Press, Cambridge (MA) 1996.

G. Teyssot, "Cancellazione e scorporamento. Dialoghi con Diller+Scofidio," *Ottagono*, no. 96, September 1990.

A. Vidler, *The Architectural Uncanny: Essays in the Modern Unhomely*, The MIT Press, Cambridge (MA) 1992.

M. Wigley, "La disciplina dell'architettura," *Ottagono*, no. 96, September 1990.

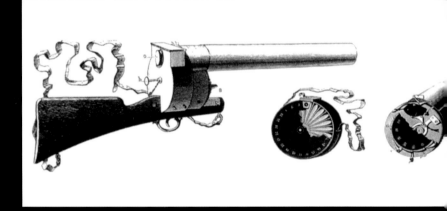

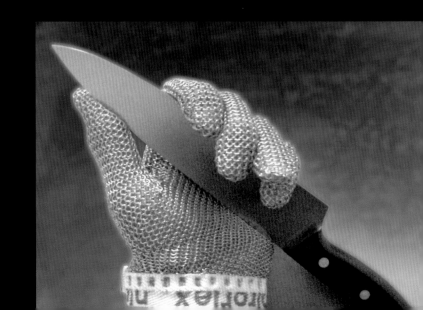

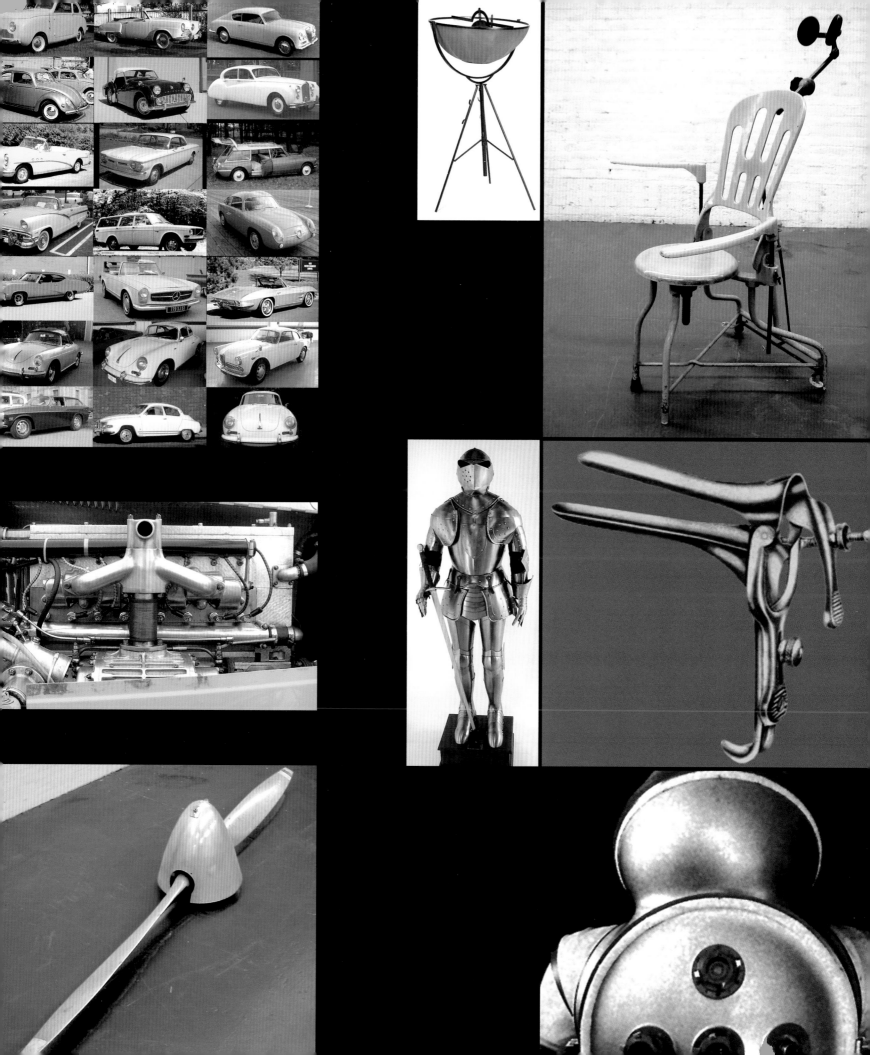

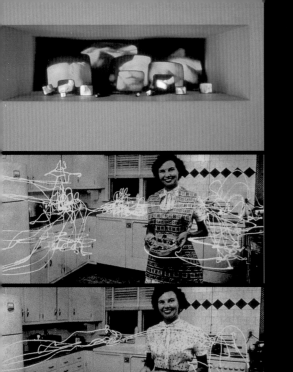

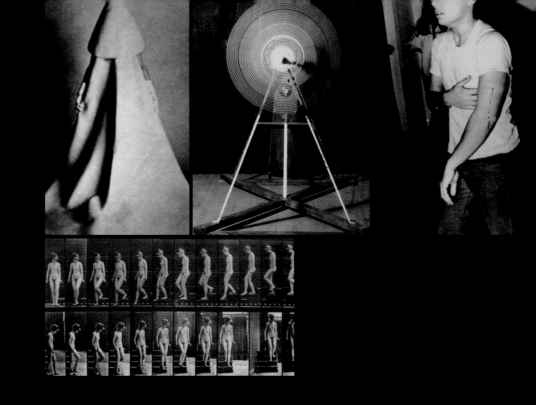

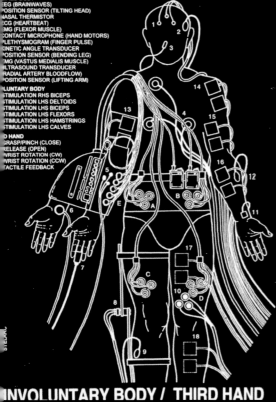

INVOLUNTARY BODY / THIRD HAND

Odd Lots
Revisiting Gordon Matta-Clark's
Fake Estates

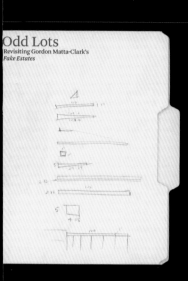

Le vol d'un pélican vu de profil.

Y ET LE VOL DES OISEAUX

premières études scientifiques des
ents des êtres vivants sont l'œuvre
ne-Jules Marey. Le rôle de Marey
recherches concernant le vol des
a été considérable.
1860 et 1880, il a essaye nombre
ils de mesure, la plupart basés sur
mbour » pneumatique transmettant
vements à un style inscripteur. Les
es de Marey ont porté également
poque sur la synthèse des mouve-

Étienne-Jules Marey, membre de l'Institut (1830-1904).

Chronophotographie avec images données
par l'emploi d'un miroir tournant (vers 1882).

appareils, en 1887, Marey obtient simultané-
ment sur fond noir trois vues : de profil,
de dessus et de trois quarts.
Marey créait en 1882 le fusil photogra-
phique à plaque circulaire mobile, puis,
en 1888, il remplaçait la plaque fixe du
chronophotographe par une bande de papier
sensible située au foyer et se déplaçant de
façon intermittente régulière avec arrêts aux
passages des trous du disque obturateur.
En 1889 et 1890, Marey perfectionnait cet
appareil par l'introduction de bandes sen-
sibles en celluloïd, puis transparentes, et,

Posé d'un canard (1882).

Phases du coup d'aile d'un goéland.

des ailes. En 1882,
une idée de Pénaud,
t le premier à réussir,
appareil chronopho-
que à plaque fixe avec
ateur, des images
es d'oiseaux en vol,
es jusqu'à cinquante
de ou espacées et
grâce à un miroir
Combinant trois

en 1892, il projetait sur un écran
les séries d'images obtenues.
Les travaux chronophoto-
graphiques de Marey forment
la base de l'invention de la
cinématographie.
À la fin de sa carrière,
Marey étudia au moyen de
fumées les remous produits
par différent corps ou pla-
cés dans un courant d'air.

Envol d'un goéland.

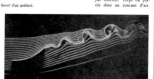

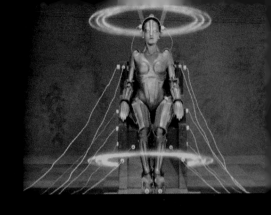

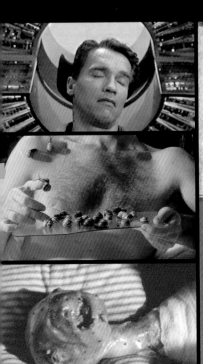

Emily Post's
Etiquette

The Blue Book of Social Usage

TO MY READERS

I have completely rewritten this new edition of ETIQUETTE because the problems of modern life demand certain changes in the forms of living. All of the fundamental principles, of course, have been left untouched. I have omitted certain non-essential customs and old-fashioned ideas; and I have added much new material in the hope that this book will continue to be as useful in its many years to come, as the old editions have been in the past.

OUR
VACATION

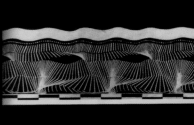

Date: July 29th, 2006
Location: Cooper Square,
New York City
Present: Elizabeth Diller, Ricardo Scofidio, Deane Simpson
(Questions formulated by Guido Incerti, Daria Ricchi, Deane Simpson)

Deane: Today I would like to primarily focus upon the formative years of the studio, your influences and your approach to practice. 1979 was an important moment for you—it was the year that you both started the studio. Could you describe the context in New York and the US at that time?

Ric: In the early and mid-1970s I had become disillusioned with architecture and dissolved a three-way partnership and more or less retired from architecture. I felt it was impossible to move the discipline forward. By 1979 there was a strange collision: I was finally ready to step back into architecture while Elizabeth was trying to find ways around it and out of it. It was also a period when the economy had collapsed and there was very little being built.

Liz: 1979 was the year I graduated from Cooper Union. I was an art student taking a course in architecture, getting progressively more interested in the discourse and deciding to linger on. I got my degree in architecture by default but never with the intention of becoming an architect. I was attracted by John Hejduk's enigmatic teaching style. After a session with him you felt like you learned something but you couldn't articulate what it was. He also had a profound distrust of the profession that was attractive to me. He felt it was corrupt and intellectually bankrupt. Students studying architecture under Hedjuk were trying to figure out how to situate architecture among other disciplines. He promoted a rigorous but a free-form type of research. It was at Cooper that I learned about interdisciplinarity. But I was a bit of a contrary in the school. While others were reading poetry, I was looking at the work of environmental artists like Gordon Matta-Clark, Robert Smithson and Dan Graham and artists at the edge of performance like Chris Burden and Vito Acconci. … also, performers like the Wooster Group and Phil Glass. I was feeding off of everything but architecture.

Ric: And I come from a music background and wanted to be a musician. I was also into B-Hollywood movies, pulp fiction and automobiles … Pop culture was very important for me.

Liz: When I graduated and Ric and I started to work together we never thought much about a trajectory. Ric was interested in rejoining architecture after a long absence; I had little interest. We found a common ground exploring public space. We did guerrilla installations on borrowed or stolen sites with no clients and no funding. We put everything on credit. It took years to pay off our credit card art debt. After some recognition, we began getting support from funding agencies back when the US government supported culture. We also made alliances with artists and alternative arts organizations like Creative Time that sponsored independent site-specific projects. They didn't have their own exhibition space but used New York City as its site. The first installation project led to a second and a third. We became progressively engaged in the art scene.

Ric: Because of the recession, there were few architectural commissions—it was a time when disaffected young architects were turning to paper architecture. The new site for architecture was the gallery wall or the printed page. It was a time when Koolhaas, Tschumi and Libeskind were showing at Max Protech. Eisenman and Graves were selling speculative houses through Leo Castelli. The "New York Five" was a loose collective formed as a promotional tool to package work for print. We took a different approach. We were anxious to test our research in real operational space, with real bodies, and real materials. But unlike architecture, the work was ephemeral. It would only be up for one or to months, and then it would become New Jersey landfill. Brevity was key. Like a Polaroid snapshot, we were able to conceive an experiment, enact it, learn from its results and then destroy it. Our practice was a laboratory.

Liz: Paper architecture seemed like a bad alternative.

Deane: In what sense was it a bad alternative?

Liz: It was a weak substitution for architecture rather than a redefinition of it. For us, the challenge wasn't just to imagine space, it was to produce new problems in space, to disrupt it. You couldn't do that on paper. At every stage along the way, our work never stood for anything other than itself. Even work we did in print was about the space of the book and the act of reading.

Ric: The critical difference between us and the others was that we had no desire to establish an architectural practice or a client base. Our independent work was not a means to an end it was an end in itself. Ours was absolutely and purely a skunkworks for an exploration of space.

Liz: We were interested in making problems in space, not solving them—especially challenging inherited spatial conventions. Each project had its logic and appropriate medium, whether it was physical materials, or video, or performance, or print. It was simply about finding the right tool for the job.

Deane: So you were never interested in giving it the name architecture? Architecture defined more the process or the tools with which to approach these issues?

Ric: We accepted that we were architects, but we weren't concerned about labels.

Liz: Well, we always wanted to be outsiders. In the art world we wanted to be thought of as architects and in the architecture world we wanted to be thought of as artists …

Ric: I don't think so … I know you like to say that … We existed in a grey area.

Liz: Yes but there was no conflict about which discipline we belonged to. It was neither.

Ric: We did architecture operating as artists …

Liz: It still didn't matter except when it came to funding. As independents, we could either find funding from an architectural source or an art source and sometimes we were able to reap the benefits of both. Other times, the art agencies preferred to regard us as architects and the architectural agencies as artists thus we got caught in a crack in the middle and got nothing. It's the same with museum exhibitions— who were we and on which floor of the museum did we belong—architecture, art, video? It didn't matter to us but it was interesting to observe how others dealt with boundaries issues.

Ric: … the border police.

Deane: There appear to be a series of issues that you are preoccupied with that define your interpretation of space. For example, a certain conceptualization of the body and how it relates to space appears to be important in your work, also a particular interest in the normative conditions of domestic space. How do you interpret space differently from predominant models (e.g. modernist ones) that exist?

Liz: We see space as scripted, not a tabula rasa. Space is inherited and is always attached to geographies, histories, and policies. So when we think about an intervention in space like an act of architecture, we always think of ourselves as visitors to a problem that existed before us, and therefore it's up to us to think backwards and forwards through contemporary filters. We were particularly interested in the everyday and tried to foreground spatial convention so culturally ingrained that blinded us by their familiarity. Sometimes the intervention was critical and other times, generative and proactive. Even our earliest works—like the entry gate installation at Art on the Beach at Battery Park—acknowledged the socio-cultural context. The site wasn't just ground, it was the ground excavated for the foundations of the World Trade Center that was to serve as a new foundation for the World Financial Center—that artists occupied temporarily to "cleanse" the site before it was swallowed by commerce. We were obsessed with recognizing a moment in space: the interface between original ground and new ground, where civic space met space reserved for culture where you had to pay admission.

Deane: This is the bowl?

Liz: Right, the bowl. We were just preoccupied with that detail. The bowl was bisected, straddling natural and manmade land. It was the moment of transaction where money changed hands from citizen to institution. We often started and still do ignite a project from a detail or the aggregation of small thoughts into a bigger whole rather than a top down approach … Like the saying goes, size doesn't matter.

Ric: That detail didn't ignite the project, it was the project.

Liz: Even though the play of property and propriety is consistent in our work, like other ongoing agendas, each project is twisted by the specificity of its site conditions. Site for us means "situation." Our work has always looked at space through a thick perception.

Ric: And as a cultural construction. "How do we perceive space?" I still struggle with what that means. Our spatial understanding comes through all of the artefacts that mediate the way we see the world, whether it's a map, whether it's a social convention. When I sit here in the studio, I place myself in relation to the East River and the Hudson River via the map I have in my brain, not by what I see. Vision occurs through the "Cyclopian Eye"—the brain. That's the seeing organ that filters how we perceive space.

Deane: Would it be possible to make a connection between the development of your understanding of space and the emergence of the discipline of Cultural Studies in the US at the time? For example was someone like Foucault particularly important for you or were there other figures that were important to you?

Liz: How far back? In school, no. Cooper at that time defined the antonym of cultural studies. Its identity was one of autonomy and purity, unaffected by the complexity of the world. It was a breach for a student to look outside the fortified walls of the school. I was a dissident. While my fellow students were leafing through Corb's *Oeuvre Complete*, I was reading Venturi's *Complexity and Contradiction* …

Ric: Undercover … (laughter)

Liz: Yes, under my desk, because if I was caught, the book would have been confiscated. (laughter)

Deane: Blacklisted …

Liz: Totally blacklisted. Cooper encouraged 19th-century and early 20th-century fiction. Gide and Proust were OK.

Ric: John Hawkes was borderline …

Liz: Yes, there were few approved contemporary writers. But to answer your question, I guess when I was a student I engaged in an unconscious form of cultural anthropology. But it was not until later that I discovered Foucault and then Marxism, gender studies, and literary and media theory. I grew up in a time of feminism and the anti-war movement. Politics was in my blood.

Deane: So it was more unconscious at the time …

Liz: In the anti-establishment climate of the 1960s and 1970s, art and activism were inextricably linked. Architecture was equated with the establishment—the seat of authority. That's why we stayed independent. We didn't want the support of the system. We could do everything on our own, within simple means, and we learned how to work the system to get our work realized.

Deane: And when you were doing this did you have some sense of where it was heading? For example, you mentioned that the paper architects were trying to more or less get clients through the exhibition of their work …

Ric: Well that's a little unfair, I don't know if they were, but clearly …

Liz: Remember, the Castelli exhibition was a speculative architecture show of houses by a selective group of architects at the margins. Collectors were buying drawings of houses to ultimately build from them.

Ric: Well, despite what others were doing, we were on our own course—it was an almost continuously forking path of research that splintered into many directions.

Deane: Technology has been a key theme in your work. How would you characterize your position in relation to technology?

Ric: No differently than we would characterize our position to pencil and paper; it's a tool, but a faster one. We did a project for print at the request of Zone Books in *Incorporations*. It was a murder mystery told through the narrative of forensic evidence like blood splatter analysis and voice recognition, similar to the aesthetics of the CSI, the no. one show on TV today. The complex story was told in many parallel registers of information. It was all done by hand, tediously layer by layer. It apparently cost Zone a fortune to produce it and they told us, "If we had known, we would have bought you a computer." Beyond expedience, new technologies have afforded new speculations. However, I have never been interested in foregrounding technology—I'm only interested in the ultimate effect. If the effect is great, it makes you forget about the technology that produced it. We've never been preoccupied with hardware for the sake of hardware or software for the sake of software—we're not nerds. But we're interested in the relation between tools and ideas: does the tool create the possibility for a new thought or does the thought require the invention of a new tool that inadvertently creates a new thought?

Liz: Though I think we have to define technology a bit better—the association with electronics is too limiting. For me, political, social and cultural technologies come first … This may be the Foucauldian influence.

Ric: Yes but …

Liz: Architecture as a technology in itself, a man-made system involving many social systems to which a new layer is now added: responsive systems, new materials, and new visualization and fabrication techniques. We should use all the tools at our disposal, old and new, for the production of space and effects. We're not interested in perpetuating a distinction between "smart" and "dumb" technologies.

Ric: It's a mix …

Liz: Because we started to work with electronic systems early, we became sceptical about the knee jerk euphoria or knee jerk panic in relation to the electronic world.

Deane: This is the position you have articulated before—between the technophile and the technophobe …

Liz: Exactly. There was a naïve notion when technologies began to leak into architecture—which was, as usual, a decade behind art—that space was dead. For some that was ecstatic for others it prompted the rhetoric of loss. It represented the end of the city, the end of tourism, the end of banking, the end of shopping, the end of sex, the end of everything. We would lose our bodies, we would lose our sexuality, we would be nothing but fingers.

Ric: Our work in new media responded critically to the evolving notion that interactivity would liberate us, democratize art, break down the separation between audience and artist and allow the audience to be part of the art-making process. Our first interactive work, *Indigestion*, came from an initiative between Banff Centre and the Pompidou, and it focused on the perceived freedoms yet limited options of interactivity. The piece pointed out that interactive art was no different than other art. The artist scripted the branching narrative and the finite options.

Liz: With *Moving Target*, a multi-media dance work, we were experimenting with real-time computing intersecting stage action. But how would the public discern between responsiveness and pre-programmed stage effects? How could the computer be a provocateur, another character on stage? Could it carry the same *liveness* that an actual performer carried?

Ric: We did over ten theater and dance works. We had a growing tendency in the stage work to replace live performers with virtual ones.

Deane: There seems to be a strong thread in your work that deliberately addresses themes associated with Modernism—in particular, those manifest in the American post-war period—themes such as standardization, efficiency, transparency, etc. How would you define your work in relation to Modernism?

Liz: Well, we've inherited the legacy of Modernism and it's still alive but in need of invention …

Deane: So you don't see yourselves as post-modern-ists? (laughter)

Ric: No. We don't like the term neo-modernist either. It's sentimental.

Liz: I would say we are post-post-modernists.

Ric: No, we are post-*post-modernist*-modernists. (laughter)

Liz: Cultural theory was maligned by the architectural term "postmodernism," an anti-modern reactionary glitch of history backed by corporate power. Our interest is in a critical extension of the modernist project. Let's take the notion of transparency for example: glass went through many iterations since early Modernism. The advent of long-span glass and curtain wall construction was introduced as an utopian material that would liberate vision and democratize space. But the global proliferation of glass and steel buildings proved it to be an expedient and economic building type. The ubiquity of glass triggered a backlash—a period of paranoia about total visibility. Yesterday's paranoia that someone may be watching led to today's paranoia that no one may be watching, which has led to a period of exhibitionism. Today's love affair with low iron super-transparent glass is not only about exhibiting behavior behind the glass but about exhibiting the glass itself as a fetish object. Glass continues to be a topic of critique and also forward speculation.

Ric: We've all been raised under the tenets and influence of Modernism—and even if we say we've stepped away, they have a much deeper influence than we're willing to admit. It's like being raised in the catholic church and then denouncing Catholicism, while its influences are there for the rest of your life. Our proximity to the 20th century can never allow us to step away far enough to see it objectively.

Liz: Also, there is no single Modernism. There's a Miesian modernism, a Corbusian modernism, an Aalto-esque modernism, a Wrightian modernism … there are Early, Mid-Century, High, and Late Modernisms. We're interested in the aggregate incorporated with cultural theory.

Deane: The Brasserie is an example of a project where you were literally working within the confines of a highly recognized modernist building. Could you talk a little bit about how you see your reaction to this …

Liz: That project was dangerous not only because it was a Mies building with Philip Johnson influence and design, but also Phyllis Lambert was the "uber"-client. The space itself had none of the qualities or aspirations of Modernism—it was totally dark, insular, and without structural or spatial interest. It was nothing but a basement in the base of the Seagram Building, a site of the Miesian unconscious.

Ric: Originally, I think it was a barber's shop and a few stores with no entrance. Then it was converted into a restaurant by Johnson. Just about anything we could do would indirectly be read as critical act on Modernism, the Seagram Building being its ultimate symbol. But we tried hard to speak to Mies indirectly.

Liz: Here, in this icon of glass and steel architecture our site was the stone base on which the tower sat. That perversity pushed us to explore attributes of glass. We produced an electronic transparency to the street to compensate for the stone interface. If glass could not be used for vision, what role could it play? We were interested in the association of glass with fragility and at the same time express its structural capacity. We displayed glass as a remnant, propped against the wall and protecting a series of artefacts while cantilevering a bank of twenty seated diners. The glass wall had a lenticular film that allowed for perpendicular vision not oblique.

Deane: So to not see it through a utopian modernist lens—transparent, democratic, and so on.

Ric: Right. Our interest in visuality extended into the social space of dining, the space of seeing and being seen. We were interested in the entrance from the street as well as the notion of "making an entrance."

Liz: The Brasserie was, in the old days before it burnt down, before it became our project, the place where the "glitter people" came from Studio 54 in the middle of the night. It was the first twenty-four-hour restaurant in New York and it was legendary. The notion of a restaurant as a social condenser urged a kind of self-conscious, perverse vision. Where you sat and what you saw from where you sat, and who do you saw were no less important now then in the 1970s.

Ric: It was amazing Restaurant Associates, the commercial restaurant client, chose us. In the interview we showed them *Indigestion*—which was about class and gender clichés. Then we talked about the great restaurants we had eaten in and the strong relation between food, space and pleasure.

Liz: But, realistically I think that Restaurant Associates had no choice because Phyllis Lambert was ultimately deciding…

Ric: But the fact that we could speak eloquently about food and that we were gourmands compensated for the fact that we were totally unqualified to do the project. (laughter)

Deane: Shifting now to another theme … the approach of the artist Marcel Duchamp appears to be a preoccupation, especially in your early work. What is the importance of Duchamp for you? And how do you see his work influencing your own?

Liz: He was a big influence and still is. Duchamp was one of those figures that didn't belong in any particular discipline or timeframe. His indeterminacy permeated everything—he was part mathematician, part artist, part woman, part man. He was very conscious and critical of the art establishment: the museum, the gallery, and the market yet he was a master of the system. He broke disciplinary boundaries between painting, sculpture and installation art, and redefined the terms of spectatorship. But maybe the most important aspect of his work was his parallel play of visual and textual languages. The work was so advanced, continues to have a strong resonance today.

Ric: I agree but for me the most important aspect of Duchampian thinking is the non-retinal. His process work and chance operations avoided aesthetic judgement, as least overtly. He invented the anti-aesthetic. It came out through his preoccupation with the ordinary, the re-contextualized, the twisted, and the assisted. We also absorbed the Duchampian notion to leave something definitively unfinished.

Liz: *A Delay in Glass* was a theater work on the occasion of the centennial of his birth sponsored by the Philadelphia Museum of Art that was loosely based on the *Large Glass*. But what we take from Duchamp is an interest in domesticity and the quotidian in general—things that are fascinatingly boring. Another influence was the early work of Chantal Ackerman.

Ric: There was a short story about a series of murders committed along a suburban block but nobody ever saw anything strange. It turned out that the murderer was the postman; no one ever sees the postman. I've always been fascinated by those things that are so familiar that we pay no attention to them, yet they deeply affect the way we behave. It has always been my impetus—to explore the invisible.

Deane: The point you raised about Duchamp, concerning the anti-aestheticization of the work is an interesting one. In earlier years you developed a quite specific formal vocabulary—particularly in the articulation of steel work common to a number of installations. How do you see the use of this vocabulary in relation to a privileging of content over form? How does this relationship play out in your work?

Liz: We had no romance with materials or construction though some people commented that we fetishized details. The high-modernist tactic was to make the pure detail, one that defied gravity, defied orientation, that neutralized material. We were interested in the potential expressiveness of architecture at the irreducible level of detail. The *Para-Site* project at MoMA is an extreme example because we took out our aggression toward the museum in a series of details between the hostile guest and the unsuspecting host. Our intervention didn't sit on a pedestal, it didn't hang from a wall as would be typical in a museum. It aggressively attached itself to the museum's surfaces and opportunistically took advantage of its systems—structural, electrical, etc. The Slow House on the other hand suppressed detail for form. Our work follows conceptual rather than formal tendencies.

Ric: Well, *Para-Site* was very literal—it clawed its way into walls and sucked onto glass surfaces. In its aggressive vocabulary, it was cartoony. Our detailing is less interested now in the expression of something that looks like what it does, than the expression of something that looks like what it shouldn't logically do.

Liz: Recently we've been challenged by observation that we were preoccupied with surface as in the Brasserie or Eyebeam. But for us the architectural language comes not out of formal proposition, it comes out of the site/situation. The Mott Street (Kopp) Townhouse façade, for instance, was prompted by a local law in Nolita which requires façades to be at least 50% masonry—suggesting punched windows. We found a way to meet the restriction with a floor-to-ceiling wall-to-wall curtain wall. In front of the glass wall we will suspend an operable screen made of glass brick units that conform to typical New York brick dimensions but are translucent.

Ric: The glass bricks are suspended in a staggered pattern that leaves 50% free area. When the glass brick panels are pulled open, they stack on each other, solids over voids, producing 50% solid masonry yet leaving a 50% free area.

Deane: Is this particular constraint being dictated to the city by the bricklayers union lobby?

Ric: No, it is a zoning regulation because of the historic identity of the area.

Liz: Well, we got what we wanted: a glass façade with a translucent operable privacy screen. The city got what it wanted: a façade made of units commensurate with the scale of the block.

Ric: Be careful. I had to convince the building department that in fact the details were exactly the same as for brick …

Liz: Except that instead of stacking the bricks, you drilled them and suspended them.

Deane: Would there be an early project (say pre-2000) that would stand as a manifesto for your preoccupations and interests in that period?

(pause)

I know it's a difficult question. (laughter)

Ric: The Slow House—which started construction but was never finished. That project brought together many important themes in our work: the changing nature of domesticity, a new intersection of leisure culture and work culture, the view as a cultural construct, and the inversion between authentic and mediated experience. We also put forth a theory about dismantling "high" and "low" distinctions between architecture and technologies. Even though construction was aborted after the foundations were poured and that it only lives on in print or exhibition, the realization of the Slow House was completed intellectually.

Liz: *A Delay in Glass* and later *Moving Target* were theater works that questioned our cultural desire for the real over the mediated and dissolved the difference. We wanted to change the terms of theater by productively confusing stage and screen and challenge the concept of liveness. Both pieces required the audience to toggle between three registers: live on stage, mediated by a mirror suspended at forty-five degrees above the stage, a pre-recorded projected imagery.

Ric: *Soft Sell* was a turning point in which our preoccupations accidentally intersected the general demography of New York—and it made us conscious of the notion of audience. A giant set of female lips was projected on the façade of an old porno theater on 42nd Street just before the district was sanitized by Disney. The lips recited improbable solicitations to the street. The general public responded—denizens of 42nd Street were used to talking back to screens, art goers appreciated the irony of seduction in the sale of empty promises. In the early days we didn't have a second thought about audience: we unconsciously attracted an art and academic following. And because demographically that audience was us, the projects were communicated using familiar and techniques. Things changed after *Soft Sell*. Blur, a bit later, learned that a successful work could have a broad appreciation without losing layers of complexity.

Deane: Both of you spent time in Italy, and you've also spent some time in Europe over the years. Did this influence your position? Could one say there is a European aspect to your work, or is it entirely American?

Liz: In these politically squalid times, I do all I can to disassociate myself with being American.

Ric: Liz spent time in Rome, I worked with Leonardo Ricci just outside Florence for over a year. Probably I was too full of myself and too young to really benefit from the experience. But I saw the city as an anti-tourist, in the cold of winter, when the piazzas were empty. You could wander the city and feel that you were back in 14th century Italy—the experience had a deep effect on me. I became attracted to the unseen, that which was outside of view.

Liz: But also you were interested in Modernist Italian architects as well right?

Ric: Yes Terragni and Nervi …

Liz: I spent some time at the American Academy in Rome. I was told before I left that I would learn more about America than I would about Italy. (laughter) It was true. The place was insular and full of scholars from the States engaged in esoteric research like watermarks on papal manuscripts of Pope Pious the … I learnt a lot about carbohydrates. I gained eighteen pounds. (laughter)

Ric: That's because the Academy had a menu of pasta and potatoes …

Liz: That's why I had to escape and spend time in the streets of Rome. It was enlightening to see the depth of architectural history yet there no developed contemporary art or architecture scene. Today, we claim we're part of a global culture—but it's not true. I just came back from Milan where we had a long discussion about the future of *Domus*. It's interesting to see how Italy resists concerns of the global in favor of its identity. Milanese culture is a phenomenon onto itself. Being a European—having moved to New York at an early age, and having lived in New York most of my life—I don't really think of myself as either European or American, but a kind of citizen of the world. These days, I crave Italy on a regular basis, like craving red meat from time to time. The culture of pleasure and low expectations about efficiency is a regular draw. (laughter)

Ric: But we're New Yorkers. I do think New York collects dissidents that can't live any place else … though I feel most at home in motion while travelling.

Deane: Would you say that your pre-occupations are not specifically local—that instead, you are addressing global phenomena?

Liz: Both. The differences are sometimes hard to make out. Global culture, connected through global economies and global ecologies, transcends national borders. And while we crave diversity, there is little left of it even if some cultures have to fabricate lost identities to re-establish tourism. One needs to look harder for the local.

"The American Mysteries," 1984

Performance in collaboration with Matthew Maguire, with Vito Ricci, Brian Eno, Clodagh Simonds, Glenn Branca and the Creation Production Company, La Mama ETC, New York

The *American Mysteries* weaves together two unrelated theatrical genres, the American detective thriller and the ancient Greek mystery. There are nine acts in nine sites: *the Writer's Room, the Detective's Office, the Office of the Mayor, the Powerhouse, the Meeting-place of the Underworld Boss, the Court Room, the Flame Club, the Boxing Ring, the Hall of Mysteries,* with nine characters: *the Mechanic, the Bodyguard, the Mayor, the Detective, the Underworld Boss, the Victim, the Waitress, the Assassin,* and *the Writer.* The set-apparatus, made up of counterweighted panels, hingeable at all sides, transforms into discrete configurations by the performers in the seamless transitions between acts. *D+S*

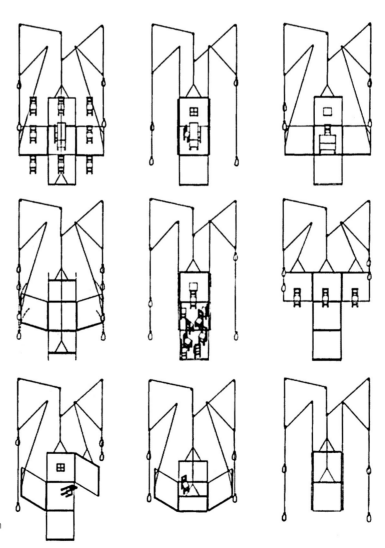

Drawing: nine stage set position

Introduction of *the Writer*

"The Memory Theatre of Giulio Camillo," 1986

Installation/performance in collaboration with Creation Production Company.
The Brooklyn Bridge Anchorage, New York

Giulio Camillo was a sixteenth-century architect/philosopher whose explorations of human memory led him to construct a "memory theater" which possessed magical powers: those who entered it would emerge with a memory of all the knowledge of the world. The labyrinthine paths of Camillo's mind are represented by the Anchorage vaults through which commedia dell'arte players guide the audience. The installation theatrically spears together three successive chambers of the Anchorage with two discrete structural units which approach one another but never meet. Exploring the aesthetics of danger, the installation produces a Janusian moment: a gap which is no longer here, but not yet there—a synapse that can only be bridged tentatively by the stride.
D+S

"The Memory Theatre of Giulio Camillo," 1986

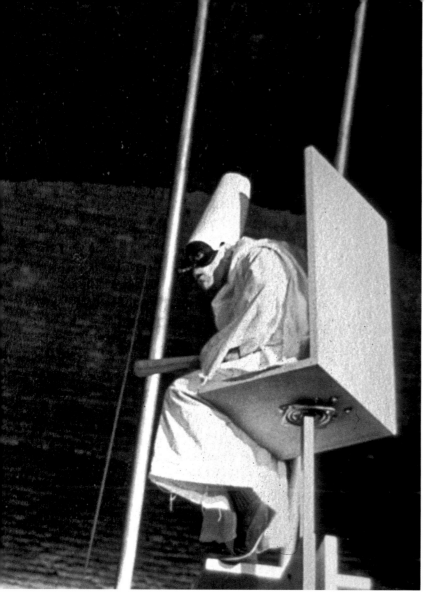

"The withDrawing Room," 1987

Installation, Capp St Project, San Francisco

A 100 year-old wood frame house renovated by sculptor David Ireland was the site for a speculation on "home." The irreducible domestic unit, the resident, intersects progressively specific conditions: *the property line*—a legal order, the resident is considered in relation to codes of privacy and publicity regarding the building envelope with its physical, optical and aural vulnerabilities… windows, doors, fences; *etiquette*—a social order, the resident is considered in relation to a set of performative conventions culturally agreed upon and enacted with a subculture… at the dinner table; *intimacy*—a private order, the resident is considered in relation to a set of codes mutually agreed upon with another body… in the bed; *the narcissistic impulse*—an internal order, the resident is considered as a maintenance project, regulated by the commodity-induced drive for uniqueness as well as conformity… the mirror.
D+S

  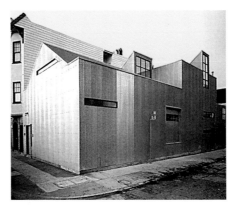 

Installation view from *Flesh*

Capp St exterior

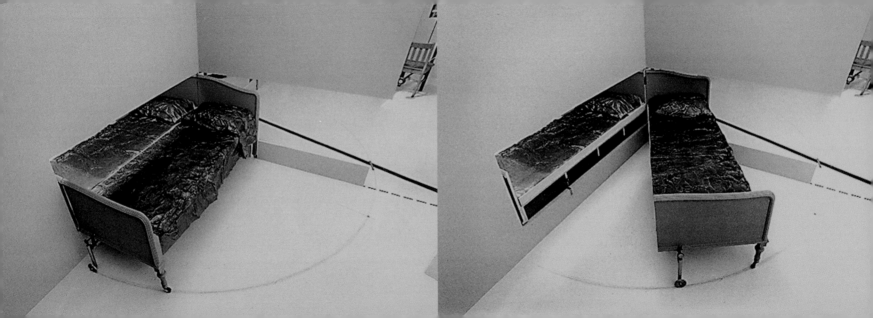

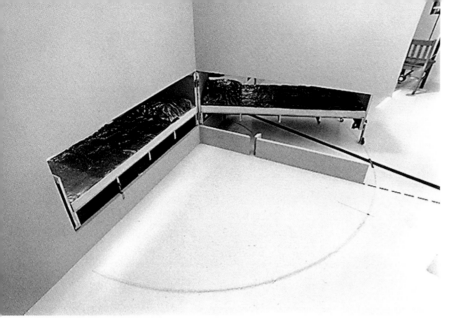

180° Bed. Occupants can adjoin body to body
or head to head

"The Rotary Notary and His Hot Plate (A Delay in Glass)," 1987

Performance in collaboration with Creation Production Company for Duchamp Centennial by the Philadelphia Museum of Art

The theater of illusion required a division, a proscenium: *pro* (in front of) + *scenium* (the scene). Based on Duchamp's *Large Glass*, the set/apparatus is an *interscenium*, bisecting the narrative space of the stage but reconciling it through artifice.

The apparatus has two constituent parts at the dividing line which separates Bride from Bachelor: an opaque panel suspended from a beam that rotates in and out of position, and a mirror suspended at 45 degrees over the rear of the stage. The concealing panel rotates 360 degrees on a pivot hinge.

A rotation of 180 degrees alternates the Bride and Bachelor domains relative to the audience; one character is always obscured but his/her image is revealed to the audience by the mirror.

The apparatus always permits the audience to see one character actually and the other virtually. The panels produce a spatial *prophylactic* and desiring mechanism, offering both temptation and denial.

Costumes

He is an automarionette, weight and counterweight. He is the tender of gravity, yet he is always out of equilibrium. He is the tender of levity, the master of irony. She is exoskeletal. Her anatomy is a hinge. She wears chastity armor with a modesty mechanism. She is well oiled.

D+S

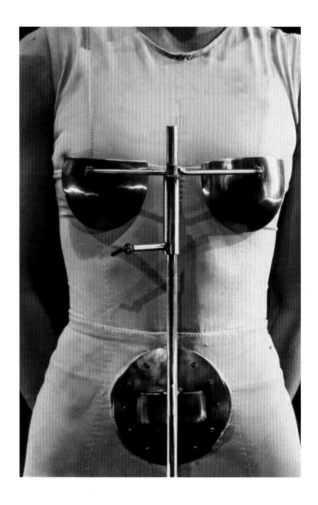

Detail, Bride armour

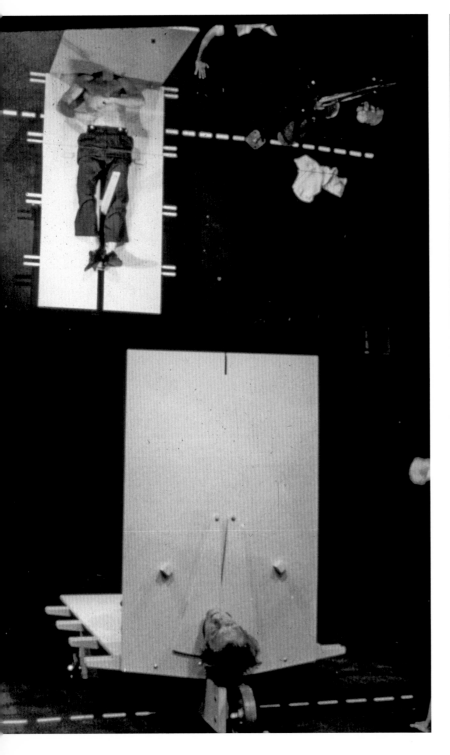

"Para-Site," 1989

Installation, Museum of Modern Art, Projects Series, New York

The installation integrates three definitions of parasite, according to Michel Serres: as the biological parasite is physically opportunistic, feeding off of its host organism, the installation steals its structural and electrical sustenance from its host site; as the social parasite entertains its host to earn welcome at the dinner table, the installation offers the entertainment value of voyeurism to a public unwittingly lured into an interrogation of vision itself; as the technological parasite creates interference in an information system, the installation interrupts the system of spectatorship in the museum to decode it. Three constructions, composed of physical and video components, exceed the designated gallery passively and aggressively into three remote sites of circulation in the museum. Within the gallery, the gazes of actual and fictional viewers, both self-conscious and unsuspecting, are reconfigured into new optical chains.
D+S

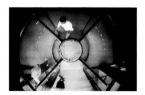

Camera view, entry

73

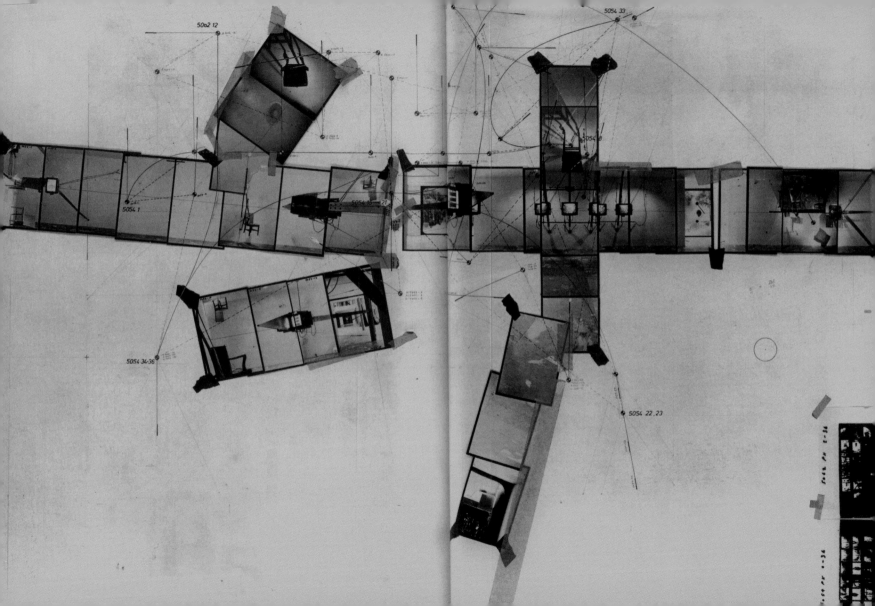

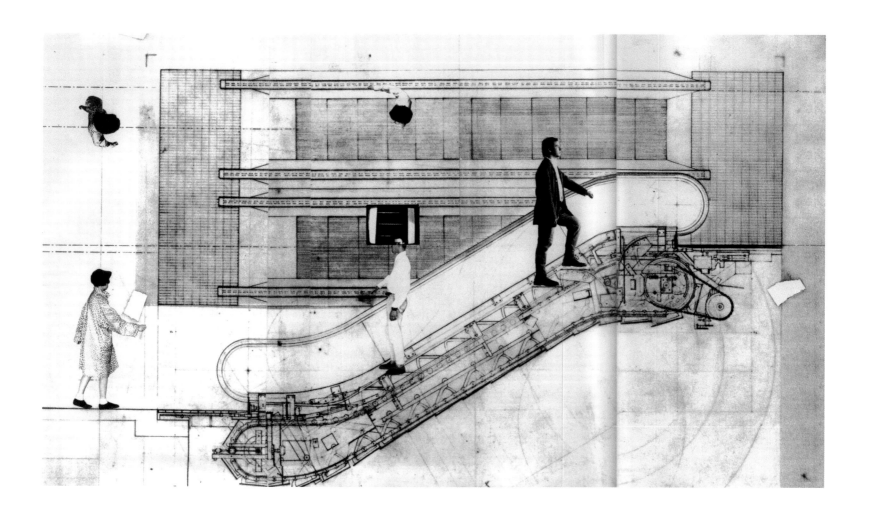

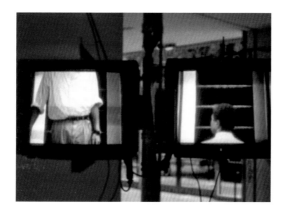

Installation, Walker Art Center, Minneapolis

Fifty identical Samsonite suitcases transport the *contents of the exhibition* and double as display cases for the *exhibition of their contents*. Each suitcase is a case-study of a particular tourist attraction in each of the fifty states in the US. Each case study critically analyzes the attraction into official and unofficial representations,

both images and texts and synthesizes them into new configurations. The project takes on national tourism, specifically travel to the past as a means to re-live national narratives. Only two types of sites are considered: famous *beds* and *battlefields*, two sites in which the subtlety of tourism's construction of *aura* most

strongly feeds the tourist's hunger for the *real*, no matter the artifice required to produce it. The installation takes on the play between *authenticity* and *authentication*.
D+S

Suitcase X-ray

Installation in travel-ready form

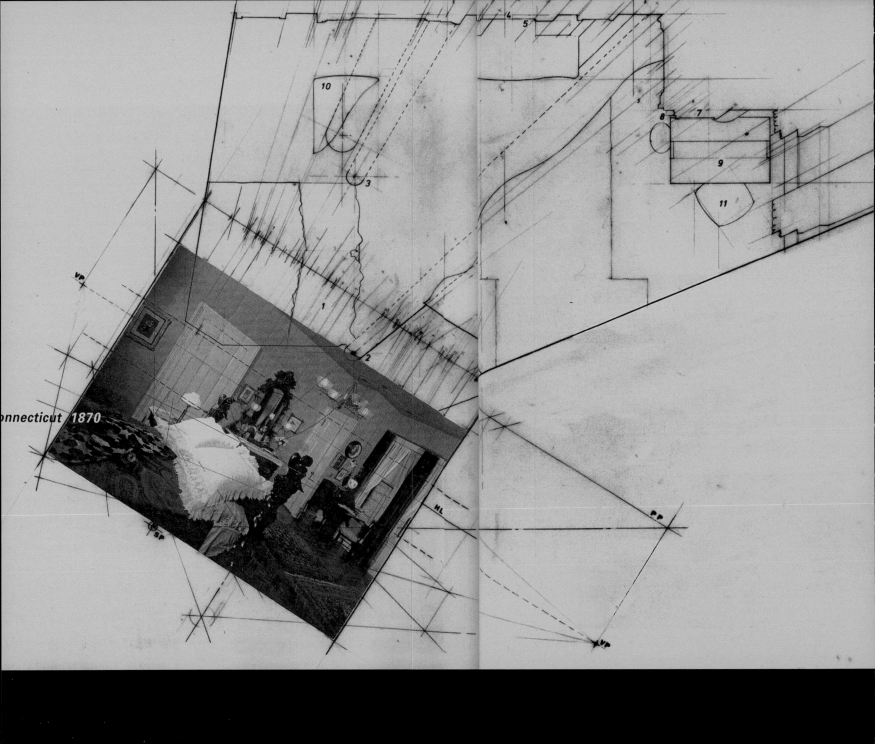

Connecticut 1870

Postcard front and back

opposite page
Postcard-plan drawing

Slow House, 1991

Vacation residence, North Haven, Long Island, New York

There is no front façade, only a front door. The house is simply a passage, a door that leads to a window; physical entry to optical departure. Beyond the door, a knife edge cuts the receding passage in plan and in section, always advancing toward the ocean view at the wide end. At the end of the 100' long passage, to either side of the picture window, are two antenna-like stacks. The chimney is to the right. At the summit of the left stack sits a live video camera directed at the water view which feeds a monitor in front of the picture window. The electronic view is operable. The camera can pan or zoom by remote control. When recorded, the view may be deferred: day played back at night, fair weather played back in foul. Nature is converted into a slow form of entertainment. In the living space, the composite view of the horizon, in two representational modes, will always be out of register.

D+S

X-ray section

Broken Horizon rendering

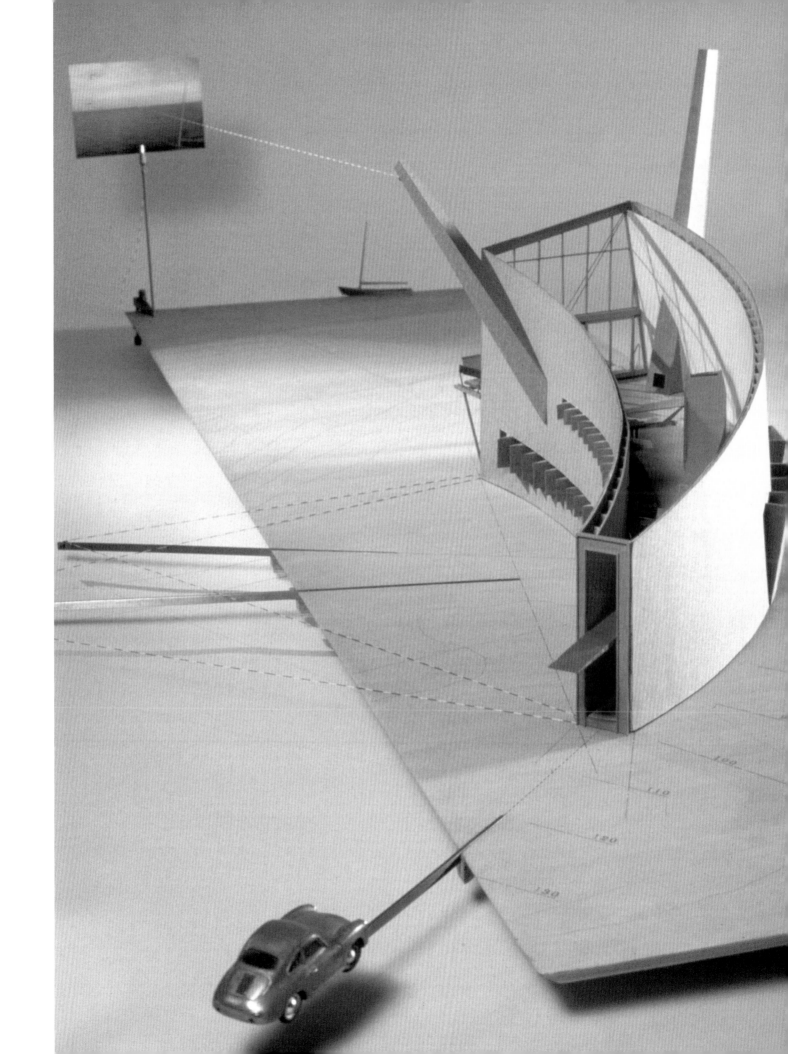

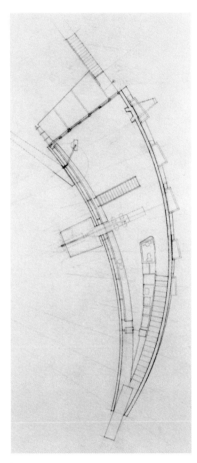

Lower level plan

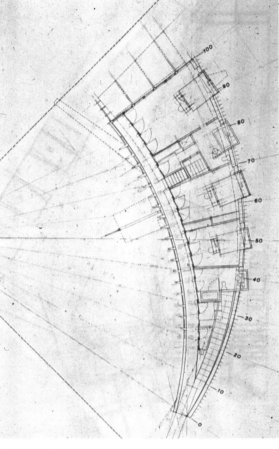

Upper level plan

Foundation, in progress

Woodblock model with X-rays

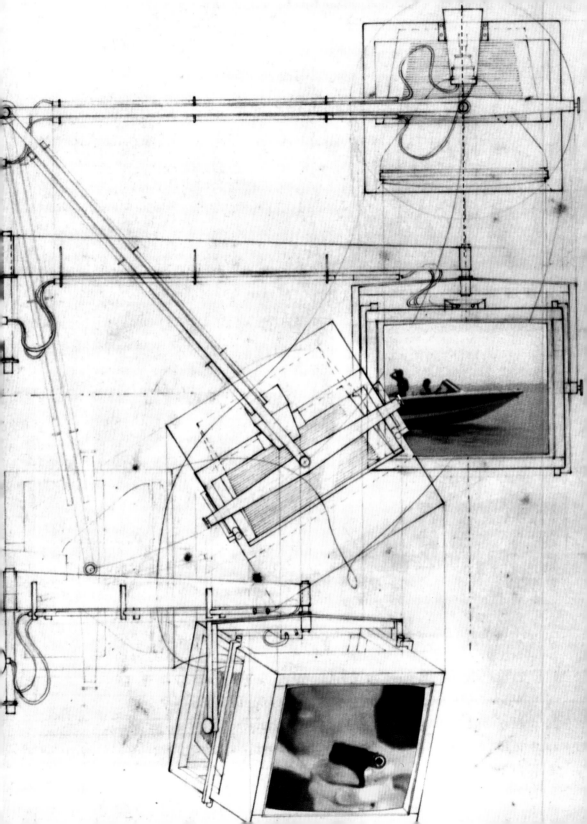

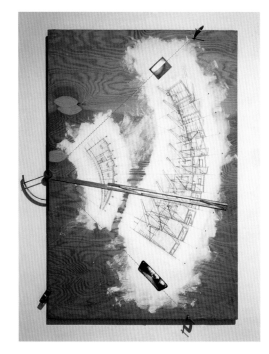

Plywood drawing

Flayed model

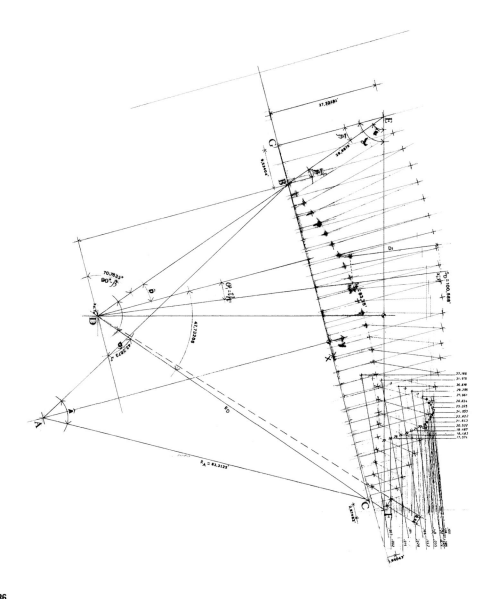

Geometry drawing

"Bad Press: Dissident Houseworks Series," 1993

Standardized boxed shirt

Bad Press examines ironing, a household task that is still guided by motion-economy principles designed by efficiency engineers at the turn of the century. In pressing a shirt a minimum of effort is used to reshape the shirt into a two-dimensional, repetitive unit which will consume a minimum of space. The standardized ironing pattern always "disciplines" the shirt into a flat, rectangular shape which fits economically into orthogonal systems of storage: the shipping carton, the display case, the dresser drawer or closet shelf, the suitcase.

When worn, the residue of the orthogonal logic of *efficiency* is registered on the surface of the body. The parallel creases and crisp, square corners of a clean, pressed shirt have become sought after emblems of refinement. But what if the task of ironing could free itself from the aesthetics of efficiency altogether? Perhaps the effects of ironing could more aptly represent the postindustrial body by trading the image of the *functional* for that of the *dysfunctional*.

Bad Press has been shown in a variety of installation formats including wall-mounted displays, hybrid ironing board-boutique table displays, shrink-wrapped and in boxes, etc. It is always accompanied by a video of a human mannequin on a small LCD monitor.

D+S

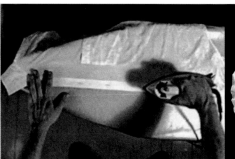

Standardized shirt on model (*center*)
Efficiency studies, 1950s (*right*)

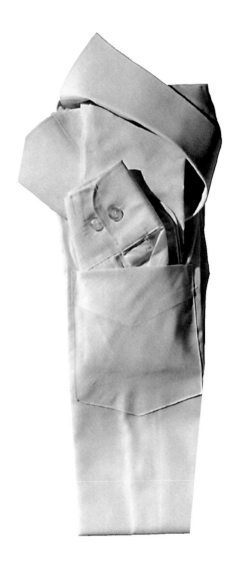
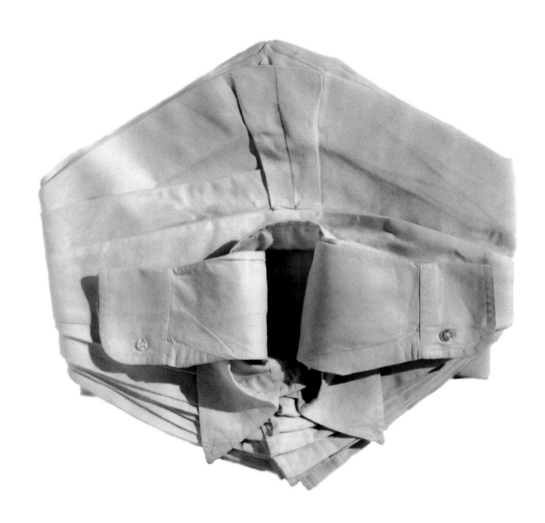

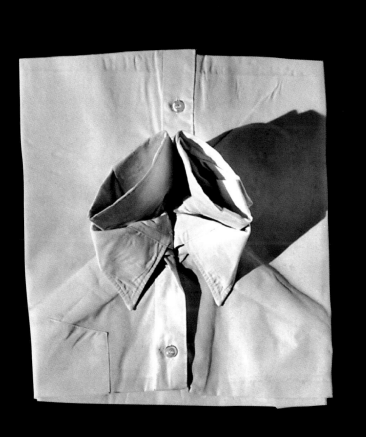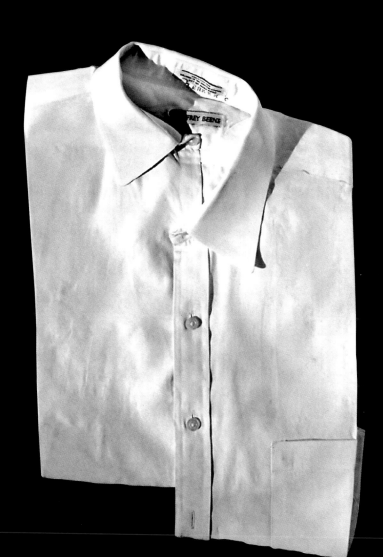

"Flesh: Architectural Probes," 1994

Princeton Architectural Press, publisher

A decade of D+S work is re-interpreted for the site-specific space of the book. The book itself is an object of inquiry: its organization, its play of textual and pictorial content, its registers of texts. The anthology of projects follows spatial conventions of the everyday and their relation to the body—as reflected in the wrap-around image of the cover. The book spine could only be legible at 1.5" thus the book was conceived from the spine outward. At the ideal paper stock, the dimension translated into 280 pages of content.
D+S

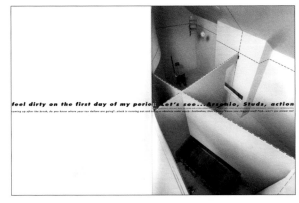

Selected spreads

PRINCETON ARCHITECTURAL PRESS

+ Scofidio

Flesh

Flesh

"Indigestion," 1995

Media installation, Banff Centre
for New Media, Canada

This interactive media installation, made in collaboration with the Banff Centre for New Media Research and Douglas Cooper (1995), intersects two electronically linked modes: an interactive video and a virtual environment. The video consists of a dining scene projected onto a horizontal screen/table that a viewer can join as a guest. An archetypal film noire narrative is played out between two characters of ambiguous relation at opposite sides of he table. A touch screen offers the viewer a choice of characters from a variety of gender and class stereotypes. The viewer can change dining partners mid-stream and, while the narratives remains continuous, it is nuanced by each new character. The narratives remain continuous, however, nuanced by differences in character. In an adjacent space, a participant using a Polhemus motion-sensing device can navigate in real time through the computer-generated, magnified space of the same dinner table. The image is split onto two large screens on opposite sides of the room for 3-D viewing. The mobile and magnified viewpoint across this mega-landscape reveals a micro-drama played out in the details. The two technologies work in tandem to produce multi-layered information. Choice is offered to lure the subject into an interrogation of the democratic aspirations of interactive technologies and to critique reductive binaries such as masculine/feminine, high class/low class, fact/fiction, and real/virtual.
D+S

Hi/Lo meals

Interface icons

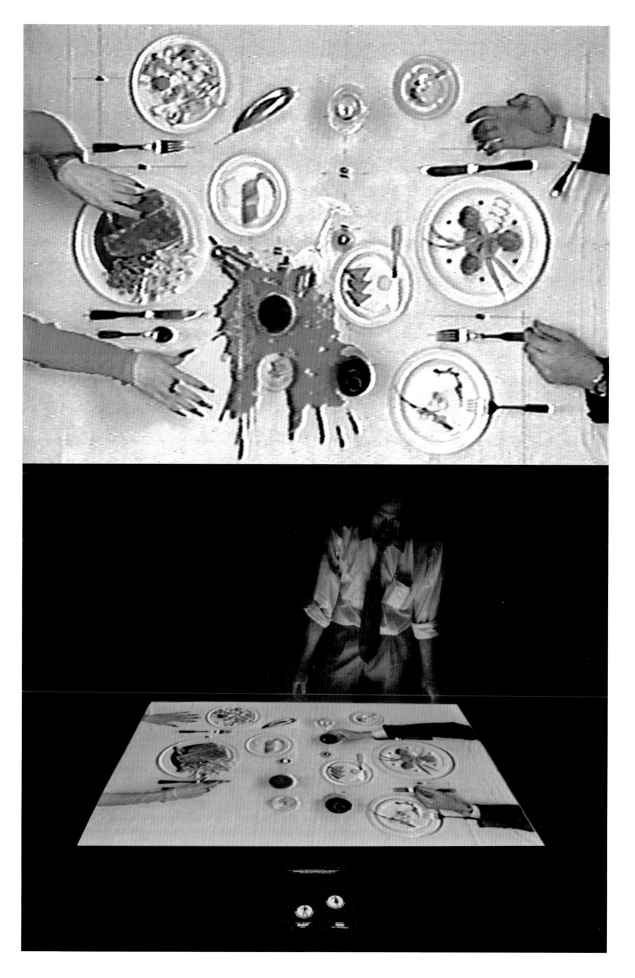

"Jump Cuts," 1995

Permanent marquee installation, United Artists Cineplex Theater, San José, California. In collaboration with Ben Rubin

A steel armature appended to the theater's glass façade supports a series of liquid crystal panels over the street. Correspondingly at the interior, one projector stationed before each of the twelve panels is fed by a string of live cameras positioned along the multiple levels of escalators in the grand lobby, either looking down in plan or across in elevation. The mechanical movement of the escalators past the stationary cameras supplies a succession of bodies on parade. As patrons zig-zag through the lobby on the moving stairs, they are electronically reconfigured to appear as if traveling across the façade. The continuous video stream of bodies is interrupted only by movie trailers.

Re-interpreting the function of the traditional theater marquee, the apparatus of *Jump Cuts* informs the passersby of events within by flipping the building inside-out, electronically. Candid views of moviegoers milling through the lobby are given equal status with more established forms of entertainment. Drawing inspiration from the tradition of grand social ante-spaces like the Paris Opera in which circulation area exceeds theater area by 5:1, the installation re-frames the question, on which side of the theater wall is the spectacle?

D+S

Live and recorded feeds

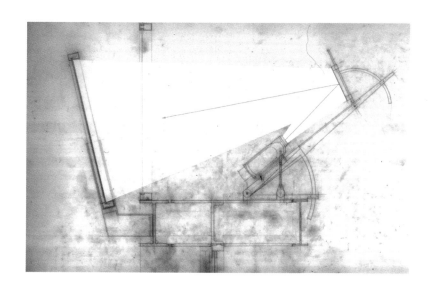

Section drawing at projector and screen

"Moving Target," 1996

Multi-media dance work in collaboration with Charleroi/Danses, Belgium

Loosely based on the recent publication of Nijinsky's uncensored diaries, *Moving Target* reinterprets the changing definitions of the "normal" and the "pathological" as well as processes of normalization.

The forty-five-degree mirror/projection screen over the stage (expanding the functionality of the mirror in *Delay in Glass*) splinters the gaze of the audience and allows for a plan view of the stage in which dance patterns and structures are more clearly visible. When combined with a video projection, the mirror synthesizes dancers into video space.

Live and pre-recorded dancers can enjoy two types of hypervirtuosity: live dancers are freed from the confines of gravity as the mirror reorients everything by ninety degrees; the pre-recorded dancers are freed from the confines of bodily physics as their actions are produced through morphing technologies. In addition, an optical tracking system follows pre-determined stimuli and draws real-time figures that are projected onto the mirror.

Spots:

Rather than the traditional division of the dance work into acts or scenes, the ninety minute dance work is interrupted periodically by commercial spots for "Normal," a faux pharmaceutical company which treats the pathologies of a post-psychoanalytic culture.
D+S

Duet for actual and virtual dancers

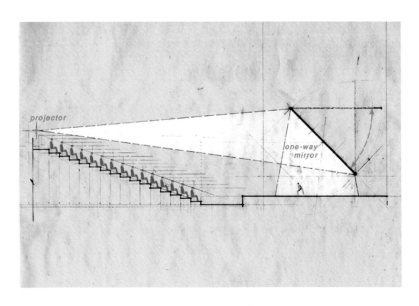

Section drawing

opposite page
Live computer tracking (*top*)
Spots, stills (*bottom*)

"Vice/Virtue Glasses," 1997

Water glasses for a post-modern culture
the *Dispensary*, the *Fountain*, the *Exhaust*,
the *Reservoir*.
The water glass series accommodates
the dual pursuits of health and hedonism
characteristic to contemporary culture.
Each glass serves one addiction.
D+S

Exhaust, Reservoir, Dispensary, Fountain

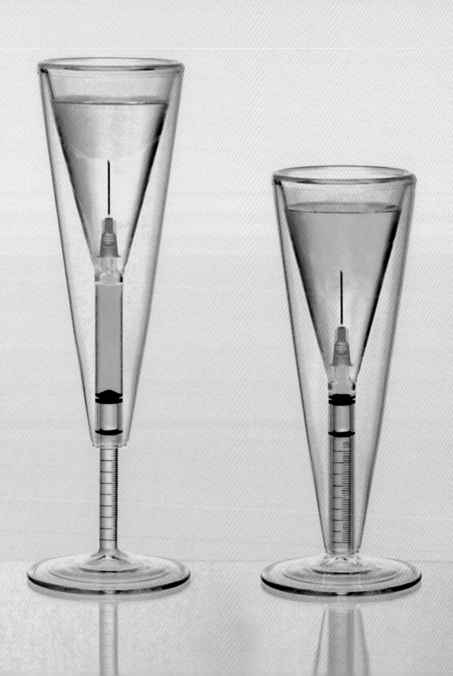

"Jet Lag," 1998

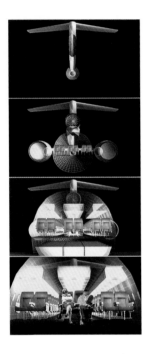

Multi-media theater work. In collaboration with The Builders Association and Jessica Chalmers

Stage action intersects live and recorded video in the presentation of two narratives:

1. In his famous interview, *The Third Window*, Paul Virilio tells the story of Sarah Krasnoff, the American grandmother, who in a period of six months flew across the Atlantic 167 times with her young grandson in an attempt to elude the pursuit of the child's father and psychiatrist. They traveled New York/Amsterdam, Amsterdam/New York, never leaving the plane or airport lounge except for the brief stop at the airport hotel. Krassnoff finally died of jet lag. In the words of Virilio, this contemporary heroine lived in "deferred time."

2. In 1969 a British eccentric named Donald Crowhurst joined the round-the-world solo yacht race sponsored by the *Sunday Times* of London. Ill-prepared but driven by the guaranteed publicity of the event, Crowhurst loaded up the film equipment provided to him by the BBC to record his journey and set sail. Within several weeks, Crowhurst encountered heavy seas in the South Atlantic. He drifted in circles on the open sea for the remainder of the race. Haunted by the specter of failure, Crowhurst broadcast false radio positions, produced a counterfeit log and documented a "successful" voyage on film. As he re-joined the race in the last leg, the fear of social humiliation finally led the troubled sailor to take his life by drowning. Crowhurst ultimately disappeared into his "deferred space."

On stage, Crowhurst appears in front of his live video camera. Just behind him is a small video backdrop of a seascape. The projector/screen assembly rocks mechanically to simulate the roll of the ocean. As Crowhurst speaks to the camera, his live image is projected onto the giant screen behind him. The audience witnesses him and his image as he produces his auto-documentary. He rewinds, makes new takes until he gets it just right.

Krasnoff appears with her grandson in the ubiquitous spaces of travel—always in surveillance videos of airport waiting lounges, sterile corridors, passport control stations, security checkpoints. On stage, the two live performers are lodged halfway between stage space and virtual backdrops, halfway between past and present.

Both true stories feature characters severed from conventions of time and space. Krassnoff is subjected to the ubiquitous, non-stop space of travel, while she produces a virtual home for her grandson in a succession of airport hotel rooms; Crowhurst simulates travel while floating in perpetual limbo. In a play of gender stereotypes, the female reproduces a static, domestic space in constant motion, while the male fictionalizes motion frozen in space, confined by the trappings of masculinity and the bravado of movement.

D+S

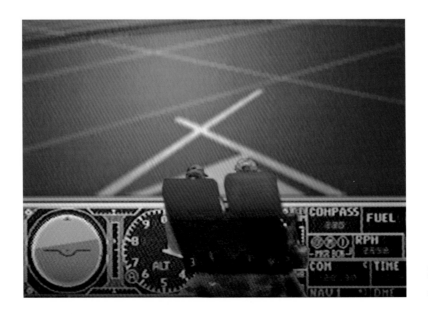

opposite page
Video stills. Introduction of Krasnoff and Grandson

CDG
23.8

"The American Lawn: Surface of Everyday Life," 1998

Co-curation, design of exhibition, Canadian Center for Architecture, Montreal

The multi-media exhibition juxtaposes historical and contemporary materials, both artistic and scientific, from high and low culture, to play out a limited set of themes about that simple platform of grass: the *American Lawn* is at once a benign, perfectly controlled, tranquil surface, and a sinister surface of repressed horror; the lawn is anything but natural—it is an engineered product subjected to laws of industry and genetic science. In federal and institutional landscape architecture the lawn is used to symbolize collective solidarity. In corporate culture it is used to represent power and control in domestic landscape. The lawn is a strategic battleground between the collective image of democracy and the property rights of the individual. *D+S*

Artificial turf samples, underside and top views

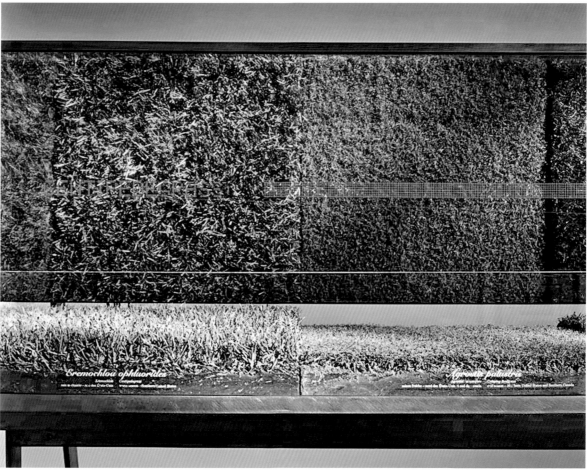

PROSECUTION
Kenney was convicted of violating
the Municipal Code.

DEFENSE
Kenney appealed his conviction on three
grounds. First, he argued that the Code
was unconstitutionally vague. The Code
demanded that homeowners' conform to
the desirable residential character of
his property without defining the
meaning of 'desirable.' The Village
explained that the alleged vagueness
simply reflected the fact that
community norms were perpetually in a
state of flux, thus requiring a

Stereoscopic images, lawn borders.
Photographs in collaboration with
Robert Sansone

Infrared aerial photographs of
American suburbs

Installation view, turf shoes

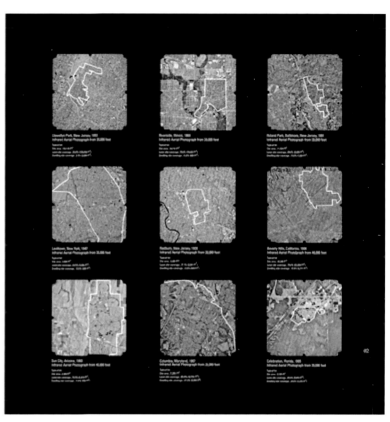

111

"Master/Slave," 1999

Installation, toy robot collection of Rolf Fehlbaum, Fondation Cartier pour l'art contemporain, Paris

In the modernist imagination, the robot served as a surrogate body that could perform menial tasks and leave man free for more important activities. This utopian fantasy turns dystopian in popular films when the robot acquires enough artificial intelligence to invert the master/slave relationship.

Rolf Fehlbaum's collection of toy robots inhabits a giant vitrine, not unlike the large glazed space of the Cartier Foundation gallery in which the display sits.

The 33' x 33' x 18"-high robot space is elevated to eye level on a grid of columns. The vitrine regulates the terms of viewing: it traps spectators between itself and the glass envelope of the gallery. It turns spectators into inspectors by keeping everyone distant enough to render the best views through imaging devices. The colony of robots parades on a 300-foot long conveyor system typically used for pharmaceutical production. The travel route, which is modeled on an unemployment office, forces the robots to line up in areas and releases them arbitrarily to engage in events. Along the parade route, the only labor the robots are expected to perform is to pose before live cameras, identify themselves, avail themselves to the scrutiny of medical devices (an airport scanner is at the base of the down ramp), and tolerate the invasive presence of the surveillance system.

D+S

Installation detail, surveillance monitor

Surveillance stillss

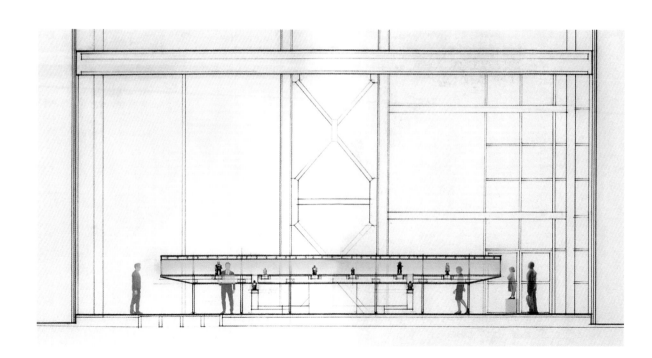

113

Robot X-ray

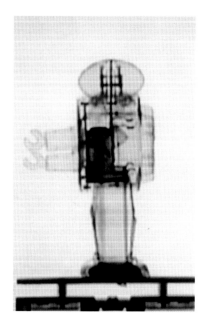 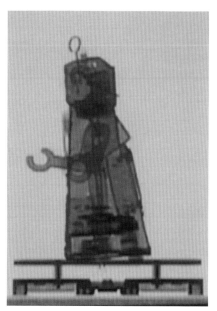

115

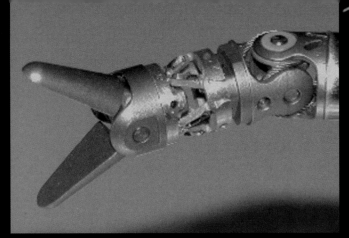

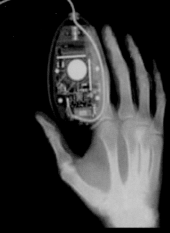

Studio iconography (2)

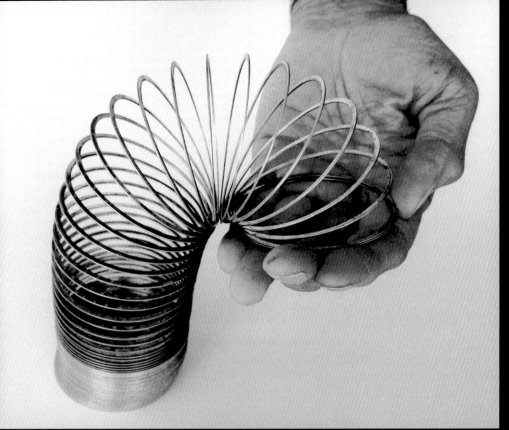
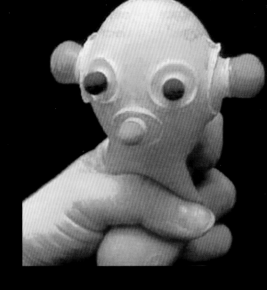

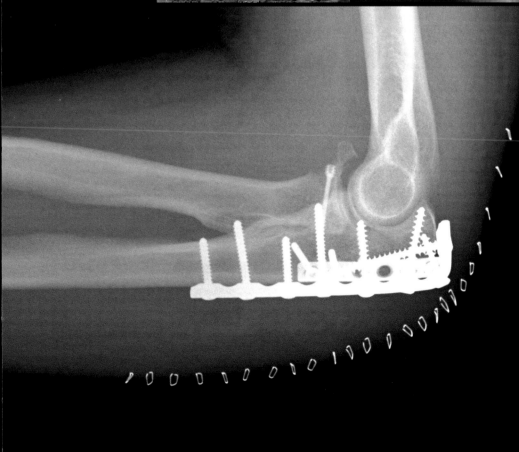

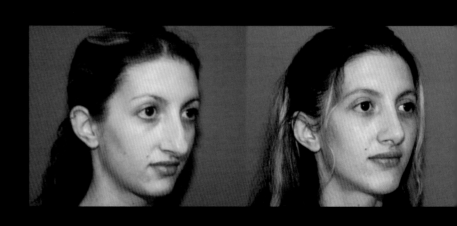

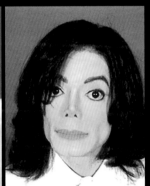

Bill Clinton's Legacy (First Draft)
By Jacob Weisberg

the hotel rooms and the airports
are the things I'll forget

Date: July 30th, 2006
Location: Cooper Square, New York City
Present: Elizabeth Diller, Ricardo Scofidio, Charles Renfro, Deane Simpson
(Questions formulated by Guido Incerti, Daria Ricchi, Deane Simpson)

Deane: So today we are going to focus more on the later work of the studio …

In recent years your work is being realized at an increasing scale. There appears to be a growing predominance of architectural and urban projects over installations and media projects. Does this represent a break or shift in the approach to, or thinking behind your work? Or is there something like a "red line" which binds all of your projects together over the years?

Liz: We've heard many remarks about the abrupt "transition in our work," from art to architecture … It seems that some of our followers feel a sense of betrayal—that we've "sold out." This reflects less on us and more on an orthodoxy hardened at the fringe that only computes old-fashioned ideas about avant-gardism and margin-

ality. There has been a smooth evolution of our work—independent projects have prompted professional ones. For example, Isozaki saw Bad Press exhibited at Gallery Ma and asked us to do social housing in Gifu. The interactive *Indigestion* installation led to the Brasserie. But the smaller projects have never stopped. Right now, we're collaborating with Mira Nair on an installation of mini-movies in Lille on xenophobia following the riots in suburban France. We're doing a performance piece with The Wooster Group at MoMA in concert with the Dada exhibition. We're building an installation in a volcanic crater in Lanzarote. Rather than transitioning from small to large work, we're just adding more trajectories to the work. All of it is bound by ongoing research.

Charles: When we present ourselves to new clients, we always start with the juxtaposition of a *Vice/Virtue* glasse and the BAM Masterplan, suggesting that there is a content link between any scale of work in the studio.

Ric: We now have opportunities to do architecture for a broader audience and bigger budgets but the content is largely the same. It's a bit like Eames's *The Powers of Ten* … there's as much complexity in a small work as a large one.

Deane: What is that content link?

Liz: It's a methodological link. The work is bound by a critical engagement with contemporary culture.

Charles: Part of the underlying issue is that all of a sudden people are seeing our buildings and saying they look a lot like buildings, conventional in a sense. As with the ICA—you have to venture more deeply into the project to encounter the investigations that we've been known for in our smaller scale work. It may look like a building, but it could be seen as a permanent and useful installation.

Ric: I disagree with the word "conventional." I don't think anything we've done is conventional.

Charles: Well, we are in an ongoing dialogue with *conventions* of space, of structure, of circulation, of domesticity, of the institution …

Liz: We are defined by a particular in-between-ness. There's no discrepancy as far as I'm concerned. Rather than characterizing our work as art or architecture, we prefer to define two more pertinent categories: moneymaking projects and money losing projects.

Deane: What's the current breakdown? (laughter)

Liz: Money-losing is definitely winning. We have a money-losing department in the studio with its own department head. (laughter)

Deane: Over the last decade your studio has also undergone considerable changes—you now have over forty employees compared to three or four in the mid-1990s, and also Charles has become a partner. How has the method of working altered between when you first started, and now? How does the studio work differently now?

Liz: I would say …

Deane: It doesn't work? (laughter)

Charles: That's what I was going to say. (laughter)

Liz: … efficiently. It doesn't work efficiently. We're not pyramidal with a strongly defined hierarchy as you would find in offices. We have something between an atelier and a democratic structure. Everyone's voice is heard though it's become a bit more chaotic because there are more and more voices. The growth equation turns out to be more work requires more people which breeds more anxiety at a slower speed. I think that's probably the change—we were once faster and more fluid and now we're multi-tasking in a slower gear.

Charles: Even though we talk about a levelling of hierarchy, the three of us still provoke the issues and make the ultimate decisions. It's a hybrid studio that thrives on research and experimentation within a formless structure regulated by schedules and budgets.

Ric: When the studio was just Liz and myself, work and home were seamless. The more people that joined the studio, the more the notion of "home" emerged.

Charles: I loved it when I first started working here—you'd have to knock on the door … (laughter) at nine o'clock—"It's you?" "Are you ready yet?" "Oh, no no. Go get a coffee—come back in five." (laughter)

Liz: A problem developed as we grew. There were more people and more charrettes on more projects, and charrettes on different projects increasingly became back-to-back. Gradually, Ric and I were going to bed at three every morning. Each team had a chance to recover but Ric and I never could. That's why we had some embarrassing moments in the mornings.

Ric: We sometimes checked into a hotel.

Liz: There was a last straw that ultimately drove us out of our live/work studio. The Fed Ex guy asked to use the bathroom. I realized that our private bathroom that I had self-consciously shared with ten staff members had suddenly gone public. (laughter) It's true.

Deane: The Blur Building seems to have been a very important project in the studio. Would you agree that the Blur Building represented a moment in which a number of your theoretical preoccupations coincided?

Liz: Our interest in tourism intersected our interest in responsive technologies as well as our interest in breaking down the nature/culture dualism. Blur allowed us for the first time to work on an environmental scale … to make a mass spectacle. We made weather!

Ric: It was our first grand fusion of art and architecture. "Blur" was an apt name.

Charles: A lot of the tedious concerns of architecture such as liability, program resolution, waterproofing, and longevity gave way to the production of a special effect. But we encountered problems with the Swiss building department that could not determine whether it was a building or an artwork and ultimately required that we install a sprinkler system. We had to convince them it was already the world's largest sprinkler system!

Ric: We had to demonstrate with data that the fog nozzles produced more water than a sprinkler system, by a large margin. Also, there was nothing combustible.

Liz: The building is nothing but structure and plumbing. (laughter)

Charles: Right, and space.

Ric: More like a habitable medium.

Deane: I want to pick up on a point that you made earlier—the question of audience. In the case of Blur what seems interesting is that it was a project that addressed both a specific art audience at the same time as being a highly popularist and publicly exposed project.

Liz: It was the next manifestation of our preoccupation with the culture of vision. Blur was an exhibition building with nothing to see and nothing to do—but reflect on our dependence on vision as the master sense. The contextlessness environment made of white noise was equally disorienting and meaningless to everyone, independent of age, race, or class. It touched a broad public.

Charles: We were not operating in an art-historical vacuum. Blur evolved from ideas that had been established in site-specific minimalist art. It merged large-scale environmental art with responsive media.

Ric: We set out to subvert the conventions of "Expo" architecture, to challenge the Expo pavilion as a tool of national self-representation. We also wanted to question the a-critical marriage of technology and progress. Judging from recent Expos and World's Fairs, especially Hanover, new media and high definition simulation technologies had become established, even expected—they had become the new orthodoxy. Expos reflected the public hunger for fidelity and more pixels per inch. Blur was decidedly low definition … yet it was smart.

Charles: Blur had an artificial intelligence that learned to perform within a set of aesthetic parameters. It was trained on actual weather events. After some weeks, it was able to think for itself and respond in real time to the vagaries of the weather.

Ric: The electronics were easier than the plumbing. When we first imagined Blur hovering over Lake Neuchâtel, we never understood the complexity of a building made of lake water. We realized we had jumped out of an airplane without a parachute. How do we make artificial weather within actual weather? There are no cloud consultants to ask so we had to face the extreme pragmatics of water collection, filtration, and distribution. We learned more than you would ever care to know about phytoplankton, the micro-organisms that live in water environments and constitute a large part of the earth's mass. As the atomized lake water was to be inhaled, it had to be purified beyond the standards of drinking water. Lungs can't fight bacteria like the intestines. If the water was not perfectly filtered, we could make an entire population sick.

Charles: With Legionnaire's Disease.

Ric: Yes. After the system was installed, we wanted to run it for several months so that emerging problems could be debugged. But because we did not get the sign-off on the water safety from the municipal health authorities, we had to run it on municipal water. There were times when the town could not flush toilets because of our consumption. We got our permit at the last possible minute on opening day, thus nobody really knew if it would work.

Deane: You had your bags packed ready to go to Brazil.

Ric: (laughter) Nowhere on earth was far enough. There was a good chance that it wouldn't work. I can remember with trepidation arriving on the morning of the opening. The contractor had turned the system on at sunrise. Monitors had arrived and were being trained. We saw the mist from far away and I could hear giddy laughter and screams from the distance. I then realized we would be touching a new sector of the population.

Charles: It was undeniably fun and sensory and that's how it engaged such diverse groups—kids and grandmas and people from different cultural backgrounds.

Liz: … as well as the art-going public and academia. We had read partial translations of *Theory of the Cloud* by the French art theorist, Hubert Damisch. In it he discusses the amorphous dynamic of the cloud against the linear order of perspective in Renaissance and Baroque painting. The book made an impact on the project. It was such a thrill to have Damisch visit Blur. We led him inside and promptly lost him. He reappeared sometime later, disoriented, full of childlike glee and a bit moist. We discussed the perceptual shifts in the fog over dinner and we've been friends ever since.

Charles: Blur was wildly popular. But it didn't start as a love fest with the Swiss. At first, they ridiculed the notion of spending $15 million to make a building of fog—fog is considered an undesirable by product of Swiss climate and in great natural supply. But in the end, we broke down their resistance. They realized how magical the man-made version could be.

Liz: In the end, they loved it so much they appropriated Blur as a national icon representing "the Swiss doubt." Blur was on postage stamps, lottery tickets, sugar packets, kirshwasser bottles, and umbrellas. They even made a Blur chocolate bar—surely the highest honor to be bestowed on an architect by the Swiss.

Ric: Like many of our earlier projects, it was ephemeral. After some attempts by the locals to preserve Blur after Expo and turn it into a science fiction museum, they mercifully blew it up and resold the steel to China.

Deane: A large proportion of your work deals with the museum, either as an installer of work within the institution, or as the designer of the building itself. How would you characterize the relationship of your work to the museum—particularly in light of your recently completed Boston ICA?

Liz: For most of our career, we came to know the museum from the artist's side of the wall. The ICA made us learn the museum from the institution's side. Ric and I came up through the era of the institutional critique in which the museum's power to create and regulate value was constantly challenged. The decision to work on site-specific projects outside the museum's walls was a critique in itself. When we accepted an invitation from MoMA to do a new installation in the Projects Series, we did so with great self-consciousness about the role of guest to host. Also, with great scrutiny about the mechanisms of the museum—the threshold between the museum and the street, the curatorial text, the holdings of the museum, its history, its board, its walls, even the whiteness of its walls. In our Whitney retrospective, we were guests playing the role of both host and guest. In the ICA, we became the inadvertent hosts. In whose voice would we speak? The ICA is a progressive place, very civic minded; it had asked us to represent them, to speak for them. Did the critique still matter? Was our voice to be a-critical or post-critical?

Ric: I don't agree. It's not about opposing sides of the wall. It's about its thicknesses and surfaces and the complex codes of the wall. We are always exploring how much of our voice has to proceed or recede. Eyebeam was an exercise in the fine line between restraint and assertive expression. In the best interest of the institution, we did not encumber it with technologies. The interior was undetermined, ready to be filled with the work of others. The signature was left to outside identity.

Charles: We reject architecture as a service-oriented profession as much as we reject the unrestrained voice of the star architect. We strive toward a self-awareness of the building in which the audience understands itself as audience and the difference between art and the building. Art and building are not competing. That is a reductive notion.

Deane: What would be an example of that in relation to the reception of the artwork in the museum? What would be a "moment" in either the ICA or another project?

Charles: The mediatheque in the ICA, for example, is an experience produced by the strong will of the architect but without signature. The view is defamiliarized. Identity is unimportant.

Ric: The building *looks* at *looking*, the primary activity in the museum. We feed off of the increased awareness that people already have in the galleries and extend it to the building itself.

Deane: Three projects that you're currently working on—the Lincoln Center, Tivoli Gardens, and the High Line engage in a scale that you haven't dealt with previously. Have the approaches to themes in the smaller scale work translated into an approach to the urban scale? Or put it another way, are you developing your own attitude about urbanism, or is it simply an extension of the smaller scale work?

Liz: Scale is not the issue, it's disciplinary boundaries. Lincoln Center and High Line require the breaking down of areas of expertise such as urbanism, architecture, landscape, media design and information design. Many scales operate at once.

Ric: I don't believe in the distinction between urban scale and architectural scale. The more meaningful distinction is between public and private space—hardened definitions that need re-examination.

Charles: There's a molecular quality in our work that connects at all scales and puts into relief the interface between the individual and the public. Like with BAM, we were interested in the way a theater audience and a citizen in the street could interface across a property divide. Lincoln Center is all about eroding the plinth that cuts civic space off from the rarefied domain of the arts.

Liz: High Line is a 1.5 mile figure-ground conundrum: at once an obsolete piece of once vibrant urban infrastructure that deteriorated into a rusting hulk slated for demolition and a newly prized historic artefact and vertebrae for new development that's driving property values to sky-rocket. It's made us consider the fluctuating distinctions between nature and culture. Why would the notion of urban ecologies and economies be any less "natural" than the micro-ecologies of flora and fauna that have thrived in the man-made environment on an elevated rail bed coursing through buildings?

Deane: You were involved to some extent in the aftermath of the events of September 11th, 2001 with the initiation and design of the temporary viewing platform at the former World Trade Center site. This was a quite different act to that of many architects involved in the later competition phases. Could this be understood as a form of activism?

Liz: It was an act of civic duty. We set out to cure a physical dilemma: crowds that were drawn to the site got in the way of the clean-up effort. There was a pathological need to see.

Ric: It was a kind of phantom limb complex where you could not accept the loss. You could feel the towers even though they were not there. Rather than proclaiming the towers had to be replaced with even bigger towers as did many of our colleagues, we just asked, "what could we do to help?" We worked with several collaborators to design the platforms; we put together a foundation, raised money, and found a builder that was willing to get started on a handshake. The city was destabilized and because of the chaos, all of the legalities and procedures of building in NY were abandoned. We did it partially under city radar or, more precisely, the city bureaucracy did not try to intervene.

Charles: They prevented us from building five viewing platforms as we set out to do. With only one, there were lines around the block. People waited for hours. So the City required the public to get tickets and observe a time limit. If we had several—one at each severed street as we had planned—visitors would have been better distributed.

Deane: It seems to be attached to an agenda around the question of vision. That vision in this situation was important, from your point of view to support a connection to what was going on at the site.

Liz: This was a particular type of vision. People were compelled to look. You'd rather not look, but you had to. But it was neither a touristic look nor a morbid desire to see wreckage and death. It was a primal need to bear witness, to verify the unthinkable.

Charles: Our mandate was to make a dignified place of reflection. It was a therapeutic architecture.

Ric: We found ourselves divorced from the architectural community. Most architects considered the site an urban *tabula rasa* for a new start, detached from its political and cultural memory. We thought it was important to have a discussion among the best thinkers in the world, to speculate on a progressive new program that would preserve the history of the site. But, we're in a city ruled by the real estate market and the new void represented financial values over cultural ones.

Deane: In recent years, your work has been appropriated by certain figures to stand for a position that has been defined as critical, in opposition to one defined as post-critical. What is your opinion on this debate and how do you see your current work in relation to it?

Liz: Ah! (laughter). I find the whole debate rather silly. Academia needs a new theory or "-ism" from time to time even though there may not be a good new idea to go with it. I've asked the proponents the question, what makes the *post-critical* any different from the *pre-critical* and I've still not gotten a response. The so-called debate is reductive and assumes that criticality and generative thought are mutually exclusive. That couldn't be more false. What has changed is people who were engaged in critical theory, a decade ago they had no means to act now have the power and means to incorporate critical thinking into generative work.

Deane: I had to ask you that. (laughter)

Ric: Yeah. (laughter) Exactly. I've seen the shift of theories over the years like flavors of the month and have to wonder, has any of this affected building? You look at the buildings that you've been touched by and see them as works by individual thinkers unadulterated by academic arguments.

Liz: No, I don't agree with you. There has been a succession of ideologies in architecture that have produced particular strains of work. We cannot claim to be individual artists acting alone in an ideologically-free context. Globalization, mono-culturalism, environmental change, technological change, and social change—all prompt responses, however unconscious. So, yes, of course there are independent brains working on independent agendas, but it's impossible to think of architecture as an autonomous discipline.

Ric: I'm not saying architecture should be autonomous … it's just the individual motor that drives change … I have a concern that today's radical idea becomes tomorrow's orthodoxy. So I tend to keep a distance from the next new thing.

Liz: There's an interesting slippage between the discipline of architecture and other disciplines. Because of mobility in academia, thinkers from multiple disciplines in critical theory entered architecture and, as well, architects freely poached from unrelated fields. This continues to be fruitful even though some academics have succumbed to the need for newness before the last project was fully digested.

Deane: Other than the Blur Building that we talked about earlier, do you feel that there is another manifesto project for you in recent years? I know this is a hard question. (laughter) By a manifesto project, I mean either a project that you saw as transforming your position, that was very important to what came after it, or in the sense of a project that was so important to you that you felt that it encapsulated your position and thinking.

Liz: Perhaps, Lincoln Center because it has forced us to rethink what is important. Even though one can look at the work and say, "well, hmm, this doesn't look as defiant as your previous work," what's significant is the enormous complexity of succeeding within multiple networks: the twelve loosely connected constituent organizations that make up Lincoln Center, the City, the State, philanthropy, historic preservation, the community …

Deane: Could you say that with the Lincoln Center, the project of negotiating your way through these institutional networks to gain approval has become its own form of project in a way …

Liz: Absolutely. This is not a project that came with unlimited freedom. Its creative challenge is navigating public and private interests as well as our own. I'm really proud of the accomplishment we've made … we've managed to get consensus around this endlessly branching project. It's going to make a change at the scale of the city—and it's that much more meaningful as it's our city.

Deane: Have you been able to somehow operate subversively within the typical structure of these institutional networks?

Liz: "Subversive" is no longer the key word. I would say, "with suppleness." There are ways of working inside the system in which you can get people where you want them through generosity, not trickery. I have to use multiple voices, however, for the diverse audiences and factions. It's a delicate work. We don't want to be among the architectural road kill that preceded us. (laughter)

Deane: How do you imagine the future direction of Diller + Scofidio (+ Renfro) after the larger projects are completed? Where is the studio heading? Do you continue to grow? Does forty become eighty? Or does forty become ten?

Ric: That assumes we have a conscious direction. We've never made long-range plans. We let things walk in the door.

Liz: Yet we know several more people would create a tipping point. The office would become a different beast. We are at the limit of what we could control with the level of involvement and intimacy we want to maintain. We purposefully moved into a new space that would run out of room immediately. As far as the direction of the office, I'm happy for the cultural work. I would love to be the Kubrick of architecture—to experiment with a different genre each time … a museum, a concert hall, a hotel, a stadium, a park … it's the challenge of learning something entirely new that keeps me going, not legacy.

Ric: We lost our flexibility because our growth. First it was Liz and I, and then, depending on the needs of a project we would expand to five or ten and once it was finished, we would reduce contract. Now we have a commitment to a staff, yet we've never had to take on a single project to keep going.

Liz: When Ric and I got together, I didn't know how to share anything—a bed or a bank account, most of all, authorship. Eventually, we formed a new identity and we were able to sign everything together. And when Charles joined us something got disturbed. The couple became a triad or three individuals or sometimes two against one, and it no longer mattered which pair.

Deane: It's streamlining your decision-making process? (laughter)

Ric: I don't know if it's streamlined it, but I think it's healthier …

Deane: Charles, when you joined Liz and Ric as a partner, what did you bring to the original "beast"?

Charles: I come from the school of Canal Street nuts and bolts architecture. It's partly because I worked with Henry Smith-Miller on Canal Street, but also because I was interested in turn-key work. You design something and make it yourself. There was an alignment of sensibilities between Liz and Ric and myself. They often built their installations in their loft. So rather than bringing something different, I think I brought something related.

Liz: When Charles joined us and then led several projects in the studio it was obvious. He brought that extra fuel we needed. He also has a neurotic anxiety that just fits with the studio … we thrive on misfits that cannot survive in the professional world. (laughter)

Charles: One doesn't normally want to talk about oneself in terms of neurotic anxiety but it's true. I'm neurotic. (laughter)

Deane: Ok, this is the final question: there has been some discussion in recent years about the possibility of a feature film coming out of the studio. When and what?

Charles: (laughter) It's one of the hardest things to do—to hold the attention of an audience for two hours.

Liz: We're coming out of an anti-narrative period and it's refreshing to think about narrative again and how new structures of story-telling can operate on new audiences. So … we have an idea that was rejected by our last performance collaborator but we realized it would be a much better fit for a feature film. It was basically …

Ric: No! Don't give it away.

Liz: No. Sorry, can't tell you …(laughter) But we're ready to trade liveness for celluloid and 3-D for flatness.

Ric: Let's say we have an itch that we're going to scratch … soon.

Brasserie, 2000

Restaurant, Seagram Building, New York City

Detail, dining room

The prospect of redesigning one of New York's legendary restaurants in one of the world's most distinguished modernist buildings was as inviting as it was daunting. The architecture of the new restaurant respectfully challenges many of the tenets of Modernism.

After removing all traces of Philip Johnson's interior, the rough concrete surfaces of the original space have been relined with new skins of wood, terrazzo, tile, and glass. These thin "liners" often lift from their surfaces to become structural, spatial and functional components. For example, the madrone floor peels up while the pearwood ceiling peels down and is molded into seating as part of a continuous wrapper around the main dining space. Pearwood skins in the rear dining room peel from the plaster ceiling and wall to become free-floating partitions which delaminate into illuminated veneers.

While the Seagram Building is the premiere 20th century glass tower, the restaurant, lodged in the stone base of the building, is entirely without glass or view. This irony prompted a series of contemplations about glass and vision. At the entry, a glass surrogate straddles the stone wall: a live video camera outside and a plasma monitor inside provide an electronic transparency to the street. In the rear dining room, a 48-foot long glass wall leans against a perimeter wall and sheaths a display of artifacts. The lenticular glass teases vision by blurring all but perpendicular views. The equation between glass and fragility is exploited as the tipped glass wall supports twenty-four seated diners along its length.

The design emphasizes the social aspects of dining. Entrance from the street is transformed into the ritual of "making an entrance." Initially, a sensor in the revolving entry door triggers a video snapshot that is added to a continuously changing display on over the bar, announcing every new patron. Along the "video beam" composed of fifteen side-by-side LCD monitors, the most recent portrait takes the first position and racks the previous fifteen to the right,

dropping away the oldest. Beyond, in a recall of the original Brasserie, the descent into the main dining room (several feet below street level), is theatricized: a glass stair of unusually gradual proportions prolongs the descent of each new patron and puts him or her on display as they enter the space.

Other features include: a slender space flanking the dining area that is sliced into private booths by a series of tall, upholstered slabs tipped up on end and propped on steel legs; men's and women's bathrooms separated physically yet connected visually by semi-transparent honeycomb panels and a cast resin sink spanning both spaces with a single drain between; dining tables of poured resin formed around stainless steel structural supports that remain visible through the material; medical gel bar seats suppoted on steel tripods.

D+S

Main dining room

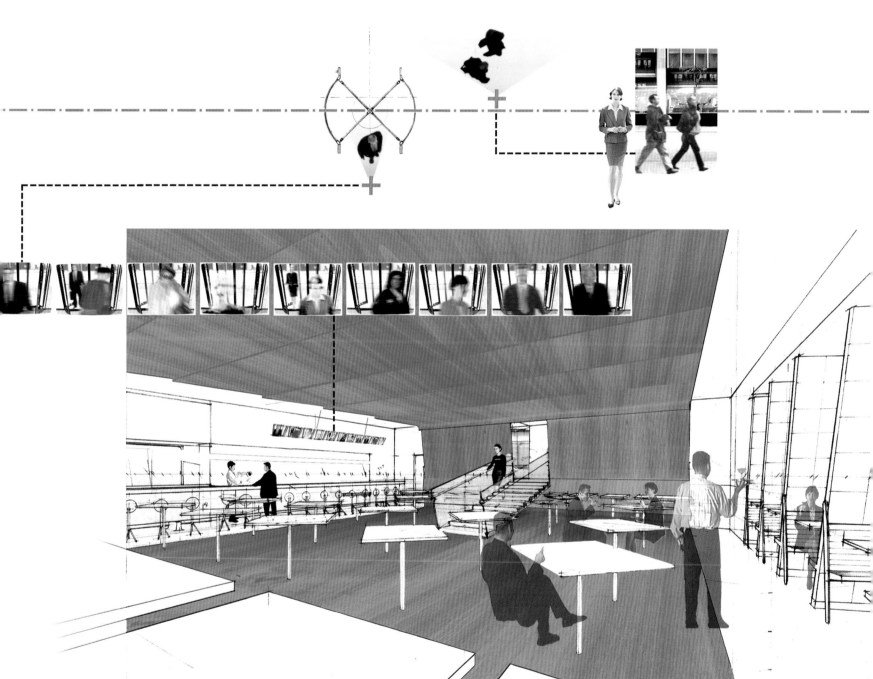

Video entry

Bar and *Bar Beam*

Slow stair

Icon pastry mould

Bathroom

Booths, main dining room

Second dining room

"Rapid Growth," 2000

Temporary installation, Philadelphia Museum of Art, 125th anniversary, Philadelphia

The computer-controlled mobile landscape supplements the classical landscape on the vast terrace of the museum. There are ten motorized grass mounds; each carries one specimen tree. The mounds move very slowly along optical guide paths. They move according to pre-programmed choreographed patterns and in response to surrounding stimuli such as density of people and light intensity, constantly reconfiguring into new topographies. At night, the mounds dock at a battery recharging station.
D+S

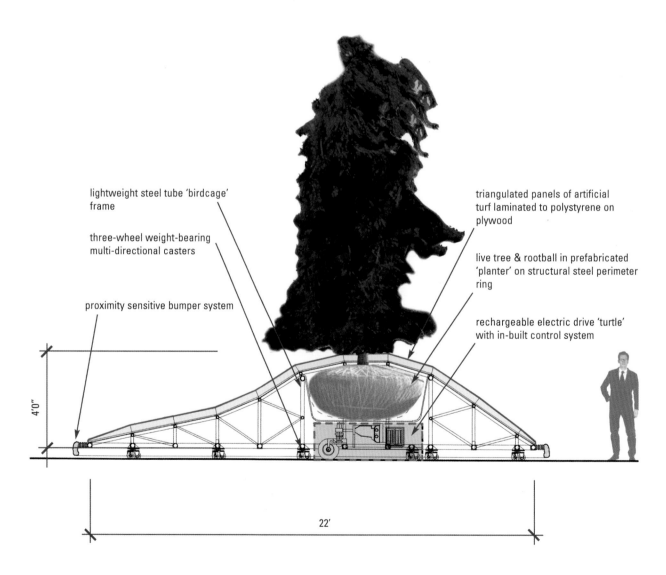

lightweight steel tube 'birdcage' frame

three-wheel weight-bearing multi-directional casters

proximity sensitive bumper system

triangulated panels of artificial turf laminated to polystyrene on plywood

live tree & rootball in prefabricated 'planter' on structural steel perimeter ring

rechargeable electric drive 'turtle' with in-built control system

4'0"

22'

Section drawing, motorized mound and tree specimen

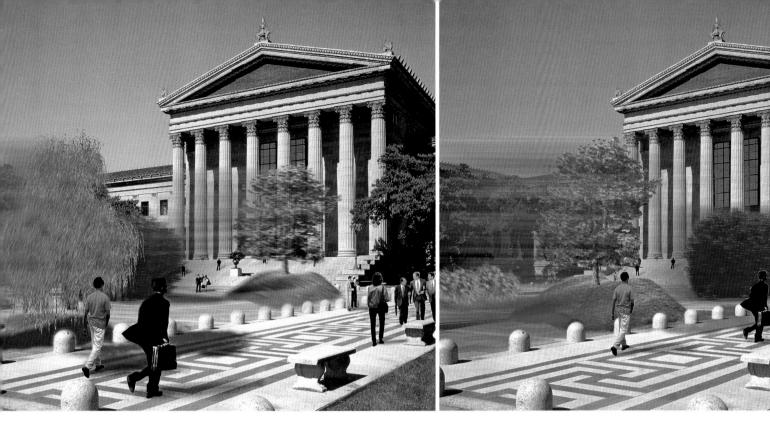

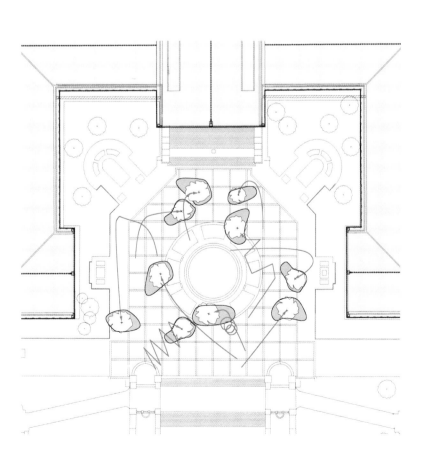

Tree behavior diagram

Slither Building, 2000

Social housing, Kitagata, Gifu, Japan

The "liberating" potential of standardization that promised variety in mass housing, was one of the myths introduced by European Modernism in the early 20th century. Unfortunately, this promise produced anonymity and thus doubt in the progressive ideals of the Modern Movement. The economic constraints which unavoidably produce the repetition of standardization in social housing, however, need not lead to the erasure of the individual dwelling. The reptilian building is made up of 105 housing units. Three disturbances are made in plan and section as a modest resistance to the inevitble repetition of the unit.

Seven units are assembled vertically into a stack. Each stack interlocks with the next stack, wedging an increment of 1.5 degrees at the joint. The accumulation of this slight angle along the building's fifteen stacks results in a shallow curve, convex to the street and concave to the communal courtyard. The long elevations are faced with diaphanous overlapping "scales" of perforated metal screening that modulate the degree of privacy at the circulation corridor and balconies.
Each unit slips 1.4 meters in plan from the next unit, thus freeing every entry door to be approached on axis. On the north side

of the building, each front door is metaphorically a private façade.
The slippage also produces a privatized balcony on the south side.
The floor slab of each unit is offset 200 mm vertically from the next unit. The circulation system of shallow continuous ramps strings together all units. No two units share the same elevational address. As the lowest unit at the west end of the building and the highest unit at the east are offset by the dimension of one full floor, the building appears to tip up from grade.
D+S

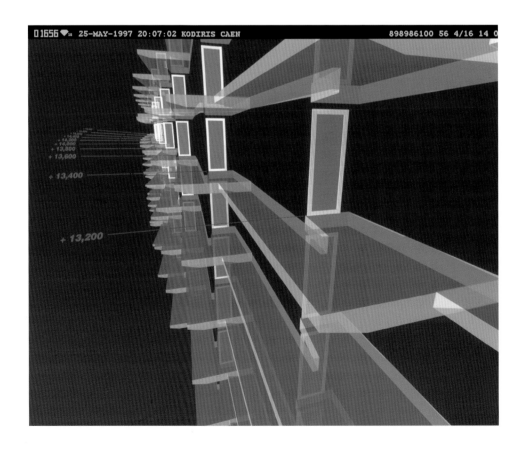

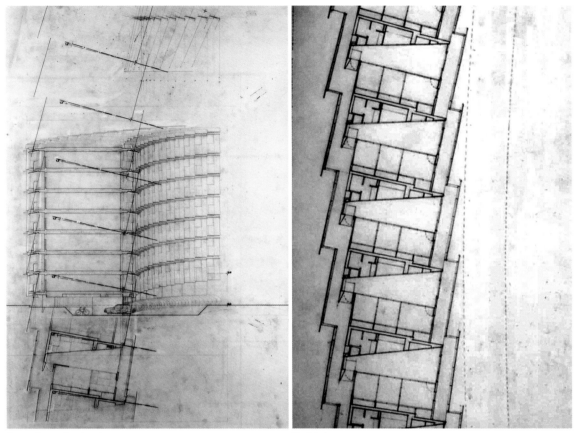

Composite section drawing

Partial plan

Flute Case Model

Model and drawings (folded to fit into carry-on
luggage compartment of a Boeing 747)

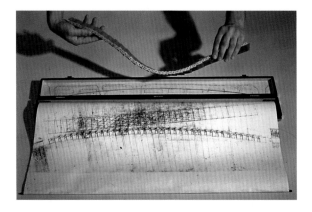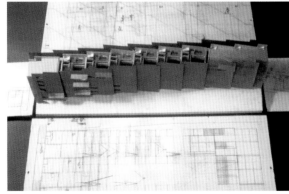

Level model

Long section drawing

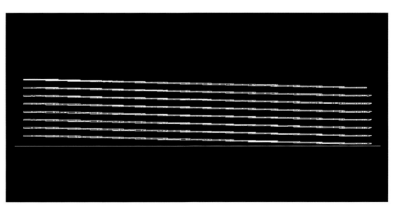

"Travelogues," 2001

Permanent installation, sterile corridors, JFK International Arrivals Building, New York. In collaboration with Tom Brigham

The sterile corridor is a space peculiar to the regulatory nature of contemporary air travel. It is a featureless non-place between jurisdictions, between the place left behind and the one about to be entered. It is a space in which diverse travelers share the status of world citizens in limbo. Defined by one-directional movement toward Customs and Passport Control, the sterile corridor is a space to pass through and not stop. Thirty-three backlit lenticular screens are evenly spaced along the 1800 linear feet of corridors of the International Arrivals Building. Each screen holds one second of action animated by the speed of the moving viewer. The succession of lenticular screens builds a sequence of micro-movies. The spaces between screens form time lapses. Thus, the traveler walking down the sterile corridor will inadvertently engage a real-time moving picture narrative in tiny installments.

Each set of panels tells a fictional narrative triggered by an anonymous traveler and their suitcase. The cases are X-rayed; contents materialize and trigger "flashback" images of a travel experience.
D+S

Production detail, rotating suitcase X-ray rig

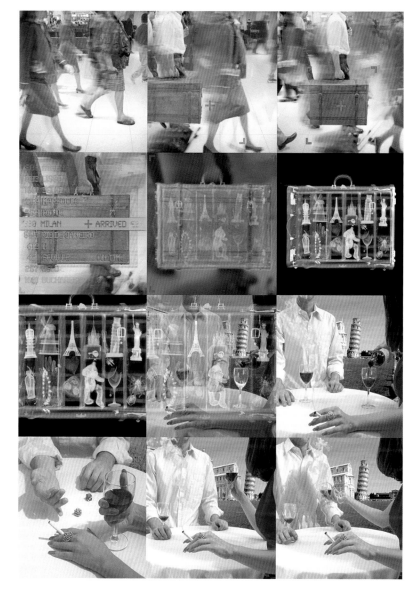

Lenticular stills, *The Collector*
and *The Prosthetic Traveller*

Plan, lenticular panel locations

Blur Building, 2002

Exposition Pavilion for Swiss Expo,
Lake Neuchâtel, Yverdon-les-Bains,
Switzerland

The Blur Building is an architecture of atmosphere. Its lightweight tensegrity structure measures 300 feet wide by 200 feet deep by 75 feet high. The primary building material is indigenous to the site, water. Water is pumped from the lake, filtered, and shot as a fine mist through a dense array of high-pressure mist nozzles. A smart weather system reads the shifting climactic conditions of temperature, humidity, wind speed and direction, and processes the data in a central computer that regulates water pressure to an array of 31,500 fog nozzles. The resulting fog mass changes from season to season, from day to day, hour to hour, and minute to minute in a continuous dynamic display of natural versus manmade forces. Upon entering the fog mass, visual and acoustic references are erased, leaving only an optical "white-out" and the "white-noise" of pulsing nozzles. Unlike entering a building, entering Blur is like stepping into a habitable medium, one that is formless, featureless, depthless, scaleless, massless, surfaceless, and dimensionless.

Contrary to immersive environments that strive for high-definition visual fidelity with ever-greater technical virtuosity, Blur is decidedly low-definition: in this exposition pavilion there is nothing to see but our dependence on vision itself. Movement is unregulated and the public is free to wander in an immersive acoustic environment by Christian Marclay. The public can ascend a stair to the Angel Deck at the summit. Emerging through the fog is like piercing a cloud layer while in flight to the blue sky. Submerged one-half level below the deck is the Water Bar which offers a broad selection of bottled waters from around the world. Water is not only the site and primary material of the building, it is also a culinary pleasure. The public can drink the building.

Note: The first fog building was made by Japanese artist Fujiko Nakaya for the 1970 Osaka World's Fair. Hers was a fog layer surfacing a geodesic dome. Nakaya was an advisor to Blur on technical and aesthetic matters.
D+S

Renderings, various atmospheric conditions

Angel Deck

Aerial view with landscape by West 8

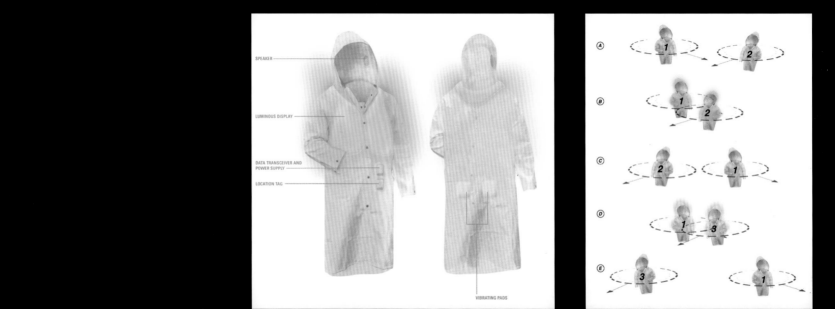

SPEAKER

LUMINOUS DISPLAY

DATA TRANSCEIVER AND
POWER SUPPLY

LOCATION TAG

VIBRATING PADS

A

B

C

D

E

Rendering, *Braincoat* media component

Screen still, nozzle control system interface

Detail, high pressure noozle

Rendering, tensegrity structural node

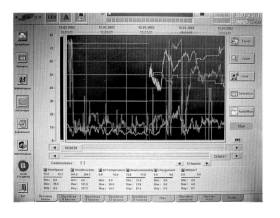

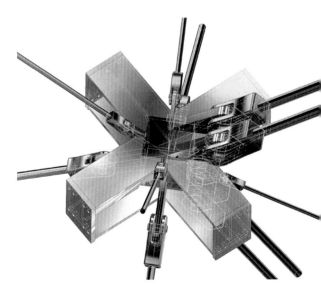

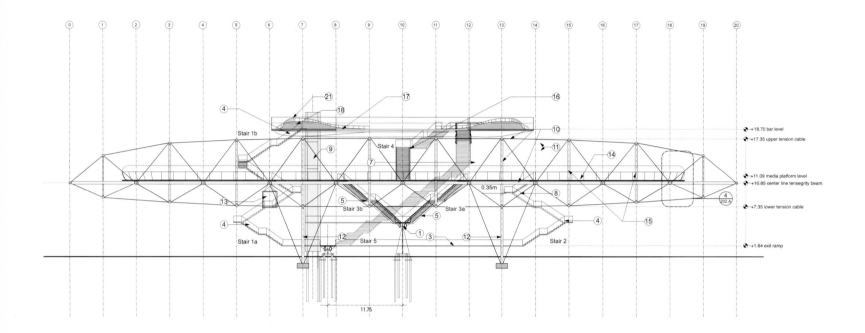

| | | | | | | | | | | | | | | | | | | | | |
|0|1|2|3|4|5|6|7|8|9|10|11|12|13|14|15|16|17|18|19|20|

21
17
4   18
16

Stair 1b   10   →+18.70 bar level
                                                              →+17.35 upper tension cable
                         9   Stair 4
                                              7   →+11.09 media platform level
                                                               →+10.85 center line tensegrity beam

13   0.35m   8
              5   Stair 3b   Stair 3a   →+7.35 lower tension cable
                            5   4
4   202.A
              0.0   1   4
Stair 1a   12 Stair 5   3   12   Stair 2   →+1.64 exit ramp

                   11.75

Section drawing

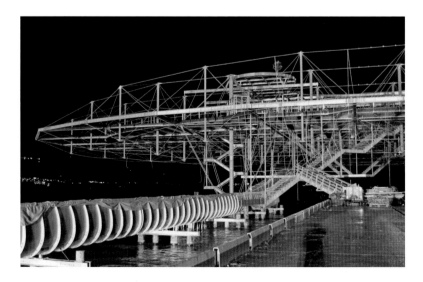

Construction view

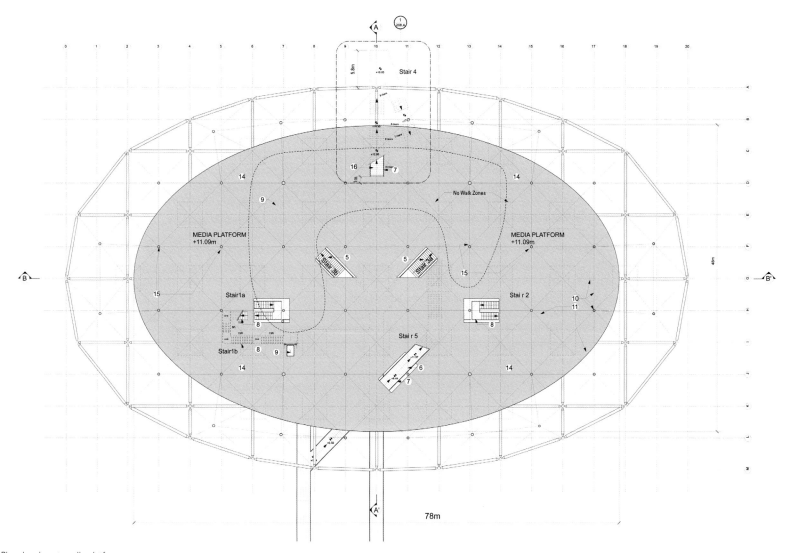

Plan drawing at media platform

"Mural," 2003

Installation, Whitney Museum of American Art.
In collaboration with Honeybee Robotics

Mural comprises a network of white walls that houses, organizes, and partitions the DS+R retrospective exhibition, *Scanning: The Aberrant Architectures of Diller + Scofidio*. Acting as both host and guest, the system of white walls is the site of the protagonist: a robotic drill sabotages the visual and acoustic isolation produced by the walls. The drill travels on a track cruising the major partition walls of the exhibition. It is guided by an intelligent navigator that randomly selects a point within a three-dimensional matrix of coverage and guides the drill to the new location. The drill pierces the drywall leaving behind a 1/2" hole.
The holes started initially as lone blemishes on the pristine white walls. As the exhibition continued, the walls became increasingly perforated. Eventually, holes on both sides of a wall would align opening views from gallery to gallery and clusters of holes randomly opened up sections of wall surface, making the wall increasingly unstable. The three-month performance work progressively contaminated the galleries with a constant background drone, visual distractions and light leaks. It perforated and eventually obliterated the curatorial text. Rather than securing a neutral background for the art works on display, the wall actively competed for attention resisting total submission of the exhibition to the collecting and mediating function of the museum retrospective.
D+S

Prototype development

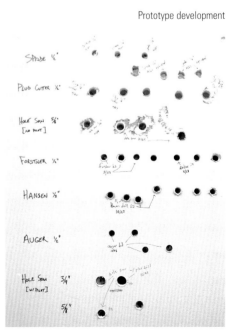

157

Eyebeam Museum of Art and Technology, 2004

Museum and Production facility, Chelsea
District, New York

New institutions breed new spatial politics
and codes of behavior. The hybrid nature
of the Museum of Art and Technology, both
museum and production/education facility,
provokes an architecture of cross-programming
and spatial interweaving. The architectural
concept begins with a pliable ribbon that
partitions the programming in two:
production spaces to one side (blue) and
presentation spaces to the other (gray).
The ribbon undulates from side to side as it
climbs from the street, floor folding into
wall, folding into floor, slipping back
gradually to fit the diminishing zoning
envelope. With each change of direction
the ribbon alternately enfolds a production
or presentation space, thus combing
together the major program divisions
and populations of the building (residents
and visitors) as well as their diverse

activities and speeds. While residents use
the east core and visitors use the west,
each must pass through the spaces of the
other when circulating between successive
levels. The ribbon is sometimes sheared and
slipped into alignment with a level above
or below, thus, conjoining a production and
presentation space. The building is designed
as a system of controlled contamination.
The ribbon is two-ply with a technical space
sandwiched between layers that house the
building's "nervous" system. The smooth
concrete ply facing the exhibition space has
a pattern of precast service jacks. The ply
of modularized panels facing the atelier
permits easy access to the interstitial space
for rewiring and servicing of exhibition
needs at specific locations below or above.
D+S

Rendering, two-ply wrapper
with nervous system

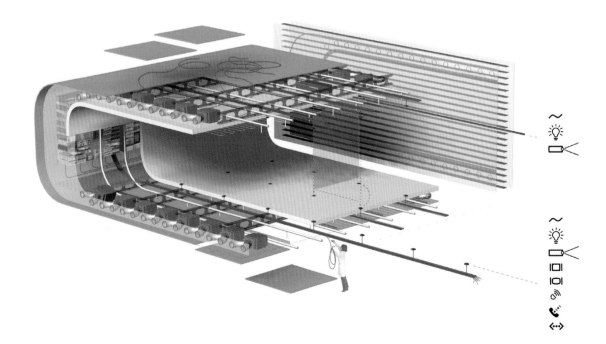

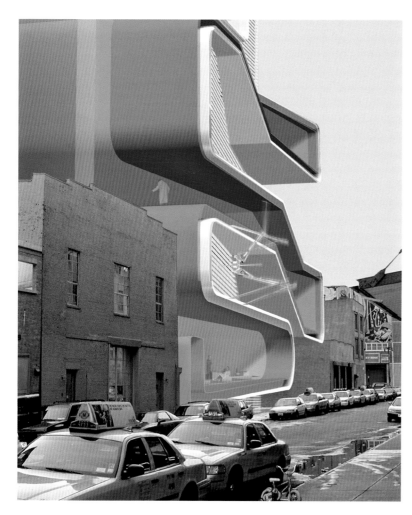

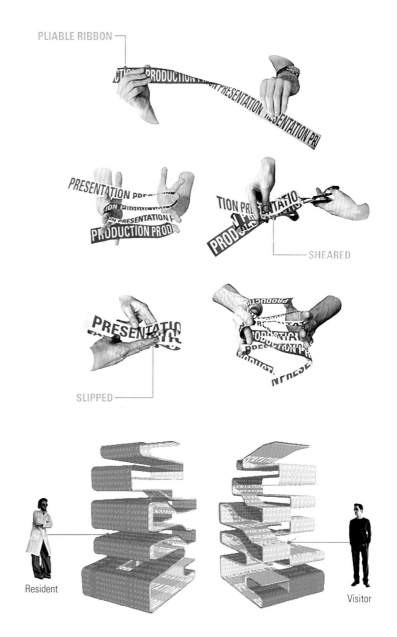

PLIABLE RIBBON

SHEARED

SLIPPED

Resident

Visitor

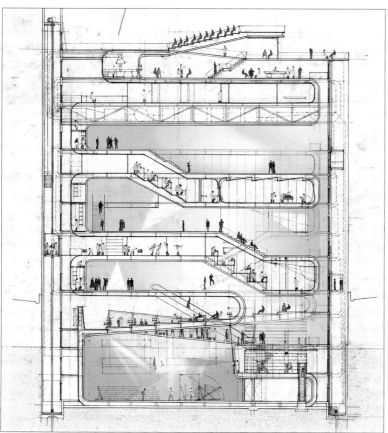

Section drawing

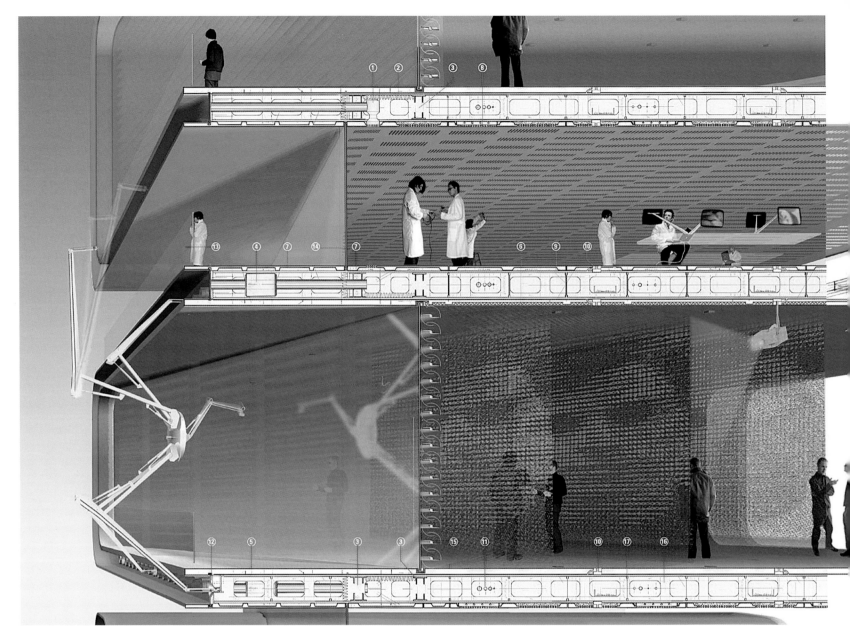

Section rendering with systems

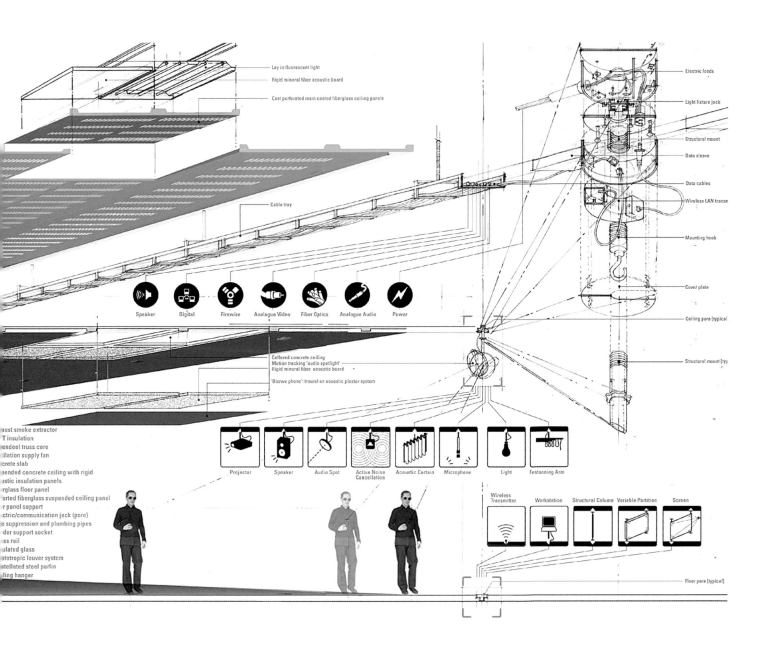

Lay in fluorescent light

Rigid mineral fiber acoustic board

Cast perforated resin coated fiberglass ceiling panels

Electric feeds

Light fixture jack

Structural mount

Data sleeve

Data cables

Wireless LAN transce

Mounting hook

Cable tray

Cover plate

Ceiling pore [typical]

Coffered concrete ceiling
Motion tracking 'audio spotlight'
Rigid mineral fiber acoustic board

'Baswa phone': trowel on acoustic plaster system

Structural mount [typ]

| Speaker | Digital | Firewire | Analogue Video | Fiber Optics | Analogue Audio | Power |

aust smoke extractor
T insulation
endeel truss core
ilation supply fan
crete slab
nended concrete ceiling with rigid
ustic insulation panels
rglass floor panel
orted fiberglass suspended ceiling panel
r panel support
ctric/communication jack (pore)
e suppression and plumbing pipes
der support socket
ss rail
ulated glass
ototropic louver system
stellated steel purlin
ling hanger

| Projector | Speaker | Audio Spot | Active Noise Cancellation | Acoustic Curtain | Microphone | Light | Festooning Arm |

| Wireless Transmitter | Workstation | Structural Column | Variable Partition | Screen |

Floor pore [typical]

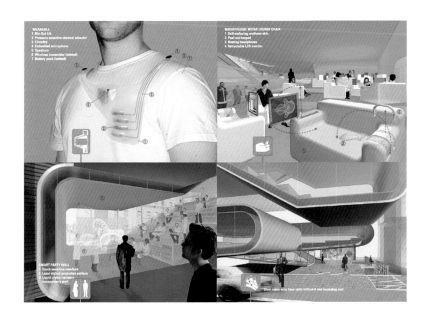

WEARABLE
1 Bio-Gel kit
2 Pressure sensitive channel selector
3 Circuitry
4 Embedded microphone
5 Speakers
6 Wireless transmitter (behind)
7 Battery pack (behind)

MEDIATHEQUE: MEDIA LOUNGE CHAIR
1 Self-enclosing urethane skin
2 Peel-out keypad
3 Nesting headphones
4 Retractable LCD monitor

SMART PARTY WALL
1 Touch sensitive interface
2 Laser etched projection surface
3 Liquid crystal rotatable transparent wall

Building media systems

161

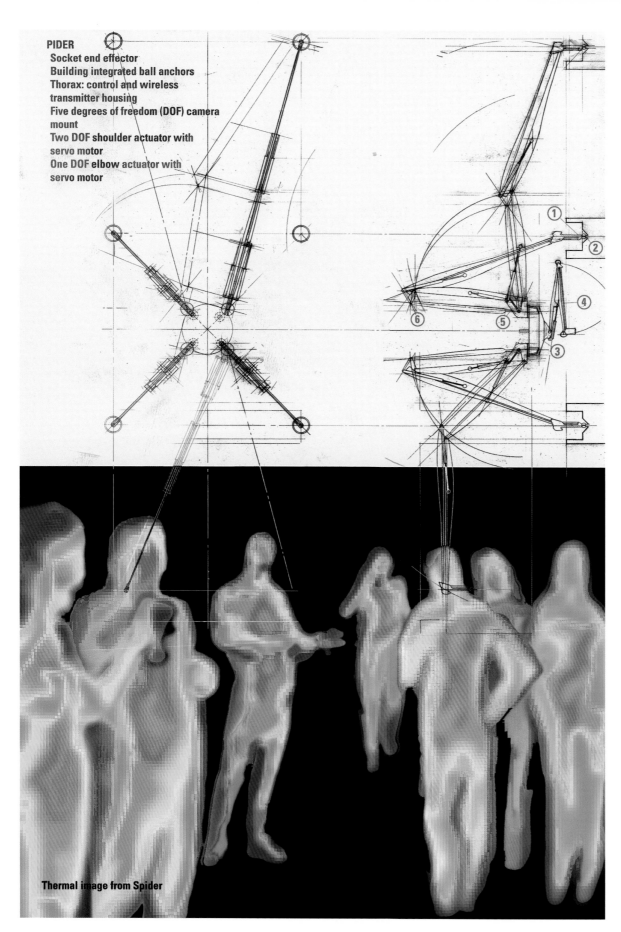

PIDER
  Socket end effector
  Building integrated ball anchors
  Thorax: control and wireless
  transmitter housing
  Five degrees of freedom (DOF) camera
  mount
  Two DOF shoulder actuator with
  servo motor
  One DOF elbow actuator with
  servo motor

Thermal image from Spider

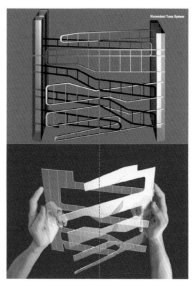

Diagram, Vierendeel structural
system and glazing

Rendering, robotic spider with thermal
imaging system

Rendering, mediateque

Rendering, computer lab

Rendering, conjoined exhibition space
and classroom

Diagram, wireless communications system

Rendering, theater

165

"Facsimile," 2004

Permanent installation, Moscone Convention Center, San Francisco.
In collaboration with Ben Rubin

A 16-foot high by 27-foot wide video monitor is suspended by a vertical armature at the parapet and soffit of the new Moscone Convention Center Expansion in San Francisco. The building is by Gensler Architects. A live video camera fixed to the armature and positioned behind the screen points into the glass building. The structure travels slowly along the surface of the building and broadcasts live views as it moves. The virtual transparency enhances the actual transparency of the glass building. While the live view naturally corresponds with the speed and direction of the scanning motion, a series of pre-recorded programs constructed to simulate the same speed sometimes replace the real view. The fictional vignettes substitute impostors for actual building occupants and spaces. The apparatus could be seen as a scanning device, a magnifying lens, a periscope (a camera at a high elevation looks toward the city), and as an instrument of deception.
DS+R

Rendering

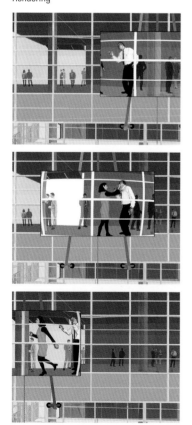

Hotel stills

Office stills

Section drawing

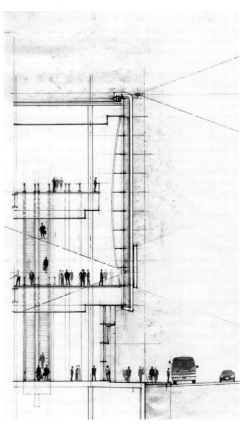

Tivoli Gardens, 2005

Masterplan, renovation and addition,
Copenhagen, Denmark

The new 1,400-foot stretch of the southern
perimeter of Tivoli Gardens, Copenhagen's
biggest attraction, adds 300,000 square feet
of commercial, recreational and cultural
programming within a porous boundary.
Included is a new entrance at the southeast
corner, retail, dining, nightlife, education
spaces, and a conference center.
The project aspires to maintain the
19th-century charm of the amusement park

while interfacing with contemporary urban
conditions. Included is a tower restaurant
with rentable dining rooms of variable sizes
accessed by chefs and servers via external
glass elevators, a name-brand shoe
store/gallery accessed by moving walkways,
amusement rides with an intersecting bar,
a paternoster of storefronts displaying
varied wares in continual rotation.
DS+R

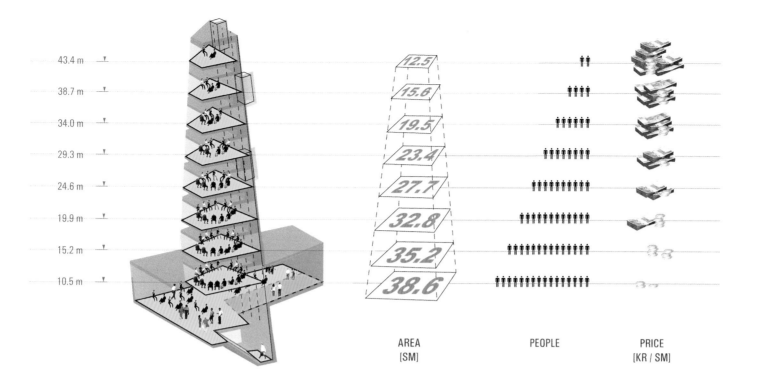

	AREA [SM]	PEOPLE	PRICE [KR / SM]

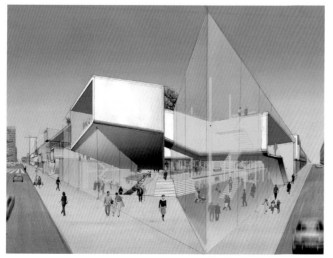

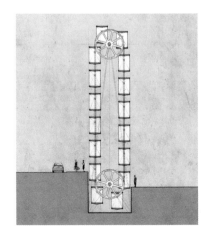

Quad House, 2005

House for couple, Camelback Mountain,
Phoenix, Arizona

The house straddles a line between two
contrasting landscapes: the flat city grid
below and the rugged mass of Camelback
Mountain above. It is divided into
quadrants of similar area and equal
programmatic value: a living space, a lawn,
a master bedroom, and a pool.
The quadrants are separated by long
sheets of glass that flip between interior

and exterior. From the living room,
a bird's eye view of the city is crisply
bisected by a zero edge swimming pool.
The contiguous spaces with no defined
circulation permit any point on the main
level to be seen from any other, thus
allowing its two residents to always stay
in visual communication.
DS+R

Institute of Contemporary Art, 2006

Museum, Fan Pier, Boston Harbor, Boston.
Associate Architects: Perry Dean Rogers
and Partners

The new ICA is the first new museum to be built in Boston in hundred years. The 65,000-square-foot building includes 18,000 square feet of galleries, a performing arts theater, a restaurant, a bookstore, education/workshop facilities, and administrative offices. The design negotiates between two competing objectives: to perform as a dynamic civic building filled with public and social activities, and as a controlled, contemplative atmosphere for individuals interacting with contemporary art. The "public" building is built from the ground up; the "intimate" building, from the sky down. The Boston Harborwalk borders the north and west edges of the ICA site. This surface, which belongs to the citizens of Boston, is metaphorically extended into the new building as a primary architectural element. The Harborwalk becomes a pliable wrapper that defines the building's major public spaces. It folds up from the walkway into a "grandstand" facing the water, it continues through the skin of the building to form a stage, then turns up to form the theater seating, then seamlessly envelopes the theater space, ultimately, slipping out through the skin to produce the ceiling of the exterior public "room." This ambiguous surface moves from exterior into interior, transforming public into semi-public space. Above the wrapper sits the "gallery box": a large exhibition space on one level that dramatically cantilevers over the Harborwalk toward the water. The flexible, column-free space is 16-foot high and partitioned into east and west galleries by the central core, and illuminated by uniform, diffused daylight filtered by a scrim below the skylight system. The 300-seat multi-purpose theater is fully glazed on its north and west faces, allowing the harbor view to become the backdrop for the stage. Light and view can be controlled in accordance with performance needs, from transparency and view, to filtered light and no view, to total blackout.

The mediatheque is suspended from the underside of the cantilevered "gallery box" and accessed from the gallery lobby. It is equipped with computer stations with on-line access and fed by a central server providing a growing database of digital art works. The building distributes the view to the harbor in small doses: compressed at the lobby entry, scanned vertically by the glass elevator, choreographed into theater performances, denied in the galleries, revealed as a panorama at the north gallery crossover, and edited to only the texture of water at the mediatheque.
DS+R

Conceptual diagram

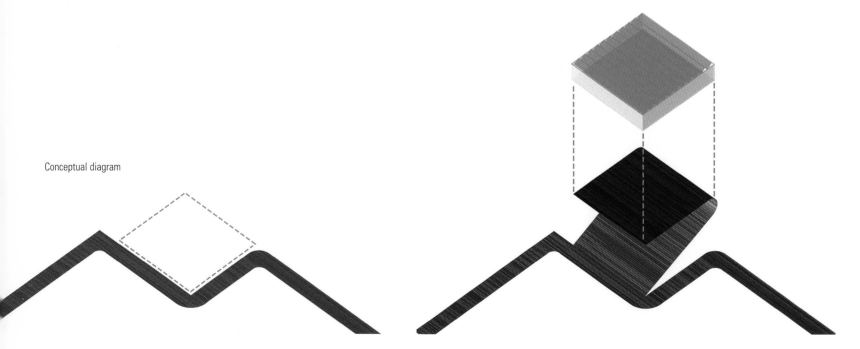

Site

Rendering northwest view

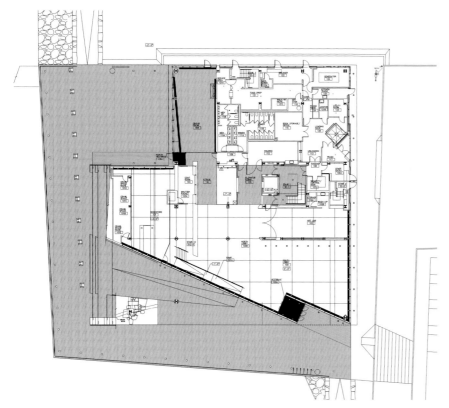

First floor plan

Second floor plan

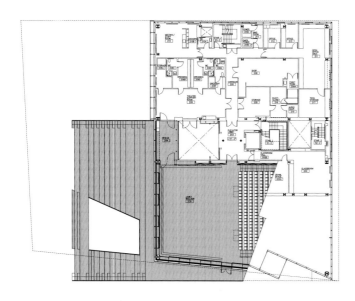

Third floor plan

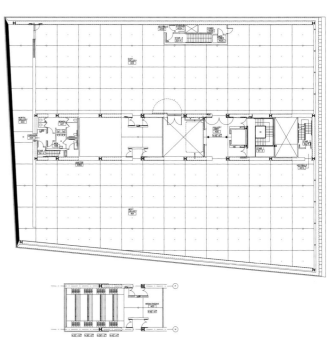

Fourth floor plan

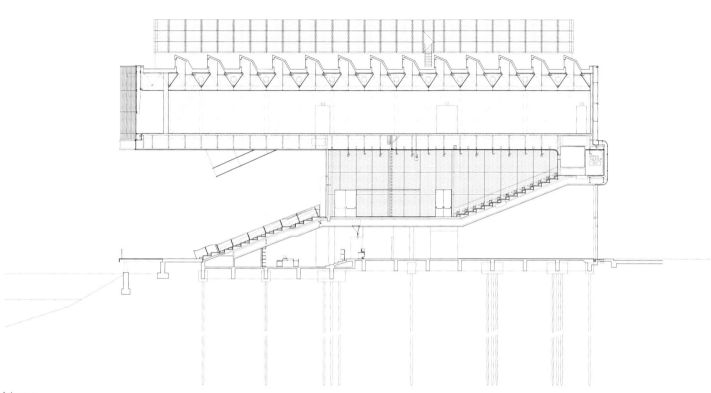

Section drawing of theater

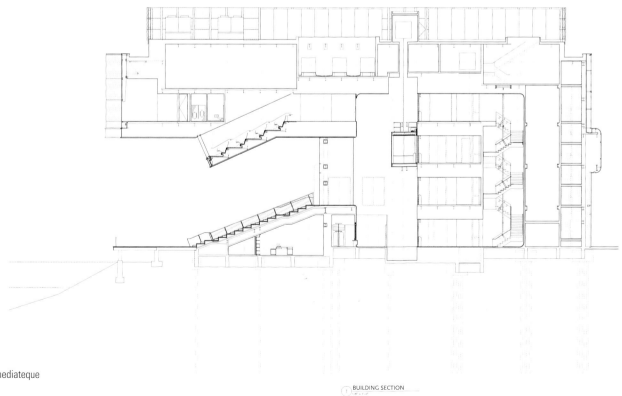

Section drawing of mediateque

179

Mediatheque view, section drawing
and rendering (*below*)

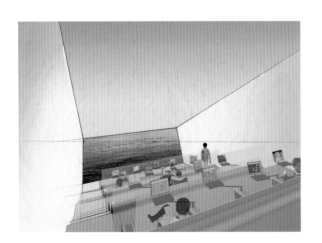

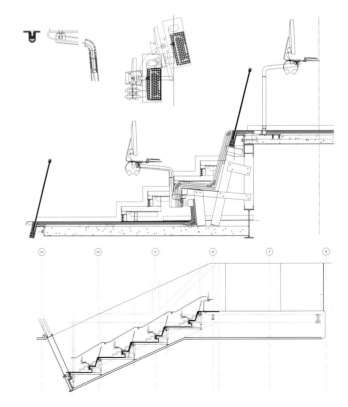

Early study models

"Who's Your Dada?," 2006

Performance, Museum of Modern Art, New York. In collaboration with The Wooster Group

Based on historical films and documents in the museum's archives, the performance work was commissioned to highlight the final week of *DADA*, an exhibition on the anti-art movement that flourished from 1916 to 1924. The performance takes place in the museum's lobby, and is conceived as a panel discussion at a long table supported on crutches. The Wooster Group's Scott Shepard moderates an unscripted panel of actors representing Dada writers and performers such as Tristan Tzara, Richard Huelsenbeck, Jean Arp and Hugo Ball. Four geriatric actors, each old enough to remember the period, join The Wooster Group principals in reminiscing about Dada's notorious Cabaret Voltaire, reciting Dada poetry and arguing theory in litigious Dada style.

The staging apparatus takes as its theme the fine line between truth and doubt, between live stage action and forms of mediation. The stage is transformed into a film production studio composed of a 24-foot long blue screen and a remotely controlled robotic camera which pans the length of the table. The camera transmits "live" video footage to three LCD monitors mounted behind the audience. The footage is edited on the fly, superimposing the actors into various pre-recorded scenes and backgrounds, docu-style. The audience is supplied with FM radio receivers, and is able to tune into four prescribed stations of Dada commentary and criticism.
DS+R

School of American Ballet, 2007

Dance studios, Rose Building, Lincoln Center, New York

The expansion project for the School of American Ballet is located in the facilities of the official training academy for the New York City Ballet. The 8,200 square foot project includes the addition of two new dance studios within the space of two existing ones. The existing 16-foot high studios are optimized by removing a deep mechanical plenum above the ceiling and reorganizing ducting into a compressed space at the periphery. The stacked studios are each 10 feet floor-to-ceiling. Like nesting dolls, each of the new studios is housed in the volume of the existing. As the new studios have a smaller footprint

and recede from the peripheral walls, they appear to float. Three steel beams bridge the loads into existing building structure. The new studios have floor to ceiling glass. Natural light and views from existing studios can be shared with the new ones. Between the two sets of stacking studios is a mezzanine lounge made of liquid crystal walls that can switch the translucent glass to transparent with the application of an electric current. At the discretion of the teachers, a view in one or both directions can be opened or denied.
DS+R

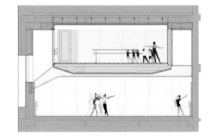

Section drawing, School of American Ballet studios

below
Interior section-perspective rendering, School of American Ballet studios

opposite page
Interiors view, School of American Ballet studios

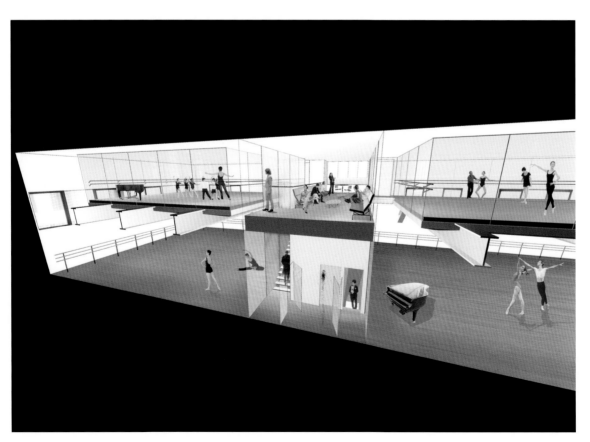

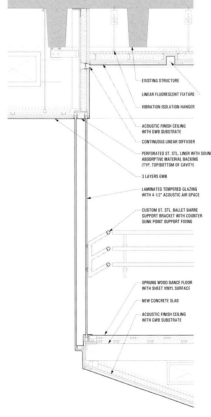

EXISTING STRUCTURE

LINEAR FLUORESCENT FIXTURE

VIBRATION ISOLATION HANGER

ACOUSTIC FINISH CEILING WITH GWB SUBSTRATE

CONTINUOUS LINEAR DIFFUSER

PERFORATED ST. STL. LINER WITH SOUND ABSORPTIVE MATERIAL BACKING (TYP. TOP/BOTTOM OF CAVITY)

3 LAYERS GWB

LAMINATED TEMPERED GLAZING WITH 4-1/2" ACOUSTIC AIR SPACE

CUSTOM ST. STL. BALLET BARRE SUPPORT BRACKET WITH COUNTER-SUNK POINT SUPPORT FIXING

SPRUNG WOOD DANCE FLOOR WITH SHEET VINYL SURFACE

NEW CONCRETE SLAB

ACOUSTIC FINISH CEILING WITH GWB SUBSTRATE

189

Lincoln Center for the Performing Arts, 2007–

Multiple projects, Lincoln Center, New York. Associate Architects: FxFowle, Beyer Blinder Belle

Once derided as an urban mistake, an "Acropolis for the cultural elite," and the embodiment of "Monumental Modernism," a term normally applied to fascist architecture, Lincoln Center has become a valued icon inextricably linked with New York City. The ensemble of buildings and public spaces that constitute the cultural campus are the product of a group of prominent architects, including Gordon Bunshaft, Eero Saarinen, Wallace K. Harrison and Philip Johnson. After unfortunate renovations in the 1980s and 1990s, and poor maintenance since its inception, Lincoln Center is undergoing a large scale multi-phase makeover. The plan includes the significant renovation and expansion of several cultural and educational facilities, the improvement of public spaces, the addition of new amenities, and the conversion of 65th Street from a service corridor into a new central spine. Rather than transforming the identity of Lincoln Center, our aim is "to make Lincoln Center more Lincoln Center than Lincoln Center," that is, to amplify its most successful attributes while teasing out its unrealized potential. The architectural challenge has been to interpret the genetic code of the architecture into a language that can speak to a diverse audience after several generations of cultural and political change. The project aims to turn the campus inside-out by extending the spectacle within the performance halls into the mute public spaces between the halls and beyond into the surrounding streets.

Some of the new architectural strategies include a ceremonial new entrance at Columbus Avenue produced by the depression of an existing drop-off road shield by a floating electronic grand stair, a floating parabolic lawn that roofs over a 250-seat glass pavilion restaurant on the North Plaza, an architectural strip-tease that exposes theaters and activities buried behind opaque travertine-clad street walls of Juilliard, and the integration of smart technologies with traditional building materials to deliver information throughout the campus.

The range of the project's scale requires an effort that dissolves boundaries between urban planning, architecture, and landscape design and information design.

The largest single part of the project is a 45,000-square-foot expansion and 50,000-square-foot renovation of The Juilliard School includes new jazz and dance studios, classrooms, practice rooms, a black box theater, and an orchestra rehearsal, a new entrance lobby and box office, administrative offices, a bookstore, lounges, a library expansion, and a scholar reading room for rare musical manuscripts. While in a new idiom, the language of the expansion interprets the DNA of the original building designed by Pietro Belluschi in the early 1960s. The top three teaching floors are extruded and cantilevered into Broadway. *DS+R*

Rendering, Columbus Avenue frontage

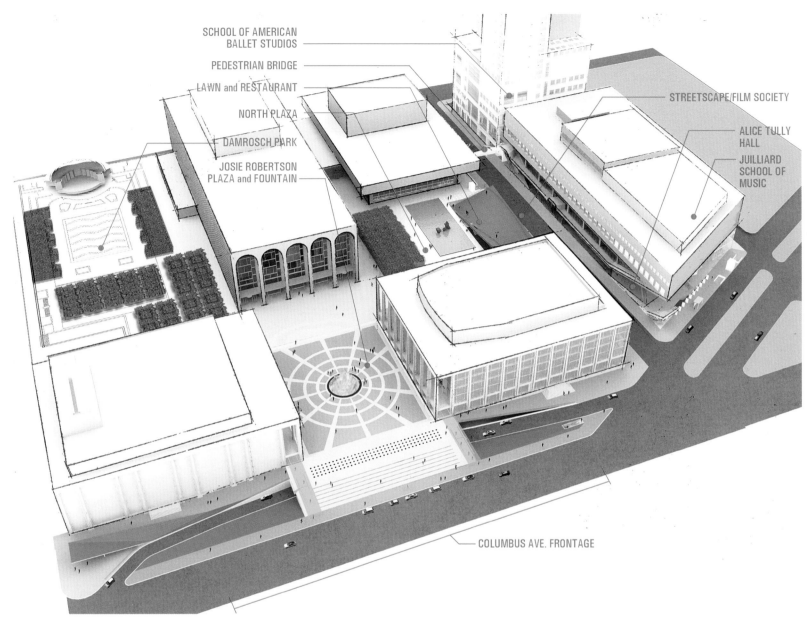

Rendering, project overview

Rendering, North Plaza
from the Lincoln Center Theater

Rendering, The Juilliard School of Music
and Alice Tully Hall

North Plaza restaurant

Renderings, North Plaza

Alice Tully Hall, 2007–

Performance Hall, Lincoln Center, New York.
Associate Architect: FxFowle

While considered a good multi-purpose hall for chamber music, film, dance and theater, Alice Tully Hall is imperfect for any particular use. The redesign is intended to improve acoustics and make Tully Hall an "intimate" chamber music venue with expanded and improved support facilities. The opaque base of the building is removed to reveal the theater within. A sloped canopy, the underside of the Juilliard expansion, frames the new lobby sheathed with a cable net glass façade.

As the hall is built adjacent to the 7th Ave subway, a partial box-in-box construction with isolating walls and slab reduces subway vibration. A high performance wood liner that wraps the interior walls, ceiling, floor and stage. This "bespoke" surface is tailored to existing hall features and incorporates new acoustic shaping to distribute sound evenly throughout the house.

The "theatricality" of a concert hall lives as much in the house as it does on stage. Thus, lighting during audience arrival, intermission, and departure is a rich part of the concert experience.

Illumination is designed into the wood skin to exude an internal glow much like a bioluminescent marine organism.

As the mandate for the redesign was to preserve every seat of the 1,100 seat hall, the architecture must be achieved within 18 inches.

DS+R

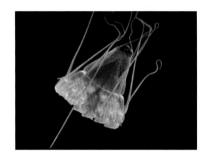

Model, Alice Tully Hall interior

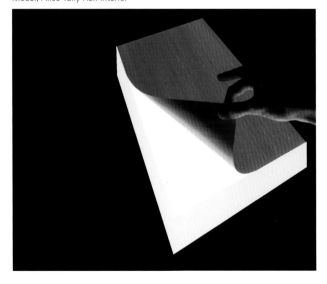

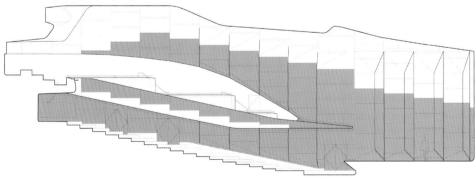

20%   ILLUMINATION WALL PANELS

80%   CONVENTIONAL WOOD PANELS

Elevation drawing, Alice Tully Hall interior, illuminated wall panel coverage

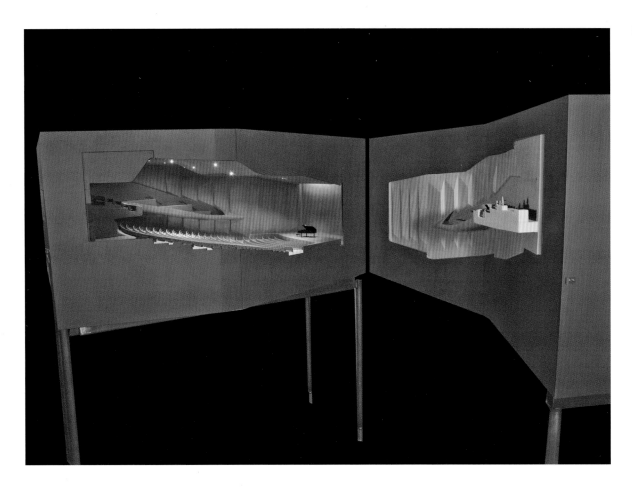

Model, Alice Tully Hall interior

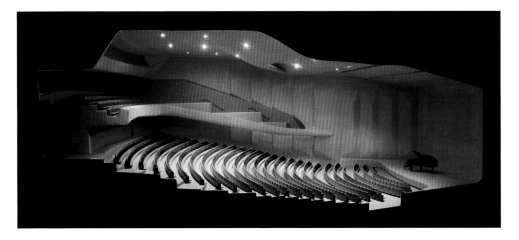

Model, Alice Tully Hall interior

Prototype, Alice Tully Hall interior,
illuminated wall panels

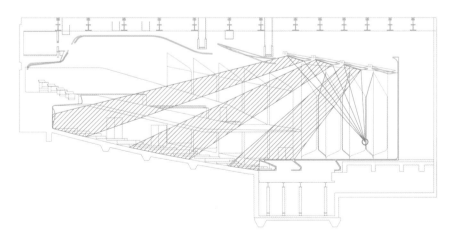

Diagram, Alice Tully Hall interior,
sound reflection

197

High Line, 2007–

Elevated public park, Chelsea District, New York. In collaboration with Field Operations

Joel Sternfeld, 2000

The High Line is a 1.5-mile long elevated industrial rail line in Manhattan stretching from the Meatpacking District to the 34th St rail yards. It has been abandoned since 1980 and is soon to be converted into a public park. Inspired by the melancholic, unruly beauty of this postindustrial ruin where nature has reclaimed a once vital piece of urban infrastructure, the new park will be an instrument of leisure reflection about the very categories of "nature" and "culture" in our time.

Through a strategy of *agri-tecture* that combines organic and building materials into a vegetal/mineral blend, the park accommodates the wild, the cultivated, the intimate, and the social. Part agriculture/part architecture the system digitizes the High Line surface into discrete units of paving and planting that could be organized in any combination from 100% hard paving to 100% soft richly vegetated biotopes or any gradation in between. The surface is built from individual pre-cast concrete planks with open joints to encourage emergent growth like wild grass through cracks in the sidewalk. The long, gradually tapering paving units are designed to comb into planting beds creating a "pathless" landscape where the public can meander in unscripted ways.

New plantings build upon the existing landscape character, working with specific environmental urban conditions and microclimates associated with sun, shade, wet, dry, wind, noise, open and sheltered spaces. Access points are durational experiences designed to prolong the transition from the frenetic pace of the city streets to the slow otherworldly landscape. Wherever possible, access points cut through the massive steel structure with slow stairs, ramps, and elevators to strategically position the body at varying elevations under, within, and above the High Line.
DS+R

Historical pohotograph

AGRI - TECTURE

Inspired by the melancholic, unrully beauty of the High Line where nature has reclaimed a once vital piece of urban infrastructure, the team retools this industrial conveyance into a postindustrial instrument of leisure, life and growth. By changing the rules of engagement between plant life and pedestrians, the strategy of **AGRI-TECTURE** combines organic and building materials into gradients of changing proportions that accomodate the wild, the cultivated, the intimate, and the hyper-social. In stark contrast to the speed of adjacent Hudson River Park, this parallel linear experience is marked by slowness, distraction and an other-worldliness to the changing needs, opportunities, and desires of the dynamic context, our proposal is designed to remain perpetually unfinished, sustaining emergent growth and change over time.

AGRI-TECTURE: A FLEXIBLE, RESPONSIVE SYSTEM OF MATERIAL ORGANIZATION WHERE DIVERSE ECOLOGIES MAY GROW.
The striated surface transitions from high intensity areas (100% hard) to richly vegetated biotopes (100% soft), with a variety of experiential gradients in-between.

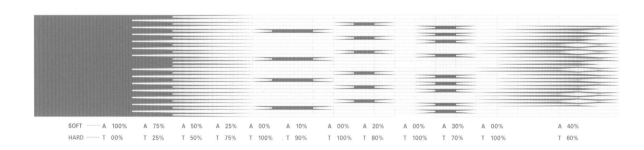

| SOFT | A 100% | A 75% | A 50% | A 25% | A 00% | A 10% | A 00% | A 20% | A 00% | A 30% | A 00% | A 40% |
| HARD | T 00% | T 25% | T 50% | T 75% | T 100% | T 90% | T 100% | T 80% | T 100% | T 70% | T 100% | T 60% |

Construction view, pre-cast concrete planks

Topside lighting

Underside lighting

Gansevoort Street entry - end view

Gansevoort Street entry - slow stair

public roof scape

gansevoort entry

vegetal balcony

LITTLE W. 12TH ST.

GANSEVOORT ST.

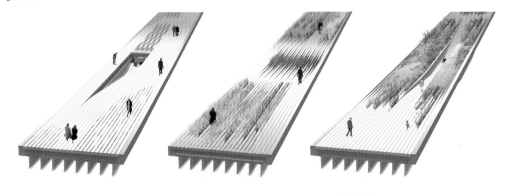

PIT
0% : 100%

PLAINS
40% : 60%

BRIDGE
50% : 50%

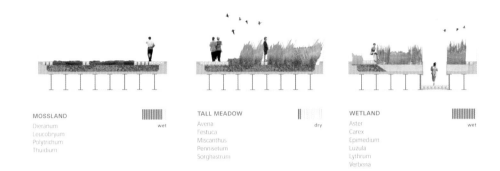

MOSSLAND
Dieranum
Leucobryum
Polytrichum
Thuidium

wet

TALL MEADOW
Avena
Festuca
Miscanthus
Pennisetum
Sorghastrum

dry

WETLAND
Aster
Carex
Epimedium
Luzula
Lythrum
Verbena

wet

MOUND
55% : 45%

RAMP
60% : 40%

FLYOVER
100% : 10%

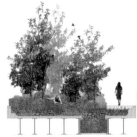

WOODLAND THICKET
Adiantum spp.
Asarum
Betula nigra 'Heritage'
Clethra barbinervis
Sassafras albidum
Osmunda spp.
Viburnum dilitatum

wet/average

MIXED PERENNIAL MEADOW
Artemisia
Eryngium giganteum
Heuchera
Monarda
Persicaria
Sanguisorba officinalis
Salvia

dry/average

YOUNG WOODLAND
Agastache
Buxus sempervirens
Cercis canadensis
Lavatera
Rhus chinensis
Salix eleagnos

average

Mott Street (Kopp) Townhouse, 2007–

Sited in a 20-foot wide lot in NoLita, the seven-story sliver building bridges the last remaining gap between twin tenements in the neighborhood. The 10,000-square-foot construction contains two duplex apartments and a simplex on upper floors and two levels of retail at the street. Local historic district zoning restrictions mandate building facades to be 50% masonry. In order to bring natural light into the narrow and deep building lot, the east-facing street façade is floor-to-ceiling glass. To satisfy zoning, the curtain wall is veiled by a system of operable, glass masonry screens. Glass bricks in a running bond pattern with staggered voids are threaded on rods like beads and suspended on tracks in front of the glass wall at every floor slab. Rigid building units are reconceived into a hefty textile screen that can be drawn by tenants like grand mineral curtains. Light and view can be regulated by overlapping the brick curtains to various degrees of porosity, always maintaining 50% masonry coverage.
DS+R

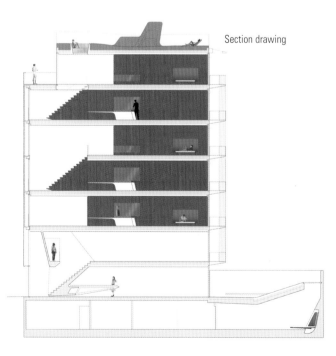

Section drawing

Detail drawings, glass masonry façade system

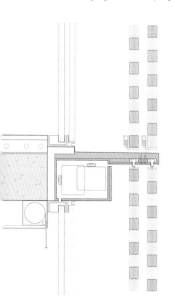
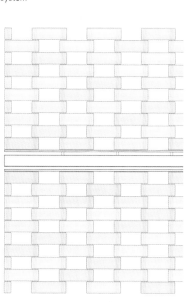

Selected Projects List

Currently in progress or completed 2007
Boulders, renovation and expansion of spa resort, Scottsdale, Arizona (to be completed 2009), project team: Michael Etzel (leader), Jesse Saylor, Sascha Delz, Frank Gesualdi.

High Line, design of park on 1.5 miles of elevated train line, New York (to be completed 2009), project team: Matthew Johnson (leader), Tobias Hegemann, Gaspar Libedinsky, David Newton, consulting engineers: Buro Happold, Robert Silman Associates, GRB Services, Inc, in collaboration with Field Operations, Piet Oudolf, L'Observatoire International.

Juilliard expansion and Alice Tully Hall expansion and renovation, New York (to be completed 2008–09) project leaders: Gerard Sullivan, Ben Gilmartin, Robert Condon, team: Ben Mickus, Anthony Saby, Sebastian Guivernau, Krists Karklins, Chiara Baccarini, Josh Uhl, Frank Gesualdi, Eric Höweler, Stefan Gruber, associate architects: FX Fowle Architects, consulting Engineers: Ove Arup, NY (in progress since 2003).

Light Sock, chandelier for Swarovski's Crystal Palace, project team: David Allin (leader), Shawn Mackinnon, Hayley Eber.

Lincoln Center 65th St Project, New York, design of 65th street, North Plaza, new restaurant pavilion, screening theaters for Film Society (to be completed 2009), project leaders: Kevin Rice, Robert Condon team: Michael Hundsnurscher, Felipe Ferrer, Pablo Garcia, Peter Zuspan, Sascha Delz, Robert Donnelly, Roman Loretan, Toshikatsu Kiuchi, associate architects: FX Fowle Architects, consulting engineers: Ove Arup NY (in progress since 2003).

Lincoln Center promenade project, New York, redesign of public spaces at Columbus Ave, Robertson Plaza, Concourse (to be completed 2009), project team: Ben Gilmartin (leader), Pablo Garcia, Laith Sayigh, Matt Peterson, associate architects: Beyer Blinder Belle, consulting engineers: Ove Arup, NY (in progress since 2005).

Mott Street (Kopp) Townhouse, New York, private residence (to be completed 2008), project team: Stefan Roschert (leader), Simon Arnold, Toshikatsu Kiuchi, Jeremy Linzee, consulting engineers: Ove Arup, NY.

School of American Ballet, New York, expansion of dance studios, project leaders: Michael Hundsnurscher, Robert Condon, collaborating engineers: Ove Arup, NY.

Completed 2006
"Have You Ever Been Mistaken for a ....?" installation in collaboration with Mira Nair, Lille 3000, France, project Leader: Hayley Eber.

Institute of Contemporary Art, Boston, Massachusetts, new museum with 18,000-square-foot galleries, black box theater, restaurant, education facility. project team: Flavio Stigliano (leader), Deane Simpson, Jesse Saylor, and Eric Höweler, collaborating engineers: Arup NY/London, associate architect: Perry Dean Rogers and Partners, Boston MA.

Who's your Dada? Performance in collaboration with The Wooster Group, MoMA, New York, NY, Project Leader: Hayley Eber.

Completed 2005
Quadrant House, Phoenix, Arizona, private residence at edge of Camelback Mountain (on hold).

Tivoli Gardens, Masterplan for 100,000-sqare-foot expansion at periphery of historic amusement park, Copenhagen, Denmark (unrealized).

Completed 2004
Eyebeam Museum of Art & Technology, New York (on hold), project team: Deane Simpson, Dirk Hebel (leaders), and Gabu Heindl, collaborating engineers: Ove Arup, NY, collaboration with Ben Rubin, Tom Igoe, Joe Paradiso.

Facsimile, Moscone Convention Center West, San Francisco, permanent installation, in collaboration with Ben Rubin and Mark Hansen, project leaders: Lyn Rice and Matthew Johnson, collaborating engineer: Les Okreglak.

Snow Show, installation Kemi, Finland.

Completed 2003
Building a Vision: Diller + Scofidio in Boston, Institute of Contemporary Art, Boston.

Diller + Scofidio Retrospective, Whitney Museum of American Art, New York.

Mural, Whitney Museum of American Art, New York, installation for *Scanning: The Aberrant*

Architectures of Diller + Scofidio, in collaboration with Honeybee Robotics, project assistants: Mark Wasiuta and Don Shillingburg.

Waterfront Park, recreational park with mixed use urban development, incorporating recreational, residential, retail and cultural programs (study, unrealized).

Completed 2002
Blur Building, Lake Neuchâtel, Yverdon-les-Bains, Switzerland, media pavilion for Swiss EXPO 2002, project team: Dirk Hebel (leader), Charles Renfro, Eric Bunge, and Alex Haw, collaborating engineers: Passera & Pedretti, advisor: Fujiko Nakaya, sound installation: Christian Marclay.

Inoui, Tokyo and Osaka, Japan, flagship store and department store prototype for Shiseido, in collaboration with Open Office, project team: Matthew Johnson, Gabriel Heindl, and Alfio Faro.

Untitled Media Landscape, Lake Neuchâtel Yverdon-les-Bains, Switzerland, media pavilion for Swiss EXPO 2002 in collaboration with Douglas Cooper, Diego Marani, and West 8, project team: Matthew Johnson and Dirk Hebel.

Completed 2001
Brooklyn Academy of Music Cultural District: Master Plan, New York, arts complex plan, in collaboration with Rem Koolhaas/OMA, project team: Charles Renfro (leader), Dirk Hebel, and Matthias Hollwich.

Buy/Sell, Palais de Tokyo, Paris, concept store for evansandwong, project assistant: Alex Haw (unrealized).

Travelogues, International Arrivals Terminal (Terminal 4). John F. Kennedy International Airport, New York, permanent installation, project leaders: Deane Simpson and Matthew Johnson.

Two-Way Hotel, Hong Kong, hotel in entertainment complex for Cirque du Soleil, project assistant: Alex Haw (unrealized).

Viewing Platforms, Ground Zero/World Trade Center site, New York, in collaboration with Kevin Kennon and the Rockwell Group.

Virtual Office for Vitra, NeoCon, Chicago, installation, project assistant: Deane Simpson, script: Ted Beunz.

Completed 2000
Bar Beam, Brasserie, Seagram Building, New York, media installation, in collaboration with Ben Rubin.

Braincoat, media component of Blur Building in collaboration with Ben Rubin and Tom Igoe.

Brasserie, Seagram Building, New York, restaurant design, project team: Charles Renfro (leader) and Deane Simpson.

Rapid Growth, Philadelphia Museum of Art, landscape installation, in collaboration with Marty Chafkin, project assistant: Deane Simpson (unrealized).

Slither Building, Gifu, Japan, 105-unit social housing complex, project team: Paul Lewis, Patrice Gardera, and Matthias Hollwich.

Completed 1999
Budget Inn Room 120, site Santa Fe, New Mexico, installation for *Looking for a Place: Third International Biennial*, project assistant: Deane Simpson.

Master/Slave, Fondation Cartier pour l'art contemporain, Paris, installation for *1 Monde Reel*, in collaboration with Lyn Rice.

Completed 1998
The American Lawn: Surface of Everyday Life, Canadian Centre for Architecture, Montreal, exhibition co-curation and design (traveled), project team: Mark Wasiuta (leader), Lyn Rice, and Gwynne Keathley.

EJM1: Man Walking at Ordinary Speed, premiere, Biennale de la Danse de Lyon, Ballet de l'Opéra national de Lyon, multimedia dance collaboration with Charleroi/Danses (international tour).

EJM2: Inertia, premiere, Biennale de la Danse de Lyon, Ballet de l'Opéra national de Lyon, multimedia dance collaboration with Ballet de l'Opéra national de Lyon.

Jet Lag, premiere, Lantaren Theater, Rotterdam, Dutch Electronic Arts Festival, multimedia theater collaboration with The Builders Association (international tour), project assistant: Paul Lewis.

Refresh, DIA Center for the Arts, New York, Internet project, project assistant: Nicholas DeMoncheaux.

Completed 1997
Interclone Hotel, Fifth International Istanbul Biennial, Ataturk Airport, Istanbul, installation, project assistant: Deane Simpson.

Non-Place, San Francisco Museum of Modern Art, installation.

Pageant, 2nd Johannesburg Biennial, South Africa, installation.

Subtopia, International Center for Communications Gallery, NTT, Tokyo, installation and Internet project, project assistants: James Gibbs and Lyn Rice.

Vice/Virtue Glasses, Internationale Glasmanifestatie, Leerdam, The Netherlands. Set of four glasses, project assistant: Mark Wasiuta.

X, Y, Kobe, Japan, permanent installation in pachinko parlor, project team: Lyn Rice and Paul Lewis.

Completed 1996
CNN Center, Turner Broadcasting and CNN headquarters, Atlanta, permanent installation in collaboration with Romm + Pearsall (unrealized).

(Monkey) Business Class, premiere, Malmö Music Theater, Sweden, multimedia theater collaboration with Hotel Pro Forma and Dumb Type (international tour).

Moving Target, premiere, Palais de Beaux-Arts, Brussels, multimedia dance collaboration with Charleroi/Danses (international tour).

Completed 1995
Cold War, Sunrise Civic Arena, Fort Lauderdale, Florida, permanent installation, project assistant: Paul Lewis (unrealized).

Food Chain, Palais des Beaux-Arts, Brussels, installation for *Diller + Scofidio: Investments*.

Indigestion, Palais des Beaux-Arts, Brussels, installation for *Diller + Scofidio: Investments*, in collaboration with Douglas Cooper, Marianne Weems, and Banff Centre for New Media Research.

Jump Cuts, United Artists Cineplex Theater, San Jose, California, permanent installation, project assistant: Paul Lewis.

Phaedra, HERE Theater, New York, stage set design in collaboration with Creation Production Company.

Skin, Palais des Beaux-Arts, Brussels, installation for *Diller + Scofidio: Investments*, in collaboration with Matthew Maguire.

Completed 1994
Feed, Metropolitan Transit Authority, 33rd Street subway station, New York, permanent installation, project assistant: Paul Lewis (unrealized).

Overexposed, The Getty Center for the History of Art and the Humanities, Los Angeles, video performance, project assistant: Paul Lewis.

Completed 1993
Bad Press, Centre d'art contemporain, Castres, France, installation (developed through 1998), project team: John Bachus, Brendan Cotter, and David Lindberg.

Case #00-17164, The New Museum, New York, installation for *The Final Frontier*, project assistant: Ted Beunz.

Forced Choice, Maison de la Magie, Blois, France. permanent installation, project assistant: Brendan Cotter (unrealized).

Soft Sell, The Rialto, New York, installation for *42nd Street Project*, presented by Creative Time, New York, project team: Brendan Cotter and Calvert Wright.

Squeeze, V2, 's-Hertogenbosch, The Netherlands, installation.

Ventilator, Museum of Contemporary Art, Chicago, permanent installation (unrealized).

Completed 1992
The Desiring Eye: Reviewing the Slow House, Gallery Ma, Tokyo, installation (traveled).

Loophole, Museum of Contemporary Art, Chicago, installation for *Art at the Armory: Occupied Territory*, project assistants: Calvert Wright and Ted Buenz.

Photo Opportunity, Walter Phillips Gallery, Banff, Canada, installation for *Queues, Rendezvous, Riots: Questioning the Public in Art and Architecture*.

Completed 1991
Slow House, North Haven, New York, residence, project team: Victor Wong, Peter Burns, and Sam Solhaug (unrealized).

Tourisms: suit(Case) Studies, Walker Art Center, Minneapolis, installation (traveled), project team: Victor Wong, Christopher Evans, Peter Burns, and Bob McAnulty.

Completed 1989
Para-Site, Projects Series, The Museum of Modern Art, New York, installation, project assistant: Victor Wong.

Completed 1988
Bodybuildings Ii, Institute for Contemporary Art, University of Pennsylvania, Philadelphia, Installation.

Completed 1987
Bodybuildings: Architectural Facts And Fictions, Storefront for Art and Architecture, New York, installation.

Hochman Properties, Tuxedo Park, New York, additions and renovations of historic Russell Sturgis house, boathouse, and gymnasium.

The Rotary Notary and His Hot Plate (A Delay in Glass) premiere, The Painted Bride Art Center, Philadelphia, theater collaboration with Creation Production Company.

The Withdrawing Room, Capp Street Project, San Francisco, installation, project assistant: Christopher Otterbine

Completed 1986
Synapse, Creative Time, Brooklyn Bridge Anchorage, New York, installation for performance of *The Memory Theatre of Giulio Camillo*, in collaboration with Creation Production Company.

Urban, Suburban, Rural Windows, Milan, Italy, installation for XVII Triennale di Milano.

Completed 1984
Gate, Creative Time, Battery Park City Landfill, New York, installation for Art on the Beach.

The American Mysteries, premiere, La Mama ETC, New York, theater work collaboration with Creation Production Company.

Completed 1983
Sentinel, Creative Time, New York, installation for performance of *Civic Plots*, in collaboration with Jim Holl and Kaylynn Sullivan.

Completed 1982
Window, Room, Furniture, Houghton Gallery, The Cooper Union, New York, installation and curation, in collaboration with Williams & Tsien.

Completed 1981
Kinney (Plywood) House, Briarcliff Manor, New York, residence.

Traffic, Institute for Architecture & Urban Studies, New York, installation in Columbus Circle.

Studio Chronology

	1979	1980	1981	1982	1983	1984	1985	1986

SELECTED PROJECTS

Urban

Architecture — ☐ Plywood (Kinney) House (1981)

Interior — ☐ (1986)

Perm. Installation — ☐ (1986)

Temp. Installation — ☐ Traffic (1981) — ☐ Window, Room, Furniture (1982) — ☐ Gate (1984) — ☐ Urban, Suburban, Ru... (1986) — ☐ (1986)

Performance — ☐ Sentinel (1983) — ☐ American Mysteries (1984) — ☐ Synapse (1986) — ☐ (1986)

Media

SELECTED EXHIBITIONS

☐ Milan Triennale (1986)
☐ (1986)
☐ (1986)

SELECTED PUBLICATIONS

☐ (1986)

AWARDS

☐ (1986)

TEACHING

Scofidio ═══════════════════════════════

Diller   ═══════════════════════

Renfro

STUDIO

☐ Diller + Scofidio formed (1979)

EVENTS

World
☐ IBM Personal Computer released (1981)
☐ Frampton: Modern Architecture: A Critical History (1981)
☐ Parc de la Villette Competition (1982)
☐ Hong Kong Peak Competition (1983)
☐ Buckminster Fuller dies (1983)
☐ First Apple MacIntosh released (1984)
☐ Chernobyl (1986)

USA
☐ Second Oil Crisis (1979)
☐ Moore, Piazzo D'Italia, New Orleans (1979)
☐ HIV first identified (1981)
☐ Reagan wins 1980 Presidential Election (1981)
☐ Michel Foucault dies (1984)
☐ Foster: The Anti-Aesthetic (1983)
☐ Iran.Contra Affa... (1986)

New York
☐ Marshall McLuhan dies (1981)
☐ John Lennon killed (1981)
☐ Eisenman steps down as Director of Institute for Architecture and Urban Studies (1982)
☐ Johnson, AT+T Building (1984)
☐ A... (1986)

Selected Exhibitions

2007

First International Architecture Triennale of Lisbon, Portugal, *Urban Voids*

Krannert Art Museum, University of Illinois, Champaign, Illinois, *Branded and On Display*

National Arts Center, Tokyo, Japan, *Skin and Bones: Parallel Practices in Fashion and Architecture*

Waino Aaltonen Museum of Art, Turku, Finland, *Wild – Fantasy and Architecture*

2006

Barbican Centre, London, *Future City: Experiment and Utopia in Architecture 1956-2006*

Center for Architecture, New York, *City of Culture: New Architecture for the Arts*

Center for Architecture, New York, *Going Public 2: City Snapshot(s) and Case Studies of the Mayor's Design and Construction Excellence Initiative*

Galerie Sfeir-Semler, Beirut, Lebanon, *Moving Homes*

Grimaldi Forum, Monaco, *New York*

La Biennale di Venezia 10th International Architecture Exhibition, Venice, Italy, *Cities*

LA MOCA, Los Angeles, *Skin and Bones: Parallel Practices in Fashion and Architecture* (traveled to The National Art Center, Tokyo)

London Biennale, London, *The World in One City – A Sketch for London*

MART, Rovereto, Italy, *Universal Experience: Art, Life and the Tourist's Eye*

Museo Nazionale Delle Arti del XXI Secolo, Rome Italy, *The 21st Century: New Museums* (traveled to Lentos Kunstmuseum Linz, Austria, Kunstsammlung Nordrhein-Westfalen, Dusseldorf, Germany; Musee des Confluences, Lyon, France; MART, Museo di Arte Moderna e Contemporanea di Trento, Italy; Caixa General de Depositos Culturgest Lisboa, Lisbon, Portugal; Staatliche Museum zu Berlin, Kulturforum, Berlin, Germany; Louisiana Museum of Modern Art, Humlebeak, Denmark; National Museum of Art, Architecture and Design, Oslo, Norway)

Museum of Modern Art, New York, *Acquisitions*

Pavillon de l'Arsenal, Paris, *Architects Scenographies*

Santa Monica Museum, Santa Monica, California, *Dark Places*

Van Alen Institute, New York, *The Good Life*

2005

Architectural Association Gallery, London, *Can Buildings Curate?* (traveled to Storefront for Art and Architecture, New York)

Centre Culturel Suisse, Paris, *Invisible Architecture*

Espai d'Art Contemporani de Castello, Madrid, Spain, *Terra Firma*

Griffin Contemporary, Los Angeles, *Weather*

Henry Urbach Gallery, New York, *Slither Building*

Museum of Contemporary Art Chicago, The Hayward Gallery, London, *Universal Experience: Art, Life and the Tourist's Eye*

Museum of Modern Art, New York, *The High Line* (solo)

Van Alen Institute, New York, *New Designs for Public Space*

2004

Beijing, China, *The 1st Beijing Biennale*

Centre Pompidou, Paris, France, *Architectures Non Standard*

Deutches Arkitecturmuseum, Frankfurt, Germany, *Post-Modernism Revisited*

Genoa, Italy, *Art & Architettura 1900-2000*

Kemi, Finland, *Snow Show*

La Biennale di Venezia 9th International Archtitecture Exhibition, Venice, Italy, *Metamorph*

Laznia Centre for Contemporary Art, Gdansk, Poland, *re(framed) locations, dis(covered) desires*

National Academy of Design, New York, New York, *179th Annual: An Invitational Exhibition of Contemporary Art*

Postbahnhof am Ostbahnhof, Berlin, Germany, *Silent Wandering, Ways of World Making Too…*

The Building Centre, London, England, *Digital Fabricators*

2003

Arena Congress Center, Verona, Italy, *Digital Scapes: Global Remix*

Association of United Architects of Israel Gallery, Jaffa, Israel, *Soft[ware Boundaries]*

Atelier Municipal 3, Lisbon, Portugal, *ExperimentaDesign*

Congress Center, Verona, Italy, *Digital Scapes: Global Remix Arena*

Editrice Compositori, Bologna, Italy, *Contemporary Museum Design Exhibit / Markitecture: Architecture and Culture*

Krasnoyarsk, Siberia, *Krasnoyarsk Museum Biennale*

La Biennale di Venezia, 50th Edition of the International Art Exhibition, Venice, Italy, *Utopia Station*

Ocularis Cinema, Brooklyn, New York, *New York Architexture*

Schusev Russian State Museum of Architecture, Moscow, Russia, *Project Classica*

Van Alen Institute, New York. *OPEN: New designs for Public Spaces* (traveled to National Building Museum, Washington, DC)

Whitney Museum of American Art, New York, *Scanning: The Aberrant Architectures of Diller+Scofidio* (retrospective)

2002

Artists Space, New York, *Infotecture*

Buell Center, Columbia University, New York, *Architourism*

Cooper-Hewitt, National Design Museum, New York, *New Hotels for Global Nomads*

Cooper-Hewitt, National Design Museum, New York, *Skin: Surface, Substance +Design*

La Biennale di Venezia, 8th International Architecture Exhibition, Venice, Italy, *Next*

National Museum of Contemporary Art, Athens, Greece, *Big Brother: Architecture and Surveillance*

Netherlands Architecture Institute, Rotterdam, *Latent Space*

2001

Archilab, Orleans, France, *Dwellings Today*

Eyebeam Atelier, New York, *Open Source Architecture: Building Eyebeam*

Henry Urbach Gallery, New York, *Third Anniversary Exhibition*

Lawrence Wilson Art Gallery, University of Western Australia, Perth, *Do It*

San Francisco Museum of Modern Art, *010101: Art in Technological Times*

Van Alen Institute, New York, *Architecture + Water* (traveled to UCLA Department of Architecture, Los Angeles, 2001; Heinz Architectural Center, Carnegie Museum of Art, Pittsburgh, 2002; San Francisco Museum of Modern Art, San Francisco, 2002)

ZKM Center for Art and Media, Karlsruhe, Germany, *CTRL [SPACE]: Rhetorics of Surveillance from Bentham to Big Brother*

2000

Artists Space, New York, *Anywhere But Here* (with The Builders Association)

FRAC Alsace, Selestat, France, *Collection 2: Curiosites Contemporaines*

K&S Galerie, Berlin, with ZKM Center for Art and Media, Karlsruhe, Germany

La Biennale di Venezia, Seventh International Architecture Exhibition, Venice, Italy, *Città: Less Aesthetics, More Ethics*

Louis Stern Fine Arts, West Hollywood, California,
Claude Parent: *An Oblique Lineage:
Drawings and Models by Architects and Artists*
Museum of Contemporary Art, Los Angeles,
*At the End of the Century: One Hundred Years of
Architecture* (traveled to Museum of Contemporary
Art, Tokyo, 1998; Antiguo Colegio de San Ildefonso,
Mexico City, 1998; Museum Ludwig/Josef-
Haubrich-Kunsthalle, Cologne, Germany, 1999;
Museum of Contemporary Art, Chicago, 1999)
New York Video Festival, Film Society, New York
White Box Gallery, New York, *After the Diagram*

1999
Centre d'Art Contemporain, Brussels, *Facettes de la
Collection du FRAC de Basse-Normandie a Caen*
Fondation Cartier pour l'art contemporain, Paris,
1 Monde Reel
Henry Urbach Gallery, New York, *Luster*
International Exhibition of Contemporary Art,
Pusan, South Korea, *Light on the New
Millennium: Wind from the Extreme Orient*
Kunstforeningen, Copenhagen, *Act 1: Stage Art
and the Visual Arts*
Ministerio de Fomento, Madrid, *Diller+Scofidio* (solo)
The Museum of Modern Art, New York,
The Un-Private House (traveled to MAK, Vienna,
1999; Walker Art Center, Minneapolis, 2000;
UCLA Hammer Museum, Los Angeles, 2000)
SITE Santa Fe, New Mexico, *Looking for a Place:
Third International Biennial*

1998
Canadian Centre for Architecture, Montreal,
*The American Lawn: Surface of Everyday
Life* (traveled to Contemporary Arts Center,
Cincinnati, 1999; Museum of Art,
Fort Lauderdale, 1999)
Creative Time, Brooklyn Bridge Anchorage,
New York, *Ret.Inevitable*
Gallery 1, RIBA Architecture Centre, London,
The Displaced Grid
International Film Festival Rotterdam,
The Netherlands
Kulturburos stadt Dortmund, Germany, *Reservate
der Sehnsucht*
Landesgalerie, Linz, Austria, *Work& Culture*
pArts, Minneapolis, *Digital Documentary:
The Need to Know The Urge to Show*
Thomas Healy Gallery, New York, *Bathroom*

1997
Barbican Art Gallery, London, and Laing Art
Gallery, Tyne and Wear Museums, New Castle,
England, *Serious Games*

Fifth International Biennial in Nagoya, Japan,
ARTEC '97
Fifth International Istanbul Biennial, Istanbul,
Turkey, *On Life, Beauty, Translations and Other
Difficulties*
Galerie Thaddaeus Ropac, Paris, *sous la manteau*
Galerie Xippas, Paris, *Prehension*
MIT List Visual Arts Center, Cambridge (MA),
*The Art of Detection: Surveillance
in Society*
Museu d'Art Contemporani de Barcelona,
Nuevos Paisajes/New Landscapes
NTT InterCommunication Center, Tokyo,
The Mirage City: Another Utopia
Sagacho Exhibit Space, Tokyo, *The Other
Architecture*
San Francisco Museum of Modern Art,
Icons: Magnets of Meaning
Second Johannesburg Biennale, South Africa,
Trade Routes
Walter Phillips Gallery, Banff, Canada,
Language Games

1996
Centre d'Art Contemporain de La Ferme
du Buisson, France, *Fluctuations Fugitives
(mutation 2)*
FRAC Basse-Normandie, Caen, France,
Espaces Construits: Espaces Critiques
Gallery Ma, Tokyo, *The 53 Origins*
Kunsthalle Wien, Austria, *Die Schrift des Raumes:
KunstArchitektur Kunst*
Kunstverein Munich, Germany, *Spaced Out*
La Biennale di Venezia Sixth International
Architecture Exhibit, Venice, Italy, *Sensing
the Future: Architect as Seismograph*
Musee des Beaux-Arts et de la Dentelle,Calais,
France, *Diller+Scofidio: Investments* (solo)
Museum of Modern Art, New York,
New Acquisitions
Neue Galerie am Landesmuseum Joanneum,
Graz, Austria, *Indigestion* (solo)
Robert Lehman Gallery, UrbanGlass, Brooklyn,
People in Glass Houses …

1995
Collegi d'Aparelladors i Arquitectes Tecnics
de Barcelona, *Arquitectures limit*
Espace d'Art Yvonamor Palix, Paris, *Fluctuations
Fugitives*
Grazer Kunstverein, Graz, Austria,
Self Made
Le Nouveau Musee/Institut d'Art Contemporain,
Villeurbanne, France, *Artistes/Architectes*
(traveled to Centre Culturel de Belem, Lisbon,

Portugal, 1996; Kunstverein, Munich, Germany,
1996; Kunsthalle, Vienna, 1997)
Palais des Beaux-Arts, Brussels, *Diller+Scofidio:
Investments* (solo)
Queens Museum of Art, New York,
City Speculations

1993
Centre d'Art Contemporain de Castres,
France, *Dysfonctionnalisme* (solo)
The Museum of Modern Art, New York,
New Acquisitions
The New Museum, New York, *The Final Frontier*
Richard Anderson Gallery, New York, *Bad Press:
Housework Series* (solo)
V2, '5-Hertogenbosch, The Netherlands,
Prothesen

1992
Arc en Reve Centre d'Architecture, Bordeaux,
France, *Diller+Scofidio* (solo)
Fondation Cartier pour l'art contemporain,
Jouy-en-Josas, France, *Machines d'Architecture*
Gallery Ma, Tokyo. *The Desiring Eye: Reviewing
the Slow House* (solo, traveled to Arc en Reve
Centre d'Architecture, Bordeaux, France, 1992;
XIX Triennale di Milano, Italy, 1994; Magasin,
Centre National d'Art Contemporain de
Grenoble, France, 1994; Palais des Beaux-Arts,
Brussels, 1995; Ikon Gallery, Birmingham,
England, 1996))
Museum of Contemporary Art, Chicago, *Art at the
Armory: Occupied Territory*
Palais Jacques Coeur, Bourges, France,
Architectures Charnieres
Richard Anderson Gallery, New York,
Love Gone Bad
Walter Phillips Gallery, Banff, Canada, *Queues,
Rendezvous, Riots: Questioning the Public in Art
and Architecture*

1991
Sadock & Uzzan Galerie, Paris, *Non Sequiturs*
(solo)
Walker Art Center, Minneapolis, *Tourisms:
suitCase Studies* (solo, traveled to MIT List
Visual Arts Center, Cambridge (MA),
1991; Wexner Center for the Arts,
Ohio State University, Columbus, 1992;
FRAC Basse-Normandie, Caen, France,
1994)

1989
Deutsches Architekturmuseum, Frankfurt, *New
YorkArchitektur: 1970- 1990*

Klostertorv 9, Galleri for design og arkitektur,
Arhus, Denmark, *Diller+Scofidio* (solo)
Museum of Modern Art, New York, *Para-Site*
(solo)

1988
Galleri Rom, Oslo, *Diller+Scofidio* (solo)
Institute of Contemporary Art, University of
Pennsylvania, Philadelphia, *Investigations*
Nature Morte, New York, *Architectural
Exhibition: Plans and Models for Alternative
Gallery Spaces*

1987
Capp Street Project, San Francisco,
The withDrawing Room (solo)
Storefront for Art and Architecture, New York,
Bodybuildings: Architectural Facts and Fictions
(solo)

1986
Artists Space, New York, *From Here to Eternity*
International Design Center, New York, *Forty
Under Forty*
XVII Triennale di Milano, Italy, *Il Progetto
Domestico*

1985
L'Institut Français d'Architecture, Paris, *Nouvelles
Directions de l'Architecture Moderne*

1984
Max Protetch Gallery, New York, *Furnishingsby
Architects: Prototypes of New Designs*

1982
Houghton Gallery, The Cooper Union, New York,
Window, Room, Furniture

Selected Awards and Fellowships

2007

American Institute of Architects Design Award
for the Institute of Contemporary Art

Architectural Lighting Magazine Outstanding
Achievement Award for the Institute of
Contemporary Art (with Arup Lighting)

Travel and Leisure Design Awards Honorable
Mention for the Institute of Contemporary Art

2006

Visionary Award, Fashion Group International

Urban Visionary Award, Cooper Union

2005

National Design Award in Architecture from
the Smithsonian Cooper-Hewitt National Design
Museum

2004

AICA-USA American Section of the International
Art Critics Award, for "Scanning: The Aberrant
Architectures of Diller + Scofidio"

High Line International Design Competition,
First Place

2003

Arnold W. Brunner Memorial Prize in Architecture,
American Academy of Arts and Letters

Citation, Progressive Architecture for Eyebeam
Museum of Art & Technology

Golden Rabbit, best building of 2002, Swiss TV
and B. Magazine

Lincoln Center, International Design Competition,
First Place

2002

Eyebeam Museum of Art &Technology, New York,
International Design Competition, First Place

2001

Institute of Contemporary Art, Boston,
commission award for new museum
MASterwork Award for Public Art, Municipal
Art Society, New York

2000

Eugene McDermott Award for Creative
Achievement, Massachusetts Institute
of Technology

I.D. Design Review, Design Distinction
in Environments, Brasserie

James Beard Foundation Award for Outstanding
Restaurant Design, Brasserie

MacArthur Foundation Fellowship
in Architecture

Obie Award, Outstanding Achievement in
Off-Broadway Theater, Special Citation for
Jet Lag (with The Builders Association)

Progressive Architecture Design Award,
Blur Building

1998

EXPO 2001, Switzerland, First Place

Graham Foundation for Advanced Studies in the
Fine Arts, Fellowship

New York Public Arts Commission Competition,
JFK Airport International Arrivals Building,
First Place

Saint-Gaudens Medal, Irwin S. Chanin School
of Architecture, The Cooper Union

1997

Chrysler Award for Innovation in Design

San Francisco Public Arts Commission
Competition, Moscone Convention Center,
First Place

1996

Fort Lauderdale Public Arts Commission
Competition, Civic Arena, First Place

1995

San Jose Public Arts Commission Competition,
United Artists Theaters, First Place

1993

Arts for Transit Competition, Metropolitan Transit
Authority, permanent installation at Lexington
Avenue and 33rd Street Station

Centre for New Media Research Media Grant
and Residency, Banff Centre, Canada and Centre
Pompidou

1991

Progressive Architecture Award, Architectural
Design, for Slow House

1990

Tiffany Foundation Award for Emerging Artists

1989

Distinguished Alumni Citation, Irwin 5. Chanin
School of Architecture, The Cooper Union

1987

Bessie Schoenberg Dance and Performance Award
for The Memory Theater of Giulio Camillo

1986

Interiors Magazine, Forty Under Forty Award

Bibliography

Selected Books and Catalogues

5th International Istanbul Biennial. Istanbul: Istanbul Foundation for Culture and Arts, 1997.

Adrìaansens, Alex, et al., eds. *Book for the Unstable Media*. 's-Hertogenbosch, The Netherlands: Stichting V2, 1992.

Alison, Jane, Marie-Ange Brayer, Frederic Migayrou and Neil Spiller. *Future City: Experiment and Utopia in Architecture, 1956-2006*. London, UK: Barbican, 2006.

Annual InterCommunication '95. Tokyo: InterCommunication Center, NTT, 1995.

Archilab Orléans 2001. Orléans, France: Ville d'Orléans, 2001.

Architects Today, London, UK: Laurence King Publishing Ltd., 2004.

Architecture & Arts 1900/2004. Milan: Skira, 2004.

Architektur und Verantwortung: 5. Internationales Architektur-forum in Prag. Cologne, Germany: Edition Arcum, 1996.

Asensio, Paco, ed. *Bars & Restaurants*. Barcelona: Loft Publications, 2001.

Azara, Pedro, and Carles Guri. *Architects on Stage: Stage and Exhibition Design in the 90's*. Barcelona: Gustavo Gili, 2000.

Bahamon, Alejandro. *New York Architecture*. daab, 2004.

Baird, George, and Mark Lewis, eds. *Queues, Rendezvous, Riots: Questioning the Public in Art and Architecture*. Banff, Canada: Walter Phillips Gallery/The Banff Centre for the Arts, 1994.

Ballesteros, Jose Alfonso, and Federico Soriano, eds. *Las Ciudades Inasibles*. Madrid: FISURAS de la Cultura Contemporanea, 1997.

Barbara, Anna, and Anthony Perliss. *Invisible Architecture: Experiencing places Through the Sense of Smell*. Milan: Skira, 2006.

Baume, Nicholas. "It's Still Fun to Have Architecture: Interview with Diller Scofidio + Renfro" *Supervision*. Cambridge (MA): MIT Press, 2006.

Betsky, Aaron. *Building Sex: Men, Women, Architecture, and the Construction of Sexuality*. New York: William Morrow and Company, 1995.

-. And K. Michael Hays. *Scanning: the Aberrant Architectures of Diller + Scofidio*. New York: Whitney Press; Germany: Steidl, Germany, Essays by Ed Dimmendberg, Jordan Crandall, Roselee Goldberg, and Ashley Schafer, and a conversation with Laurie Anderson, 2003.

-. *Violated Perfection: Architecture and the Fragmentation of the Modern*. New York: Rizzoli International Publications, 1990.

Bodybuildings: Architectural Facts and Fictions. Diller + Scofidio. New York: Storefront for Art and Architecture, 1987.

"The Blur Building," *Verb Matter: Architecture Boogazine*. Actar, 2004.

Bonami, Francesco. *E. Diller & R. Scofidio, Interclone Hotel/Suitcases Studies, Universal Experience: Art, Life and the Tourist's Eye*. Chicago: Museum of Contemporary Art, 2005.

Bouman, Ole. *The Invisible in Architecture*. London: Academy Editions, 1994.

Brayer, Marie-Ange, and Beatrice Simonot, eds. *Archilab's Futurehouse: Radical Experiments in Living Space*. New York: Thames & Hudson, 2002.

Busquets, Joan. *Speculative Procedures, Cities X Lines*. GSD – Nicolodi, 2007.

Carter, Brian, and Annette Lecuyer. *All American: Innovation in American Architecture*. London: Thames & Hudson, 2002.

Chance, Julia, and Torsten Schmiedeknecht. *Fame and Architecture*. New York: John Wiley & Sons, 2002.

Christ, Ronald, and Dennis Dollens. *New York: Nomadic Design*. Barcelona: Gustavo Gili; New York: Rizzoli International Publications, 1993.

Coates, Stephen, and Alex Stetter. *Impossible Worlds*. Basel, Switzerland, and Boston: Birkhauser, 2000.

Crary, Jonathan, and Sanford Kwinter, eds. *Incorporations*. New York: Urzone, 1992.

Davidson, Cynthia C., ed. *Anybody*. Cambridge (MA): MIT Press, 1997.

-. *Anyplace*. Cambridge (MA): MIT Press, 1995.

-. *Anything*. Cambridge (MA): MIT Press, 2001.

-. *Anyway*. New York: Rizzoli International Publications, 1994.

Deamer, Peggy. *Elizabeth Diller – The Slow House, The Millenium House*. Yale School of Architecture, 2004.

Desmoulins, Christine. "Foundation Cartier pour l'art contemporain: Master/Slave Collection De Robots De Rolf Fehlbaum." *Scenographies D'Architectes / Architects' Exhibition Designs*, June 2006.

Diller+ Scofidio. Madrid: Ministerio de Fomento, 1999.

Diller + Scofidio. Tokyo: Gallery Ma, 1992.

Diller, Elizabeth, and Ricardo Scofidio. *Blur: The Making of Nothing*. New York: Henry N. Abrams, 2002.

-. *Flesh: Architectural Probes*. New York: Princeton Architectural Press, 1994.

-. *Visite aux Armées: Tourisms de Guerre/Back to the Front: Tourisms of War*. Caen, France: FRAC Basse-Normandie; New York: distributed by Princeton Architectural Press, 1994.

Dimenberg, Edward. "Architecture Inside Out: Urban Thresholds and the Digital Image." *Metamorph 9th International Architecture Exhibition Focus*. Venezia: La Biennale di Venezia, September 2004.

Ducros, Franqoise. *Diller+ Scofidio: les "architectures dissidents" de Diller et Scofidio*. Caen, France: FRAC Basse-Normandie, 1999.

EJM1/EJM2. Lyon, France: Ballet de l'opéra national de Lyon, 1998.

Enwezor, Okwui. Trade *Routes: History and Geography: 2nd Johannesburg Biennale*. Johannesburg, South Africa: Greater Johannesburg Metropolitan Council; The Hague, The Netherlands: Prince Claus Fund for Culture and Development, 1997.

Fast Forward >> Hot Spot Brain Cells. Beijing: Architecture Biennial, 2004.

Fausch, Deborah, Paulette Singley, Rodolphe el-Khoury, and Zvi Efrat, eds. *Architecture: In Fashion*. New York: Princeton Architectural Press, 1994.

Feireiss, Kristin, ed. *The Art of Architecture Exhibitions*. Rotterdam, The Netherlands: NAi Publishers, 2001.

Flachbart, Georg, and Peter Weibel. "Elizabeth Diller and Ricardo Scofidio: Architecture as a Habitable Medium," *Disappearing Architecture: From Real to Virtual to Quantum*. Birkhauser, 2005.

Frampton, Kenneth, and Michel W. Kagan. *Nouvelles Directions de l'Architecture Moderne*. France: Electa Moniteur, 1985.

Fung, Lance. "Experimental Processes," *The Snow Show*. 2005.

Gallery Ma 1992. Tokyo: Gallery Ma, 1993.

Galofaro, Luca. "Transforming Landscape," *Artscapes: Art as an approach to contemporary landscape*. Ed. Gustavo Gili, Barcelona: 148–57, 2003.

Goldberger, Paul. *Portraits of the New Architecture*. Assouline, 2004.

Graham, Beryl. "Diller + Scofidio," *Directions in Art: Digital Media*. UK: Heineman Library Press, 2003.

Greub, Suzanne, and Thierry Greub, "Diller Scofidio + Renfro, Museum of Art and Technology," *Museums in the 21st Century: Concepts, Projects, Buildings*. Basel: Art Centre, 2006.

Hejduk, John, et al. *The Education of an Architect*. New York: Rizzoli International Publications, 1991.

Hodge, Brooke. *Skin + Bones: Parallel Practices in Fashion and Architecture*. London: Thames and Hudson, 2006.

Hughes, Francesca, ed. *The Architect: Reconstructing Her Practice*. Cambridge (MA): MIT Press, 1996.

Iijima, Yoichi. "Discussing Borderlines: Interview with Diller + Scofidio." *Gallery Ma 1992*. Tokyo: Gallery Ma, 1993.

Il Progetto Domestico: XVII Triennale di Milano. Milan: Electa, 1986.

Isenstadt, Sandy. *The Modern American House: Spaciousness and Middle Class Identity*. Cambridge (MA): MIT Press, 2006.

Isozaki, Arata. *The Mirage City: Another Utopia*. Tokyo: NTT InterCommunication Center, 1997.

Jodido, Philip. "Diller Scofidio + Renfro #4," *Architecture in the United States*, November. Taschen, 2006.

- . *Architecture; Nature*. Prestel, 2006.

- . "Diller Scofidio + Renfro, The High Line," *Architecture Now! 4*. Cologne, Germany: Taschen, 2006.

- . "Diller + Scofidio," *Architecture Now! 3*, Cologne, Germany: Taschen, 2004.

- . *Architecture Now!* Cologne, Germany: Taschen, 2001.

Kahn, Robin. *Time Capsule: A Concise Encyclopedia by Women Artists*. New York: Creative Time/Distributed Art Publishers, 1995.

King, John. "A Matter of Perception; Escalators, Moving Sidewalks, and the Motion of Society," *Up, Down, Across: Elevators, Escalators, and Moving Sidewalks*. National Building Museum, 2003.

King, Sarah S., ed. *Looking for a Place: SITE Santa Fe Third International Biennial*. Santa Fe, New Mexico: SITE Santa Fe, 1999.

Klotz, Heinrich, and Luminita Sabau, eds. *New York Architektur 1970 - 1990*. Munich: Prestel, 1989.

Koshalek, Richard, and Elizabeth A.T. Smith, eds. *At the End of the Century: One Hundred Years of Architecture*. Los Angeles: The Museum of Contemporary Art; New York: Henry N. Abrams, 1998.

Kubo and Salazar. "*A Brief History of the Information Age*," *Matters, VERB*. Barcelona: Actar, 2005.

Lleo, Blanca. "La Casa Futura: un oasis a la carta," *Sueno de habitar*. Barcelona: Gili, 2005.

Levin, Thomas Y., Ursula Frohne, and Peter Weibel, eds. *CTRL [SPACE]: Rhetorics of Surveillance from Bentham to Big Brother*. Karlsruhe, Germany: ZKM Center for Art and Media; Cambridge (MA): MIT Press, 2002.

Lim, Cj, and Ed Liu, eds. *Realms of Impossibility*. Water, West Sussex, England: Wiley-Academy, 2002.

Liu, Yu-Tung. "Diller Scofidio + Renfro: Eyebeam Museum of Art and Technology," *Diversifying Digital Architecture: 2003 FEIDAD Award*. Basel: Birkäuser, 2003.

Lupton, Ellen. *Skin: Surface, Substance + Design*. New York: Princeton Architectural Press and Smithsonian Institution, 2002.

Machines d'Architecture. Paris: Fondation Cartier pour l'art contemporain/Techniques & Architecture, 1992.

Marotta, Antonello. *Diller + Scofidio: Il Teatro Della Dissolvenza*. Rome: Edilstampa, 2005.

McAnulty, Robert. "Body Troubles." *Strategies in Architectural Thinking*. Cambridge (MA): MIT Press, 1992.

Metamorph 9th International Architecture Exhibition Trajectories. Venice: La Biennale di Venezia, September 2004.

Miller, Susan. *Capp Street Project, 1987- 1988*. San Francisco: The Capp Street Project, 1989.

Mitnick, Keith. "Diller + Scofidio: Eyebeam Museum of New Media: the 2002 Charles and Ray Eames Lecture," *Michigan Architecture Papers*, 2004.

Morel, Philippe. "Diller + Scofidio: The Slow House," *Architectures Experimentales: 1950-2000* (Collection du Frac Centre). HYX, 2003.

Mostaedi, Arian. *New Apartment Buildings*. Barcelona: Instituto Monsa de Ediciones, 2001.

Moving Target. Charleroi: Charleroi/Danses. Brussels: Plan K, 1996.

Muybridge: Man Walking at Ordinary Speed. Charleroi, Belgium: Charleroi/Danses, 1998.

Nesbit, Molly. "4th Window." *Dreams and Conflicts: The Dictatorship of the Viewer*. Venice: Venice Biennale of Art (2003), 2004.

Nikolovska, Lira. "Ambient Environments," *The New Everyday: Views on Ambient Intelligence*. Uitgeverij 010, 2003.

Noever, Peter, and Francois Perrin, eds. "Tangents." *Yves Klein: Air Architecture*. Hatje Cantz Publishers, 2004.

Nuevos Paisajes: New Landscapes. Barcelona: Museu d'Art Contemporani de Barcelona; Actar, 1997.

Obrist, Hans-Ulrich. *Do It*. New York: Independent Curators, 1998.

Ockman, Joan, and Salomon Frausto. "Travelogues, Blur Building" *Architourism: Authentic, Escapist, Exotic, Spectacular*. Prestel, 2005.

Papadakis. Andreas, ed. *The End of Innovation in Architecture*. Windsor, England: Andreas Papadakis, 1998.

-. Geoffrey Broadbent, and Maggie Toy, eds. *A Free Spirit in Architecture: Omnibus Volume*. London, UK: Academy Editions, 1992.

Peran, Martí. "The Builders Association and Diller+Scofidio" *See How They Move*, 2005.

Phillips, Patricia C., ed. *City Speculations*. New York: Princeton Architectural Press; Queens, New York: Queens Museum of Art, 1996.

Préhension. Paris: Galerie Xippas, 1997.

Rambert, Francis. *Architecture Tomorrow*. Paris, France: Terrail, 2005.

Rattenbury, Kester. "Diller + Scofidio" *Architecture Today*, London, UK: Laurence King Publishing, 2005.

Reed, Christopher, ed. *Not at Home: The Suppression of Domesticity in Modern Art and Architecture*. New York: Thames & Hudson, 1996.

Rendell, Jane, Barbara Penner, and Lain Borden, eds. *Gender Space Architecture: Interdisciplinary Introduction*. London: Spon Press; New York: Routledge, 1999.

Reservate der Sehnsucht. Dortmund, Germany: Kulturbüro Stadt Dortmund; hARTware projekte e.v.; Kultur Ruhr, 1998.

Rice, Peter, et al. *Columbia Documents of Architecture and Theory*, *Vol. 1*. New York: Columbia University Graduate School of Architecture, Planning, and Preservation, 1992.

Riddell, Jennifer, and Timothy Druckrey. *The Art of Detection: Surveillance in Society*. Cambridge (MA): MIT, List Visual Arts Center, 1997.

Riley, Terence. *The Un-Private House*. New York: Museum of Modern Art; Harry N. Abrams, 1999.

Rogoff, Irit. *Terra Infirma: Geography's Visual Culture*. London and New York: Routledge, 2000.

Ruby, Andreas, and Philip Ursprung, "Diller + Scofidio." *Minimal Architecture*, Basel: Prestel, 2005.

Schittich, Christian, ed. *Interior Spaces: Space Light Materials*. Munich: Institut für Internationale Architektur-Dokumentation; Birkhaüser, 2002.

"Sensi Contemporanei in Campania." *Biennale di Venezia Catalogue 2004*. 2004.

Sensing the Future: The Architect as Seismograph: 6th International Architecture Exhibition. Venice: La Biennale di Venezia; Milan: Electa, 1996.

Serious Games: Art, Interaction, Technology. London: Barbican Art Gallery, 1996.

Shamiyeh, Michael. "Elizabeth Diller & Ricardo Scofidio - The Blur Building," *What People Want: Populism in Architecture and Design*. Birkäuser, 2005.

Simmons, Dan. *Robots: Collection Rolf Fehlbaum*. Paris: Fondation Cartier pour l'art contemporain, 1999.

Soriano, Federico, ed. *Under the Table Table-Talk*. Madrid: FISURAS de la Cultura Contemporánea, 2001.

sous le manteau. Paris: Galerie Thaddaeus Ropac, 1997.

Sporre, Dennis J. "The Blur Building," *The Creative Impulse*, Seventh Edition, 2005.

Teyssot, Georges, ed. *The American Lawn*. New York: Princeton Architectural Press, 1999.

-. "Erasure and Disembodiment." *Book for the Unstable Media*. V2_Publishing, 1992.

-. *Interior Landscapes*. Milan: Electa, 1987.

Tichá, Jana, ed. *Architektura na prahu informacního veku*. Prague: Zlatýrez, 2001.

Toy, Maggie, ed. *The Architect: Women in Contemporary Architecture*. Victoria, Australia: The Images Publishing Group, 2001.

Twenty Years from the Fondation Cartier pour l'Art Contemporain. Cartier, 2004.

Ursprung, Phillip, Ilka & Andreas Ruby, and Angell Sachs. *Diller + Scofidio, Minimal Architecture*. London, UK: Prestel Publishing, 2003.

Vidler, Anthony, ed. *The Architectural Uncanny: Essays in the Modern Unhomely*. Cambridge (MA): MIT Press, 1992.

Weibel, Peter, ed. *Olafur Eliasson: Surroundings Surrounded: Essays on Space and Science*. Karlsruhe, Germany: ZKM Center for Art

and Media; Graz, Austria: Neue Galerie am Landesmuseum Joanneum, 2000.

Whiteman, John, Jeffery Kipnis, and Richard Burdett. *Strategies in Architectural Thinking*. Cambridge (MA): MIT Press 1992.

Wigley, Mark, and Catherine de Zegher, eds. *The Activist Drawing: Retracing Situationist Architectures from Constant's New Babylon to Beyond*. New York: The Drawing Center; Cambridge (MA): MIT Press, 2001.

Williams, Tod, and Ricardo Scofidio. *Window Room Furniture*. New York: Rizzoli International Publications, 1981.

Wright, Beryl J., Robert Bruegmann, and Anne Rorimer. *Art at the Armory: Occupied Territory*. Chicago: Museum of Contemporary Art, 1992.

Selected Articles and Reviews

Abrams, Janet. "Art at the Armory." *Frieze*, no. 9 (March/April 1993): 47–48.

-. "Cine City: Film and Perceptions of Urban Space." *Archis* (1994): 10–12.

-. "Diller + Scofidio: Jump Cuts: Between Space and Surveillance." *Rethinking Design*, no. 4 (October 1997): 2–3.

-. "The Avante Garde Grows Up." *Blueprint*, no. 35 (March 1987): 34–40.

-. "The Restaurant as Performance." *Domus*, no. 830 (October 2000): 118–20.

Affleck, Gavin. "National Velvet: The Canadian Centre for Architecture locates the American Eden in a patch of grass." *Metropolis 18*, no. 3 (November 1998): 121–23.

Alfaro, Andru. "Institute of Contemporary Art: Diller & Scofidio contruirán el nuevo ICA de Massachusetts." *Pasajes: Arquitectura y Critica*, no. 43 (January 2003): 17.

Amelar, Sarah. "Diller Scofidio + Renfro Fold the ICA into Boston's Waterfront." *Architectural Record* (March 2007): 108–15.

Anderegg, Roger. "Die Wunder-Wolke." *SonntagsZeitung*. (May 19, 2002): 17.

"Architecture au Magasin." *La Lettre Grenoble Culture*, no. 26 (March/April 1993).

Arnardottir, Dr. Halldora. "Móòu-byggingin i d'Yverdon-les-Bains i Sviss." *TMM Magazine*, Iceland (2003): 30–31.

"Artists of the Floating World: The Lakeside Pavilions of Switzerland's Expo." *World Architecture* (June 2002): 40–49.

Atkins, Robert. "State of the (On-line) Art." *Art in America 87*, no. 4 (April 1999): 89–93.

Backlund, Nicholas. "Living Architecture Diller and Scofidio." *I.D. 36* (November/December 1989): 14.

Bahçekapili, Nalan. "Sanat ve Mimarlikta Bulaniklaan Sinirlar." *Arredamento Mimarlik* (June 2006): 36–56.

Barliant, Claire. "Extreme Entertaining." *Food & Wine* (March 2006): 128–35.

Barnhill, Robert J. "Jet Lag: A Diller + Scofidio Performance in Rotterdam." *Archis* 4 (1999): 66–69.

Barrenche, Raul. "Set Pieces." *Architectural Record* (September 2003): 111–18.

Bartle, Andrew, and Jonathan Kirschenfeld. "L'analogo e l'anomalo: Architettura e il quotidiano." *Ottagono*, no. 86 (September 1987): 20–47.

Batchen, Geoffry. "Book Reviews: Back to the Front: Tourisms of War." *AA Files*, no. 28 (Autumn 1994): 90–91.

Beret, Chantal. "Non-Sequiturs." *Art Press*, no. 175 (December 1992): 41.

Berson, Misha. "'Jet Lag' about perpetual motion of humans." *Seattle Times*, May 13, 2000, sec. D: 3.

Betsky, Aaron. "Diller + Scofidio: Under Surveillance." *Architecture 89*, no. 6 (June 2000): 128–47.

-. "Freed Form." *Wired 7*, no. 9 (September 1999): 169–73.

-. "Urbane Sprawl." *Tate: The Art Magazine*, no. 22 (Summer 2000): 30–35.

Blanco, Ricardo. "Blur. Edificio como paisaje." *Contextos 12: Naturaleza y Paisajes* (October 2003): 130–39.

Blincoe, Nicolas. "Pop Philosophy: Urban Pleats and Folds." *Black Book* (Winter 2000/2001): 112–17.

Blume, Harvey. "Q&A with Elizabeth Diller." *Boston Globe*, February 18, 2007.

Bohlen, Celestine. "Being Met at the Airport by New Art." *The New York Times*, May 24, 2001, sec. E: 1, 5.

Bouman, Ole. "Quick Space in Real Time." *Archis*, no. 7 (1998): 74–77.

Boyer, Charles-Arthur. "Elizabeth Diller & Ricardo Scofidio." *Galeries Magazine*, no. 59 (Spring 1994): 104.

"Brasserie en Nueva York." *DiseñoInterior*, no. 103 (January 2001): 150–59.

Brayer, Marie-Ange. "Diller & Scofidio." *Forum International*, no. 12 (March 1992): 84.

-. "Art/Architecture, constructions d'atmosphere." *Artpress+: l'architecture contre-attaque* (May 2005): 48–54, 60–63.

Bruckner, D.J.R. "Technology as a Setting for Isolation and Defeat." *The New York Times*, January 14, 2000, sec. E: 4.

Brunson, Jamie. "A House Divided Up: Capp Street Project, San Francisco." *Artweek 18* (September 5, 1987): 5–6.

Budick, Ariella. "Drilling Into Illusions; Diller + Scofidio and the Deceptiveness of Looking." *Newsday*, March 28, 2003.

"Building a Following." *New York Newsday*, September 22, 2004, Part 2, sec. B: 233.

Burke, Gregory. "Diller/Scofidio: Propelling Social Changes." *Monument 1*, no. 4 (1994): 32–41.

Calzavara, Michele. "Diller Scofidio + Renfro: ICA, Boston." *Abitare* (February 2007): 122–29.

Campbell, Robert. "Designers' Plans for New ICA Reflect Changing Landscape." *Boston Sunday Globe*, August 26, 2001, sec. L: 5.

Campbell, Robert. "People, Places and Postcards: 'Suitcase Studies' at MIT." *Boston Globe*, May 7, 1991: 61, 63.

-. "A floating palace for art." *The Boston Globe*, December 6, 2006.

-. "A Vision Fulfilled at Harbor's Edge." *The Boston Globe*. Friday, December 1, 2006. sec. A: 1, 26.

-. "Alone on the Waterfront in South Boston, the Unfinished ICA is a Bold Presence." *The Boston Globe*, no. 3 (May 28, 2006).

-. "By standing out, it's a perfect fit." *The Boston Globe*, December 10, 2006.

-. "New ICA building emerges into the light." *The Boston Globe*, November 30, 2006.

-. "They Built a Body of Incisive Artwork." *The Boston Globe*, April 6, 2003.

Cappellieri, Alba. "'Blurring Architecture' by Diller + Scofidio." *Domus*, no. 838 (June 2001): 33.

Carlisle, Isabel."Cames with a Magic Edge." *The Times* (London), June 26, 1997: 39.

Carter, Brian. "Harbour Master." *The Architectural Review* (February 2007): 40–51.

"Casa Kinney." *Arquirectura*, no. 244 (September/October 1983): 62-63.

Casals, Conzalo. "Ladrillos + Pixels: Entrevista a Elizabeth Diller, Diller + Scofidio, arqs." *Summa+ 48* (April/May 2001): 68–73.

Cassin, Alessandro. "La Renovacion del Lincoln Center." *Arquine* (2004): 11–12.

Celant, Germano. "Diller + Scofidio: Progettare l'inconsistente." *Interni* (January 2005): 42–49, 74–79.

Chalmers, Jessica. "A Conversation about *Jet Lag*. Between Diller & Scofidio. Jessica Chalmers, and Marianne Weems." *Performance Research 4*, no. 2 (Summer 1999): 57–60.

Chaplan, Julia. "Bar Codes: From Grunge to Grolsch: Brasserie." *Paper* (March 2000): 158.

Chaplin, Sarah, and Eric Holding. "Consuming Architecture." *Architectural Design 68*, no. 112 (January/February 1998): 6–8, 46–47.

Chasin, Noah. "Blurring Boundaries." *Time Out New York*, March 13-20, 2003: 72.

Cohn, David. "Visiones trastocadas: La arquitectura de Diller & Scofidio." *Arquitectura Viva*, no. 26 (September/October 1992): 70–73.

Colomina, Beatriz. "Domesticity at War." *Assemblage 16* (1992): 14-41.

-. "Domesticity at War." *Ottagono*, no. 97 (December 1990): 24-46.

Colontonio, Allex. "Nas dobras da evolução." *Casa Vogue*, no. 249 (2007): 76-77.

"Concurso Learning Center Lausana Diller y Scofidio/Renfro – Finalista." *av proyectos*, (June 2004): 36-37.

Conde, Yago. "Inspectors of Space; Jugglers of Gravity." *Arquitectura*, no. 280 (Fall 1989): 108–15.

Cortes, Jose Miguel. "Tienen Género?." *ArteContexto*, Actar (2005): 22–29.

Couder, Antoine. "Le nouveau théatre des operations." *Renez-vous* (2005): 42–43.

Cramer, Ned. "All Natural: Diller + Scofidio's Blur building for the Swiss Expo 02 in Yverdon-les-Bains." *Architecture* (July 2002): 53–65.

Csaba, Varjasi Farkas. "Diller + Scofido: Test." *Octogon* (June 1999): 107–12.

Cuozzo, Steve. "Brasserie II: a design to die for." *New York Post*, February 9, 2000: 32.

Czarnecki, John E. "Diller + Scofidio challenge assumptions in first major American exhibition." *Architectural Record* (April 2003): 103–04.

Czarnecki, John E., and Clifford Pearson. "Diller + Scofidio Chosen For Its First Major U.S. Project: Boston's ICA." *Architectural Record 189*, no. 5 (May 2001): 38.

Damisch, Hubert. "Effacer l'architecture? Une fable." *Les Cahiers du Musee national d'Art Moderne*, no. 87 (2004): 19–33.

Davidson, Justin. "Abandoned Rail's an Urban Dream." *Newsday*, April 19, 2005.

-. "Challenging Assumptions." *Newsday*, September 22, 2005, sec. B: 2–3, 70.

-. "Lightness of being." *Newsday*, April 14, 2004, sec. A: 8.

-. "The Illusionist." *The New Yorker*, May 14, 2007: 126–37.

Davis, Douglas. "The Museum of the Third Kind" *Art in America* (June/July 2005): 75–81.

de Bonfils, Virginie. "50 valises dans tous leurs états." La Manche Libre, February 6, 1994: 5.

Decter, Joshua. "A Strangely New New York: From Viewing Platform at WTC/Ground

Zero to Prada Epicenter Store." *Flash Art 34*, no. 223 (March/April 2002): 53–55.

-. "Architectural Exhibition: Gallery Nature Morte, New York." *Arts Magazine 63* (November 1988): 112.

Delbene, Giacomo. "The High Line Masterplan." *Area no. 79, Infrastructure Landscape* (April 2005): 83–103.

"Desenfocado, Edificio Blur." *Oeste*, no. 14 (2001): 32–61.

Dheere, Jessica. "Climate Changers." *Art News 100*, no. 11 (December 2001): 109.

"Die letzte Zielscheibe von Frédéric Flamand." *Ballett International/Tanz Actuell*, no. 4 (April 1996): 44–47.

Dietmar, Steiner. "Architecture for the New Haus Museum." *Oris* (June 2004): 62.

Dietz, Steve. "Interactive Publics." *Public Art Review* (Fall/Winter 2003): 23–29.

"Diller + Scofidio." *Binyan Vediur*, no. 76 (October/November 2001): 150–56.

"Diller + Scofidio: Only Blue Skies." *At Cooper* (Spring 2002): 14–16.

"Diller + Scofidio: SuitCase Studies: la Production d'un Passé National." *Art Présence*, no. 8 (January/February 1994).

"Diller + Scofidio: The Brasserie, The Seagram Building, New York." *A+U*, no. 368 (May 2001): 70–77.

"Diller et Scofidio à Grenoble." *Techniques et Architecture* (February/March 1993): 8.

"Diller+ Scofidio Profile." *Oculus 56*, no. 10 (1995): 6–7.

"Diller+ Scofidio: Blur Building. PA 2000 Award." *Architecture 89*, no. 4 (April 2000): 90–95.

Diller + Scofidio, "Blur Building Expo 2002." *Lotus International: Liquid Architecture*, no. 125 (2005): 76–79.

Diller + Scofidio, "Blur Building/Eyebeam." *Era 21* (2005): 30–35.

Diller + Scofidio, "The Brasserie." *Bob, International Magazine of Space Design*, (May 2005): 152–57.

Diller + Scofidio, "Urban Readymades." *Interni* (January 2005): 42–49.

Dithmer, Monna. "Det gode og det dårlige ubehag." *Politiken*, November 14, 1998.

-. "Jet Lag i hyperspace." *Politiken*, November 10, 1998.

Dollens, Dennis. "Para-Site: Elizabeth Diller and Ricardo Scofidio at MoMA." *Telescope* (Autumn 1989): 20–21.

-. "The Storefront for Art and Architecture." *Sites*, no. 20 (1989): 29–33.

Domino, Christophe. "La Balade de Diller & Scofidio. Fonds Régional d'Art Contemporain

Basse Normandie, Caen, France." *Beaux Arts Magazine*, no. 121 (March 1994): 107.

"Dossier: Vitesse et mémoire." *Nouvelles de danse*, no. 27 (Spring 1996): 15–64.

Drewes, Caroline. "A house that is art." *San Francisco Examiner*, September 3, 1987, sec. F: 1, 4.

Drobnick, Jim. "Interactivity and Real Time-Envy: An Interview with Diller + Scofidio." *Parachute*, no. 86 (April-June 1997): 10–13.

Dussol, Dominique. "Un regard acide." *Sud Ouest*, October 27, 1992.

Dyckhoff, Tom. "Boston's New Gallery is a Real Tease," *The Times*, London, December 12, 2006.

-. "Suitcase Studies: The Production of a National Past." *Studio Art Magazine*, no. 58 (November/December 1994): 48–55.

"Elizabeth Diller and Ricardo Scofidio: Jump Cuts." *Architectural Design 68*, no. 112 (2005): 46–47.

Elton, Lars. "Arkitekturteater." *Aftenpoften*, November, 14, 1988.

Ernst, Wolfgang. "Reviews Visite aux Armées: Tourismes de Guerre." *Mediamatic 8*, no. 2/3 (1995): 152–54.

"Estrutura Quimérica." *Casa Vogue* (Brazilian edition), no. 214 (August 2003): 162–65.

Etherington, Daniel. "Serious Games." *Art Monthly*, no. 203 (February 1997): 32–34.

-. "Serious Games." *Mute* (Winter 1997): 22.

Evans, David. "Machines d'Architecture." *AA Files*, no. 24 (Autumn 1992): 86–93.

"Expo .02 Yverdon-les-Bains Arteplage: The Cloud." *A+U*, no. 383 (August 2002): 28–35.

"Facsimile." *Via Arquitectura 8* (September 2000): 136–37.

"Facsimile: San Francisco." *Metropolis* (April 2003): 106.

Field Operations-Diller Scofidio + Renfro, "The High Line Project." *Lotus, Camouflage* no. 126 (2006): 106–11.

Filler, Martin. "New Beacon for Boston." *House & Garden* (February 2007): 68-70, 156.

Fillon, Odile. "Les aberrants." *Architecture Interieure* (April/May 2003): 80-83.

"Finalist: Eyebeam Atelier/Museum of Art and Technology Competition 2001." *Dialogue*, no. 57 (April 2002): 68–73.

Fischer, Ole. "Alle reden vom Wetter..." *Arch Plus*, No 178 (June 2006): 76–81.

Fitoussi, Michele, and Philippe Tretiack. "Le Couple, Oeuvre Cart." *Elle* (France), June 7, 1993: 23.

Flagge, Ingeborg and Romana Schneider. "Life

Without Nostalgia." *Post-Modernism Revisited* (October 2004): 174–89.

Flamand ,Frédéric. "Dance and Architecture." *Lotus International* 122 (November 2004): 17–21.

Forgey, Benjamin. "The Heirs Aberrant of Architecture." *Washington Post*, March 30, 2003, sec. G: 01.

Foster, Hal. "Architecture-Eye." *Art Forum* (February 2007): 246–53.

Frampton, Kenneth. "In (de)Nature of Materials: A Note on the State of Things." *Daidalos*, no. 56 (August 1995): 16–18.

"Frederic Flamand – Diller + Scofidio Moving Target." *Lotus* no. 122 (November 2004): 18–19.

Freedman, Adele. "Baggage on the Battleground." *The Globe and Mail*, June 11, 1994, sec. C: 2.

Frei, Hans. "L'Intérieur: Les Champs de Bataille de la Vie Privée." *Faces*, no. 23 (Spring 1992): 4–7.

Friedman, Mildred. "Tourisms: suitcase Studies." *Design Quarterly*, no. 152 (1991): 35–40.

Frith, Ed. "Reviewing 'The Desiring Eye: Reviewing the Slow House.' Ikon Gallery, Birmingham, England." *Architectural Design 66* (September/October 1996): 16.

Fuchs, Claudia. "Expo.02 in der Schweiz." *Detail*, no. 41 (2001): 1474–75.

Galvin, Terrance. "Architecture as Probe: Elizabeth Diller in Conversation with Terrance Galvin." *Fifth Column 8*, no. 2 (1992): 27–35.

Gardner, James. "Correcting a Half-Century's errors in Urban Development." *The New York Sun* (2004): 16.

Geibel, Victoria. "Harbingers of Change." *Metropolis 7*, no. 4 (November 1987): 46–57.

"Gifu Kitagata Apartments Second Phase." *Shinkenchiku*, no. 5 (2000): 92–109.

Gilmartin, Ben, Amanda Reeser, and Ashley Schafer. "Technological Landscape." *Praxis*, no. 4 (Fall 2002): 94–107.

Giovannini, Joseph. "Blithe Spirits." *New York Magazine*, March 17, 2003, 50–51.

Glancey, Jonathan. "I Have Seen the Future and it's Wet." *Guardian*, June 10, 2002: 12.

Gleiniger, Andrea. "Stand de Dinge: Expo.02: eine neue Landesausstellung fur die Schweiz." *Baumeister 98*, no. 11 (November 2001): 14.

Glueck, Grace. "Engaging Experiments Transform a Sandy Site." *The New York Times*, July 31, 1983, sec. H: 25–26.

Goldberger, Paul. "Comfort Zone." *Metropolis 19*, no. 8 (May 2000): 130, 140.

-. "West Side Fixer-Upper." *The New Yorker*, July 7, 2003, 36–40.

Gordon, Meryl. "Table Stakes." *New York Magazine*, January 10, 2000, 34-39.

Grimes, William. "Out of the Ashes: New Look, Old Spirit." *The New York Times*, March 15, 2000, sec. F: 10.

Grout, Catherine. "Tony Brown / Diller + Scofidio." *Arqefactum*, no. 48 (June-August 1993): 36–37.

Guiney, Anne. "In Detail: School of American Ballet." *Architects Newspaper*, February 14, 2007: 9.

Hall, Peter. "Art's Next Generation." *Architecture 90*, no. 9 (September 2001): 71–73.

Harwood, John. "More Lincoln Center than Lincoln Center" in *DoCoMoMo Journal* (2005).

Hawthorne, Christopher. "Flood of Ideas on Boston Harbor," *The Los Angeles Times*, December 11, 2006.

Hejduk, John. "Kinney House: A Design by Ricardo Scofidio and Elizabeth Diller." *Lotus International*, no. 44 (1984): 58–63.

Hejduk, John. "Kinney House. Westchester, New York." *Casabella 47*, no. 496 (1983): 28–29.

Helfand, Glen. "Subversive Living: A House Divided." *San Francisco Sentinel*, September 4, 1987: 23, 28.

Hess, Alan. "Cybercity to Get Its Own Sign of the Times." *The San Jose Mercury News*, June 17, 1994, sec. C: 1, 5.

-. "That's Entertainment: High-tech on the Streets." *The San Jose Mercury News*, October 23, 1994, sec. F: 1, 3.

Hess, Elizabeth. "Museum Bytes Dog." *Village Voice*, June 15, 1993: 93.

Hogben, Gavin. "Ritual. Recent Architectural Installations by Diller and Scofidio." *The Architectural Review*, no. 185 (February 1989): 54–57.

Holg, Garrett. "For Armory Show, Artists Find Territory." *Chicago Sun-Times*, October 18, 1992, sec. E: 7.

Horn, Gillian. "Cross-border Architecture." *Blueprint*, no. 126 (March 1996): 24–26.

Hossli, Peter. "Expo im Nebel." *SonntagsZeitung*, April 2, 2000: 59, 61.

Hubert, Christian. "Site-seeing. Back to the Front: Tourisms of War." *Design Book Review*, no. 35–36 (Winter/Spring 1995): 89-90.

Hunt, David. "Faraway and Nearby: the Province of Telepresence." *Camerawork 26*, no. 1 (Spring/Summer 1999): 26–29.

Hüster, Wiebke. "Offener Vollzug: Auftakt für die Berner Tanztage." *Basler Zeitung*, August 23–24, 1997.

Huxtable, Ada Louise. "Down-to-Earth Masterpieces of Public Landscape Design." *The Wall Street Journal*, May 4, 2005, sec. D: 10.

-. "The Hub of Architecture: Boston and a Neighbor Embrace the New With Fervor." *The Wall Street Journal*, July 31, 2003, sec. D: 8.

"Inside Out: Finestra Sul Giardino." *Domus*, no. 671 (April 1986): 62.

"InterClone Hotel." Maja Estonian *Architectural Review*, no. 32 (January 2002): 46–47.

"Institute of Contemporary Art," *l'Arca* (June 2007): 14–21.

"Institute of Contemporary Art/ Boston," *A+U* (July 2005): 76–85.

Iovine, Julie V. "An Avant-Garde Design for a New Media Center." *The New York Times*, March 21, 2002, sec. E:1, 5.

Isozaki, Arata. "Architecture that Redefines Architecture: New Strategies of the Body and Space." *InterCommunication*, no. 11 (Winter 1995): 35–47.

Isozaki, Arata. "Kitagata Apartment Reconstruction Project, Gifu." *Dialogue*, no. 40 (September 2000): 36, 46–47.

-. "The Kitagata Housing Complex, Gifu." *Lotus International*, no. 100 (1999): 40–59.

Jacobs, Karrie. "The Softer Machine." *Dwell 1*, no. 4 (April 2001): 15–16.

Jankovic, Nikola. "Parages in extremis: Art et Architecture." *Art Présence*, no. 18 (April-June 1996): 44–53.

Jodidio, Philip. "Prendre le Plaisir au Sérieux." *Connaissance des Arts*, no. 563 (July-August 1999): 92–97.

Kennicott, Philip "Museum Sticks Its Neck Out – But Only So Far." *The Washington Post*, December 24, 2006.

Kim, Min. "Eyebeam Atelier's New Museum of Art and Technology." *Concept* (May 2002): 10–25.

Kipnis, Jeffrey. "InFormation/DeFormation." *Arch+*, no. 131 (April 1996): 66–81.

Kisselgoff, Anna. "Discovering a Cool Esthetic for Burning Issues." *The New York Times*, September 24, 1998, sec. E: 1.6.

Klein, Richard. "Diller + Scofidio, Maîtres d'œuvre." *Sans Titre*, no. 35 (April-June 1996).

Lacayo, Richard. "Architecture: The Outsiders." *Time Style & Design* (Summer 2007): 43.

-. "First Thinking, Then Building." *Time Magazine*. December 4, 2006.

215

-. "Walk on the Wild Side," *Time Magazine*, January 18, 2007.

Lambert, Phyllis. "Blotting out Architecture? A Fable in Seven Parts." *Log* (Fall 2003): 9–26.

Lanks, Belinda. "Bodies & Space." *Metropolis* (March 2007): 116–19.

Lanz, Isabella. "Gemis aan bezieling spelt ook Moving Target parten." *De Voorkant*, October 1, 1997.

Larson, Kay. "On the Beach." *New York Magazine*, September 5, 1983: 52–53.

Lavin, Sylvia. "Toward an Even Newer Architecture." *Log* (Winter 2005): 20–26.

Leland, John. "Letting the View Speak for Itself." *The New York Times*, January 3, 2002, sec. F: 1.

Levinson, Nancy. "View Masters." *I.D.*, (March/April 2007): 91–92.

Lixenberg, Dana. "Mind over Matter." in *Blueprint*, London (March 2005): 46–49.

Logullo, Eduardo."Estrutura Quimérica." *Casa Vogue*, 214. (2004):162–65.

Lootsma, Bart. "Flesh. Visite aux armées: Tourismes de Guerre." *Archis* 2 (1997): 85–86.

-. "Wonen op het slagveld: Theorie en praktijk van Diller & Scofidio." *De Architect* (April 1994): 46–69.

-. "Indeed, Diller+ Scofidio are Not Elephants: A Reaction to Michael Stanton's 'Dissipated Scandals'." *Archis* 8 (1998): 74–77.

-. "Towards an Architecture of Entrapment: Recent work by Diller + Scofidio." *Archis* 8 (1996): 45–53.

Lowery, Ethan. "Smart Cameras." *Cluster on Innovation*, issue 03 (2004): 56.

Lubow, Arthur. "Architects, in Theory." *The New York Times Magazine*, February 16, 2003: 36–41.

-. "Vorsicht: Architekten!" *Architectural Digest* (German Edition), no. 40 (June 2003): 36–40.

Luscombe, Belinda. "People to Watch. Liz Diller and Ricardo Scofidio." *Time* 155, no. 6, February 14, 2000: 85.

MacDonough, Todd. "Education of the Senses." *Art in America* (March 2007): 122–27.

MacNair, Andrew. "Forty Under Forty." *Interiors*, no. 146 (September 1986): 149–210.

Maguire, Matthew. "Architectural Performance." *Midgård*, no. 3 (1987): 127–40.

-. "The Site of Language." *The Drama Review* 27, no. 4 (Winter 1983): 54–69.

Mancia, Paolo G. Ed. "Eyebeam Institute in Architecture & PC La rivoluzione digitale in architecttura." *Hoepli* (2004): 116–21.

Mancini, Daniele. "Building as Interface." *Cluster on Innovation*, issue 03 (2004): 59–64.

Marcelis, Bernard. "Gender-4e Biennale Charleroi/Danses via '99: divers lieux, Charleroi/Maubeuge." *Art Press*, no. 247 (June 1999): 69–70.

-. "Virtual Imagery, Real Tension." *Art Press*, no. 215 (July/August 1996): 70–71.

Margolis, Lynn. "Mist Opportunities: When Water is Part of the Architecture." *Christian Science Monitor*, March 14, 2002: 18.

Marks, Peter. "Diller + Scofidio: Architects Building Castles in the Clouds." *The New York Times*, May 23, 2001, sec. E: 1, 4.

Martin, Reinhold. "The American Lawn: Surface of Everyday Life." *Journal of the Society of Architectural Historians* 58, no. 2 (June 1999): 196–98.

Mathews, Stanley. "The Body Politic." *Dialogue* (January/February 1993): 12–13.

Matsuzaki, Yata. "Diller + Scofidio." *Q-plus Magazine*, Japan (2003): 19–23.

Mays, Vernon. "The Art of Building for Art." *Architect* (March 2007): 72–79.

McCormick, Carlo. Design Issue. "Shadows and Fog." *Paper* (May 2006): 86–87.

McDonough, Tom. "Diller + Scofidio: Critical Structures." *Art in America* (October 2003): 90–95 and 147.

McGuigan, Cathleen. "Down From the Clouds." *Newsweek*, March 17, 2003: 64.

McKee, Bradford. "Off the Wall." *Harper's Bazaar* (December 2000): 230, 253.

McLaren, Brian. "Architectural Tourism at the Walker Art Center, Minneapolis." Architecture. no. 80 (March 1991): 27.

Menking, William. "Notes from New York." *Building Design*, November 10, 1989: 28.

Meredith, Michael. "Scanning: The Aberrant Architectures of Diller + Scofidio." *A+U*, 03: 06, No. 393 (2004).

Merkel, Jayne. "The Museum as Artifact." *Wilson Quarterly* 26, no. 1 (Winter 2002): 66-79.

-. "Word of Mouth: Diller + Scofidio in Conversation with Jayne Merkel." *Architectural Design* 71, no. 6 (2001): 58–65.

"Méta-maquettes. Galerie Sadock et Uzzan, Paris." *Connaissance des Arts*, no. 479 (January 1992): 18.

Meyhofer, Dirk. "Bauwerk: Institute of Contemporary Art, Boston." *Deutsche Bau Zeitschrift* (January 2007): 24-31.

-. "Gedurfde Eersteling." *De Architect* (February 2007): 68–73.

"Mies en mente: Restaurante en el edifcio Seagram, Manhattan." *Arquitectura Viva*, no. 76 (January/February 2001): 52-53.

Millard, Bill. "Boston's First New Museum in a Century." *Icon.* (February 2007): 66–72.

Mirapaul, Matthew. "Office Webcams Provide Raw Material for Art Project." *The New York Times*, October 1, 1998, sec. E: 10.

"Modern Ikone." *Architektur Innenarchitektur Technischer Ausbau* (June 2000): 86–89.

Montaner, Josep Maria. "La tentación vanguardista." *La Vanguardia*, March 1, 1994.

Moreno, Shonquis. "Cloud Control." *Surface*, no. 30 (2001): 49-50, 164.

-. "Conversation Pieces." *Frame* 25 (March-April 2002): 38-47.

-. "Rewriting the Museum." *Frame* 24 (January/February 2002): 116–27.

-. "Disco au go go." *Pol Oxygen*, no. 6 (December 2003/January 2004): 114–21.

-. "Paper Architecture." *Off The Wall* (2006): 210–15.

Morley, Andrew. "Serious Games." *Contemporary Visual Arts*, no. 15 (1997): 66–67.

Morrissey, Simon. "Seeking New Ways to Present Architecture." *Architect's Journal* 203, February 15, 1996: 54–55.

"Moving Target." *Alternative Théâtrales* 51 (May 1996): 49–60.

Mozas, Javier, and Aurora Fernandez Per. "Field Operations." *In Common | Collective Spaces*, a+t ediciones, no. 25 (Spring 2005): 98–111.

Muschamp, Herbert. "A Highbrow Peep Show on 42nd Street." *The New York Times*, August 1, 1993, sec. H: 34.

-. "An Elegant Marriage of Inside and Outside." *The New York Times*, October 21, 2001, sec. 2: 34.

-. "For All You Observers of the Urban Extravaganza." *The New York Times*, November 10, 2002, sec. 5: 34.

-. "Outside the Avant-garde." *Terrazzo* (1988): 44–50.

-. "Updating a Brasserie with Pizazz." *The New York Times*, August 29, 1999, sec. 2: 28.

-. "A New Face For Lincoln Center." *The New York Times*, April 13, 2004, sec. E: 1–5.

-. "The Classicists of Contemporary Design." *The New York Times*, Feb 28, 2003, sec. E: 41–43.

-. "Architecture + Water: Just Add Water to Instant Inspiration." *The New York Times*, April 6, 2001, sec. E: 33.

-. "Exploring Space and Time, Here and Now." *The New York Times*, February 6, 2000, sec. 2: 37, 39.

-. "Leaping from One Void Into Others." *The New York Times*, December 23, 2001, sec. 2: 1.

-. "Looking at the Lawn, and Below the Surface." *The New York Times*, July 5, 1998, sec. 2: 1–32.

-. "Vacation Checklist: Socks, Passport, Architecture." *The New York Times*, July 10, 1994, sec. H: 30.

-. "With Viewing Platforms, a Dignified Approach to Ground Zero." *The New York Times*, December 22, 2001, sec. B: 8.

"New York, Electric City." *A+U*, no. 344 (May 1999): 3–115.

Nobel, Philip. "Let it Be, Architects can't resist the lure of buildings-even if the brief doesn't." *Metropolis* (October 2004): 82–86.

Noiret, Michele. "Charleroi, la danse à mille Temps." *Libération*, May 3, 1996.

"NY ? D+S." *Arquitectura y Critica*. no. 37 (May 2002): 6–10.

Ockman, Joan, and Nicholas Adams. "Forms of the Spectacle." *Casabella* 63, no. 673/674 (December 1999/January 2000): 4-8, 162–63.

Ouroussoff, Nicolai. "Expansive Vistas Both Inside and Out." *The New York Times*. December 8, 2006, sec. E: 31.

-. "Competing Visions for Governors Island." *The New York Times*, June 20, 2007, sec. E: 1, 5.

-. "Gardens in the Air Where the Rail Once Ran: Architects Selected to Make Over the High Line." *The New York Times*, August 12, 2004, The Arts, sec. E: 1, 7: 22–33.

"PA Awards." *Architecture Magazine* (January 2003): 76–77.

Papadakis, A & A., eds. "Diller + Scofidio Eyebeam School." *Newarch 07, Innovation* (2004): 99.

Papadakis, A. "Eyebeam School." *New Architecture*, no. 7 (December 2003): 98–101.

Park, Haeyoun and Graham Roberts. "Reconstructing Alice Tully Hall." *The New York Times*, May 1, 2007, sec. E: 5.

Park, Kyong. "Diller + Scofidio: The Architecture of Entrapment." *Flash Art* 29, no. 188 (May/June 1996): 92–96.

Payne, Andrew. "Review of Back to the Front: Tourisms of War." *Columbia Architecture, Planning, Preservation Newsline* (November/December 1994): 8.

Phillips, Patricia C. "Art at the Anchorage." *Artforum* 25 (November 1986): 139–40.

-. "Boston: Elizabeth Diller and Ricardo Scofidio." *Artforum* 30 (November 1991): 140–41.

-. "Diller and Scofidio (Of) Of Bodies and Technologies." *Columbia Architecture, Planning, Preservation Newsline* (October 1990): 5.

-. "A Parallax Practice: A conversation with E. Diller and R. Scofidio." *Art Journal* (Fall 2004): 62–79.

-. "Art on the Beach." *Artforum* 23 (November 1984): 98.

-. "Elizabeth Diller and Ricardo Scofidio. Museum of Modern Art, New York." *Artforum* 28 (November 1989): 145–46.

-. "Hinged Victories." *Artforum* 26 (Summer 1988): 106–09.

Piccoli, Cloe. "Diller +Scofidio." *D: la Repubblica delle Donne*, March 15, 2003: 117.

Plaut, Jeannette. "Diller + Scofidio: Hacia La Expansion Espacial." *Ambientes* 37 (2004): 40–43.

Poels, Jan-Willem. "Feel-Good Factor." *Frame* 14 (May/June 2000): 89–97.

Pogrebin, Robin. " More Room to Pirouette at Lincoln Center Studios," *The New York Times*, January 19, 2007, sec. B: 2.

-. "Alice Tully, Could That Really Be You?" *The New York Times*, Arts and Leisure, November 13, 2005: 40.

-. "An Intermission for Renovation Begins at Alice Tully Hall." *The New York Times*, April 30, 2007, sec. E: 2.

-. "Couples Who Build More Than Relationships." *The New York Times*, April 22, 2007: 28.

-. "For Lincoln Center's Plaza, a Gracious Entry Point." *The New York Times*, June 12, 2006, sec. E: 1, 6.

-. "Lincoln Center Proceeds, Modestly." *The New York Times*, May 8, 2003, sec. E: 1, 5.

-. "Plans Turn a Neglected Alley Into a More Welcoming Space." *The New York Times*, April 13, 2004, sec. E: 1-5.

Porcu, Michele. "Dancing with Architecture: Frédéric Flamand." *Abitare*, no. 401 (December 2000): 126–27, 191.

Posner, Ellen. "Architecture Without Building, at MoMA." *The Wall Street Journal*, August 8, 1989, sec. A: 8.

Price, Claire. "Home and Away at the Ikon." *Building Design*, March 1, 1996: 17.

-. "I Sing the Body Electric." *Building Design*, July 11. 1997: 12.

Princenthal, Nancy. "Architecture's Iconoclasts." *Sculpture* 8, no. 6 (November/December 1989): 18–23.

Pugh, C. "Museum Quality – Wanted: An Architect to Rebuild Houston's Reputation." *Zest*, April 3, 2005: 11.

R. F. "Museums – und Ateliergebäude für 'Eyebeam.'" *Bauwelt*, May 17, 2003: 9.

Rankin, Mary, "Investigation '88." *Art Matters* 7, no. 10 (July/August 1988).

Rappaport, Nina. "The Gallery: Visions of a Shapeshifting Museum." *The Wall Street Journal*, October 10, 2001, sec. A: 14.

Rattenbury, Kester. "Real, Live, Technophilia." *Building Design* (May 16, 1997): 2.

Rendell, Jane. "Women in Architecture: What is a Feminist Aesthetics of Space?" *Make: The Magazine of Women's Art*, no. 89 (September-November 2000): 20–22.

Rhee, Pollyanna. "Flux = Rad." *Loud Paper*, Volume 4, Issue 3 (2004): 62-63.

Richardson, Tim. "Look But Don't Touch." in *Domus International* (September 2005): 24–29.

Rietstap, Doorine. "Schizofreen Moving Target van Flamand is alles tegelijk." *NRC Handelsblad*, September 30, 1997.

Riley, Terence. "Det o-privata huset." *MAMA*, no. 27 (2000): 70–104.

Robinson, Marc. "A Long Journey Into Flight." *The Village Voice*, January 12-18, 2000: 68.

Rochat, Henri. "Eine kunstliche Dunstwolke." *Schweizer Ingenieur und Architekt*, no. 33/34, August 22, 2000: 12–16.

Ross, Val. "Lawn and Order." *The Globe and Mail*, July 11, 1998, sec. C: 1, 5.

Rothkopf, Scott. "Diller + Scofidio." *Artforum International* (Summer 2003).

Rubenstein, Hal. "Mod Swing." *New York Magazine*, February 21, 2000: 107–08.

Rutkowski, Roman. "Blur." *Architektura & Biznes* (February 2003): 44–51.

Ryan, Raymond. "Letter from America." *The Plan* (February/March 2007): 18–31.

Ryan, Zoe. "Aberrant Architecture." *Contemporary*, No. 49 (2003): 62–65.

Saltz, Jerry. "Architectural Follies." *The Village Voice*, April 16-22, 2003: 51.

Scanlon, Jessie. "Making it Morph: Elizabeth Diller and Ricardo Scofidio want Architecture to Change Everything." *Wired* 8, no. 2 (February 2000): 152–59.

Schafer, Ashley, and Don Shillingberg, "Exhibit to Exhibition: Tracing the Design of D+S from within The Museum to the Museum." *Praxis* no. 7 (2005): 50–59.

Schindler, Susanne. "Ein Wonderbra für Boston." *Bauwelt* (January 2007): 28–33.

Schlagenwerth, Michaela. "Elegante Anstrengung vor schrägem Spiegel." *Berliner Zeitung*, August 18, 1997: 25.

Scott, Felicity. "Involuntary Prisoners of Architecture." *October Magazine*, M.I.T, (Fall 2003): 75–101.

Silva, Vânia, and Ricardo França. "Blur Building: Diller + Scofidio." *AU* 16, no. 90 (June/July 2000): 26–29.

Silver, Joanne. "'Tourisms' Examines Rites of Travel." *Boston Herald*, May 24, 1991, sec. S: 26.

Sirefman, Susanna. "Three's Company." *Surface* (November 2006): 131, 149–53.

Smith, P.C. "Diller & Scofidio at Richard Anderson." *Art in America* 82, no. 5 (May 1994): 114.

Smith, Roberta. "Architectural Gadgetry In Installation at the Modern." *The New York Times*, July 21, 1989, sec. C: 30.

-. "In Installation Art, a Bit of the Spoiled Brat." *The New York Times*, January 2, 1993, sec. B: 31.

-. "Art Center Has Room for the Big and the New." *The New York Times*, June 2, 1999, sec. E: 1, 5.

Sokol, David. "Viewing Pleasures." *Azure* (March/April 2007): 60–65.

Sozanski, Edward J. "ICA highlights artists who are conceptualists." *The Philadelphia Inquirer*, June 19, 1988, sec. E: 1,6.

Speaks, Michael. "Views of the Observer: Dubbeldam, Diller + Scofidio." *Space: Arts & Architecture: Environment*, no. 9 (September 1995): 48–59.

-. "Views of the Observer: Flesh: Architectural Probes." *Columbia Architecture, Planning, Preservation Newsline* (September/October 1995): 2.

Stanton, Michael. "Of Mice and Monsters. A Response to Bart Lootsma." *Archis* 10, (1998): 66–69.

Stec, Barbara. "O fatdowaniu w architekturze." *Archivolta* 1 (January-March 2000): 14–18.

Steen, Karen E. "Friends in High Places." *Metropolis Magazine* (December 2005): 118–123, 149–157.

Stegner, Peter. "Von der Choreographie der Räume und Menschen," *Baumeister* (August 2003): 60–65.

Steinberg, Claudia. "Zwei, die um die Ecke denken." *Architektur & Wohnen*, Germany (June/July 2003): 150–53.

Sternbergh, Adam. "The High Line: It Brings Good Things to Life." *New York Magazine*, May 7, 2007: 26–33, 107.

"Storefront: Iconoclasm. Invention and the Ideal." *A+U*, no. 197 (February 1987): 71–98.

Strutt, Rachel. "The Visionary." *The Boston Globe*, December 31, 2006.

Sutavee, Kevin. "Diller Scofidio + Renfro."

Prophecy Magazine no. 8 (Autumn 2005): 28–35.

Suzuki, Akira. "The Desiring Eye: Reviewing the Slow House." *Telescope* (Autumn 1992): 68–70.

"Swiss Expo 2002." *Assemblage*, no. 41 (April 2000): 25.

Talarico, Wendy. "The Brasserie, Seagram Building." *Openings: Graphic Standards Details* (2005): 92-99.

Taylor, Kate. "At Lincoln Center, 'Street of the Arts' Is the Goal." *The New York*, May 2, 2007.

Taylor, Rebecca. "Public housing with a woman's touch." *The Japan Times*, June 21, 1997: 15.

Temin, Christine. "Waterfront Colors: Boston's Modern Update." *The Washington Post*, December 8, 2006.

Temko, Allan. "Cutting Up the House." *San Francisco Chronicle*, September 3, 1987: 66.

Teyssot, Georges. "The American Lawn: The Spectacle of Suburban Pastoralism." *Lotus International*, no. 101 (1999): 92–115.

-. "Lawnmowers and Machine Guns." *Blueprint*, no. 152 (July/August 1998): 30–31.

-. "Erasure and Disembodiment." *Ottagono*, no. 96 (September 1990): 56-88.

Theissen, Bennett. "Creation's the American Mysteries." *The Drama Review* 27, no. 2 (Summer 1983): 83–86.

"The Institute of Contemporary Art." *Detail* (March 2007): 32–41.

"The Meaning of Mowing." *The Economist* 348, no. 8078 July 25-31, 1998: 82.

"The Slow House. North Haven, N.Y." *Progressive Architecture* 72 (January 1991): 88–90.

Timm, Tobias. "Die Stadt als Bühne, die Bühne als Haus." *Die Zeit*. December 20, 2006: 47.

Titz, Walter. "Mythen und Stereotypen." *Kleine Zeitung*, June 22, 1996: 14.

"Toss A Bone into the Sky." *Black Book* (Spring 2001): 128–33.

"Tourisme des Guerres." *La Chronique d'Amnesty International*, no. 90 (May 1994): 35.

"Toward a New Living Environment: Gifu Kitagata Housing Project." *Space Design* (August 1997): 93–116.

"Travelogues: Diller + Scofidio." *Dialogue*, no. 58 (May 2002): 82–87.

Turner, Matthew. "Pilgrim's Progress." *Building Design*, January 12, 2007.

Turner, Nicola. "Gin Palace." *World Architecture*, no. 88 (July/August 2000): 86–91.

Ulam, Alex. "Taking the High Road." *Landscape Architecture* (2005): 62–69.

Umeni, Muzeum. "Blur Building." *Era* no. 21, (June 2004): 30–35.

Urbach, Henry. "Avant Stars: Diller + Scofidio's Blueprint for Success." *W30*, no. 10 (October 2001): 222–24.

Ursprung, Philip. "Exhibition Landscapes: Project for the Swiss National Exposition 2001." *Diadalos*, no. 73 (October 1999): 60–65.

Van de Walle, Lucie. "Danse, mensonges et vidéos." *L'Express*, September 11, 1998: 82.

Verdaguer, Carlos. "Género urbano: Vivendeas sociales en Gifu, Japón." *Arquitecutra Viva*, no. 62 (September/October 1998): 88–97.

Vernay, Marie-Christine. "Flamand ne fait pas de sentement." Libération, September 18, 1998.

Vidler, Anthony. "Broken Homes." *Public* 6 (1992): 119–24.

-. "Homes for Cyborgs, Domestic Prostheses from Salvador Dalí to Diller and Scofidio." *Ottagono* 96 (September 1990): 36–55.

-. "Homes for Cyborgs." In *Not at Home: The Suppression of Domesticity in Modern Art and Architecture*, Christopher Reed ed. (1996): 161–78.

Vidler, Anthony. "Robots in the House: Surveillance and the Domestic Landscape." *Diadalos*, no. 73

Vogel, Carol. "A Passport to the Arts." *The New York Times*, Feb 12, 1999, sec. E: 36.

-. "In Times Square, Art Conquers Kung Fu." *The New York Times*, July 7, 1993, sec. C: 13.

Vossoughian, Nader. "ICA, Baby – Shakin' That Art." *Tank*. Volume 4, Issue 9 (2007): 82–85.

Wagner, Michael. "Diller + Scofidio Blend Architecture and Theatre at the Brooklyn Bridge Anchorage." *Interiors*, no. 147 (December 1987): 160–61.

Wehle, Philippa. "Live Performance and Technology: The Example of Jet Lag." *PAJ: A Journal of Performance and Art* 24, no. 1 (2002): 133–39.

Wesemann, Arnd. "Images Dance Better: Frédéric Flamand's 'EJM 1' and 'EJM 2' in Lyon." *Ballet International/Tanz Aktuell*, no. 11 (November 1998): 46–47.

Whiting, Sarah. "Tactical Histories: Diller + Scofidio's Back to the Front: Tourisms of War." *Assemblage* 28 (December 1995): 70–85.

Whoriskey, Peter. "Art of the American Lawn: Mower Power to It." *The Miami Herald*, September 2, 1999, sec. A: 1, 18.

Widder, Lynnette. "Against Self-Disciplining." *Daidalos*, no. 56 (August 1995): 35–47.

Wines, Suzan. "Go with the Flow: Eight New York-Based Artists and Architects in the Digital Era." *Domus*, no. 801 (February 1998): 84–91.

Wines, Suzan. "Architettura inaspettata." *Domus* no. 858 (April 2003): 27–29.

Wright, Bruce N. "Postcards from Diller + Scofido at the Walker Art Center." *Progressive Architecture*, no. 72 (March 1991): 21.

Wynants, Jean-Marie. "Le Corps Médiatisé." *Le Soir*, April 17, 1996.

Yang, Andrew. "The Stealth Designers." *The Architects Newspaper* no.10, June 8, 2004: 8–9.

Yood, James. "Art at the Armory: Occupied Territory. Museum of Contemporary Art, Chicago." *Artforum* 31 (December 1992): 98.

Zapatka, Christian. "Home Turf." *Architecture* 87, no. 8 (August 1998): 27–28.

Zeiger, Mimi. "Now on View." *Architecture* (September 2006): 68–77.

Selected Artist's Writings, Portfolios, and Illustrations

"The American Lawn, Surface of Everyday Life." *Lotus International*, no. 101 (1999): 116–31.

"Autobiographical Notes." In *The Activist Drawing: Retracing Situationist Architectures from Constant's New Babylon to Beyond*, edited by Catherine de Zegler and Mark Wigley, 131–33. New York: The Drawing Center; Cambridge (MA): MIT Press, 2001.

"Bad Press: Housework Series." In *Anyway*, edited by Cynthia C. Davidson, 152-61. New York: Rizzoli International Publications, 1994." Bad Press." Arch+, no. 131 (April 1996): 72–73.

"Bad Press." In *The Architect: Reconstructing Her Practice*, edited by Francesca Hughes, 74-94. Cambridge (MA): MIT Press, 1996.

"Bad Press." In *Architecture: In Fashion*, edited by Deborah Fausch, et al., 404–10. New York: Princeton Architectural Press, 1994.

"Bad Press." *BAU*, no. 15 (1997): 106–09.

"Bad Press." *Prototypo*, no. 3 (January/February 2000): 32–39.

"Bad Press: The Politics of Dress." *Suitcase 2*, no. 112 (1997): 98-103.

"Bad Press." *Zehar*, no. 44 (November 2000): 14–25.

"Bad Press: Diller + Scofidio." *A+U*, no. 375 (December 2001): 78–81.

"Blur/Babble." In *Anything*, edited by Cynthia C. Davidson, 132–39. Cambridge (MA): MIT Press, 2001.

"Blur Building." In *Olafur Eliasson: Surroundings Surrounded: Essays on Space and Science*, edited by Peter Weibel, 176–80. Karlsruhe, Germany: ZKM Center for Art and Media; Graz, Austria: Neue Galerie am Landesmuseum Joanneum, 2000.

"Blur Building." *transReal*, no. 7 (November 2000): 50–55.

"Blur Building." *Via Arquitectura* 10 (December2001): 114–17.

"The Body, The Daily Life." *Art Press*, no. 175 (December 1992): 19–21.

"Bodybuildings: Architectural Facts and Fictions." *A+U*, no. 222 (March 1989): 57–64.

"Case No. 00-17163." In *Incorporations*, edited by Jonathan Crary and Sanford Kwinter, 344–61. New York: Urzone, 1992.

"Case No. 00-17164." In *Anyplace*, edited by Cynthia C. Davidson, 180-89. Cambridge (MA): MIT Press, 1995.

"CNN Center Proposal: Diller + Scofidio/ Romm + Pearsall." *Art Papers* 20, no. 2 (March/April 1996): 26–7.

"A Delay in Glass." *Assemblage* 6 (1998): 63–71.

"A Delay in Glass." *Daidalos*, no. 26 (December 1987): 84–101.

"A Delay in Glass: Architectural Performance from a Work by Marcel Duchamp." *Lotus International*, no. 53 (1987): 23–31.

"Diller Scofidio + Renfro." *Area no. 79, Infrastructure Landscape* (April 2005): 96–99.

"Desecrated Flags." Assemblage 20 (1993): 34–35.

"Diller + Scofidio: Architecture and Interactivity." *Revue virtuelle* 14. Paris: Centre Georges Pompidou, 1995.

"Diller + Scofidio: Bad Press." In *Genderspace Architecture: Interdisciplinary Introduction*, edited by Jane Rendell, Barbara Penner, and Iain Borden, 385-96. London: Spon Press; New York: Routledge, 1999.

"Diller + Scofidio: Delay in Glass." *A+U*, no. 307 (April 1996): 80–83.

"Diller + Scofidio: Permanent Installation, San Francisco." *Casabella* 63, no. 673/674 (December 1999/January 2000): 104–06.

"Diller + Scofidio: Permanent Installation, Sunrise." *Casabella* 63, no. 673/674 (December 1999/January 2000): 101–03.

"Diller + Scofidio." *Prototypo*, no. 6 (December 2001): 50–83.

"Diller Scofidio + Renfro Miracle Library." Eun Kyoung Lee, *Space* (November 2004): 140–52.

"Docket." In *The American Lawn*, edited by Georges Teyssot, 205-19. New York: Princeton Architectural Press, 1999.

"An Eco-House for the Future." *The New York Times Magazine*, May 20, 2007: 84-90.

"Foto Opportunity: Eight Strategies of Niagara Falls." In Queues, Rendezvous, *Riots: Questioning the Public in Art and Architecture*, edited by George Baird and Mark Lewis, 99–106. Banff, Canada: Walter Phillips gallery/The Banff Centre for the Arts, 1994.

"Fourth Window." *Forum* 38 (May 1995): 53–56.

Hard Pressed. Castres, France: Centre d'Art Contemporain de Castres, 1993.

"His/Hers." In *Time Capsule: A Concise Encyclopedia by Women Artists*, edited by Robin Kahn, 310–11. New York: Creative Time/Distributed Art Publishers, 1995.

"Homebodies on Vacation." *Center*, no. 9 (1995): 32–41.

"Holiday Home Survival Kit." In "They Did Windows," *The New York Times Magazine*, December 22, 1996: 34.

"Household Artifacts: Codes of Property and Propriety." *AI*, no. 1 (Fall/Winter 1996): 20–29.

"Implementing Architecture: Blur Building Yverdon-les-Bains, Switzerland." (Charles Renfro) *A+U* (May 2006): 62–73.

"Indigestion." In *Anybody*, edited by Cynthia C. Davidson. 138–43. Cambridge (MA): MIT Press, 1997.

"Indigestion." In *Under the Table Table-Talk*, edited by Federico Soriano, 102-64. Madrid: FISURAS de la Cultura Contemporánea, 2001.

"In Plain View."Any, no. 18 (1997): 30–35.

"The Institute of Contemporary Art, Boston MA." *IW: Humanity Space Furniture 54*. (2007): 32–41.

"Institute of Contemporary Art." *l'Arca*, (June 2007): 14–21.

"Jet Lag." In *:éc/art S:#I-99*, 119-45. Roanne, France: éc/art S, 1999.

"Jetlag." *Performance Research* 4, no. 2 (Summer 1999): 109–10.

"Jump Cuts." In *Las Ciudades Inasibles*, edited by Jose Alfonso Ballesteros and Federico Soriano, 108-11. Madrid: FISURAS de la Cultura Contemporánea, 1997.

"Jump Cuts." *Prototypo*, no. 1 (January 1999): 132–39.

"Post-Paranoid Surveillance." In *CTRL[SPACE]: Rhetorics of Surveillance from Bentham to Big Brother*, edited by Thomas Y. Levin, Ursula Frohne, and Peter Weibel, 354–57. Karlsruhe, Germany: ZKM Center for Art and Media; Cambridge (MA): MIT Press, 2002.

"Pretext Machine." *Ottagono*, no. 96 (September 1990): 89–104.

"Projects." *Journal of Philosophy and the Visual Arts: Architecture, Space, Painting*, no. 2 (1992): 58–67.

"Property Lines." In *Self Made*, 44-46. Graz, Austria: Grazer Kunstverein, 1995

"reViewing." In *Columbia Documents of Architecture and Theory*, Vol. 1, Peter Rice, et al., 29–50. New York: Columbia University Graduate School of Architecture, Planning, and Preservation, 1992.

"The Rotary Notary and His Hot Plate." *AA Files*, no. 14 (Spring 1987): 54–61.

"Slow House." *Global Architecture Houses*, no. 28 (1990): 27–29.

"Soft Sell." *Architectural Design* 64 (November-December 1994): 68–73.

"Soft Sell." In *City Speculations*, edited by Patricia C. Phillips, 26–29. New York: Princeton Architectural Press; Queens, New York: Queens Museum of Art, 1996.

"Soft Sell." In *Las Ciudades Inasibles*, edited by Jose Alfonso Ballesteros and Federico Soriano,162–65. Madrid: FISURAS de la Cultura Contemporánea, 1997.

"Subtopia." In *The Mirage City: Another Utopia*, 215–28. Japan: NTT InterCommunication Center, 1997.

"Suitcase Studies: The Production of a National Past." *Suitcase 1*, no. 1/2 (1995): 10–27.

"This is Not Now." In *Theater Etcetera*. Munich: Theaterfestival Spielart, 1999.

"This is Not Now." *Architektur Aktuell*, no. 239 (March 2000): 72–79.

"This is Not Now." *La Mazarine*, no. 12 (March 2000): 40–43.

"The withDrawing room: a probe into the conventions of private rite." *AA Files*, no. 17 (Spring 1989): 15–23.

"Tourisms: SuitCase Studies." In *Semiotext(e)*, edited by Sylvere Lotringer, 6–18. NewYork: Semiotext(e) and Hraztan Zeitlian, 1992.

Acknowledgements

This volume came out of a chance constellation of characters and events that took place in New York, Venice, Milan, Florence and Zurich. It all could not have been possible without Skira's Luca Molinari, whose enthusiasm for the work of Diller Scofidio (+ Renfro), trust in the authors, and patience in seeing the material assembled was crucial, and tremendously appreciated. We are grateful for the hard work and patience of Emma Cavazzini, Laura Guidetti, Marcello Francone, Paola Ranzini Pallavicini and Flavio Ranzini at Skira for managing, editing and designing the book respectively. It was also a pleasure to work with Reinhold Martin, whose preface graces this volume.

The authors would like to thank the following members of the studio of Diller Scofidio + Renfro who assisted in assembling a wide variety of material: Matthew Johnson, Hayley Eber, Ben Gilmartin, Gerard Sullivan, Frank Gesualdi, Stefan Röschert, Kathryn Crawford, Tami Kinsler and Denise Fasanello. Eamon Tobin of Diller Scofidio (+ Renfro) deserves special thanks for his patient and diligent attention to our frequent badgering over the past eighteen months.

Guido Incerti would like to personally thank Beatrice and his family. Thanks also to his partners in nEmoGruppo who patiently supported him throughout this project. Many thanks to Marcello Mamoli for his constant perpetual stimulation in recent years, and to Laura Andreini who continues to control him. Thanks to Antonella Radicchi and Lisa Casucci for their remarks and kind criticism, and also to Margherita for her new energy.

Daria Ricchi expresses her gratitude to Giulia Pellegrini and Beatrice Papucci who have as usual followed every step of the writing. Thanks to Note Blu. Many thanks also to Antonio Pizza and Ezio Godoli for the professional remarks in the last reading.

Deane Simpson would like to convey his sincere thanks to Ida Richter Braendstrup, Marc Angélil, Dirk Hebel, Jörg Stollmann, Jesse Le Cavalier, Cary Siress, Paul Lewis and Hans Frei. Special thanks also to Mark Campbell for his incisive editing and criticism.

Last but certainly not least, heartfelt thanks go to Elizabeth Diller, Ricardo Scofidio and Charles Renfro who supported this project from its inception. We hold great admiration for the passion and commitment they have for their work. It knows no bounds and offers inspiration to many.

Photograph Credits

LEGEND

1. living
2. dining
3. kitchen
4. bathing/wc
5. sleeping
6 fold-up bed
7. work desk
8. meeting table
9. bookcase/shelves
10. workshop
11. string bass
12. tv/monitor
13. photocopier/ plotter

1980

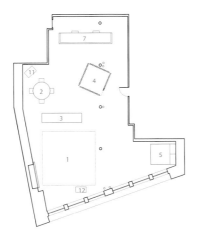

1985

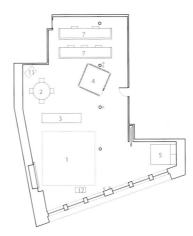

1990

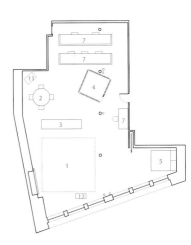

1995

2000

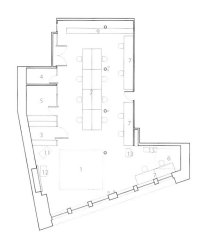

2005

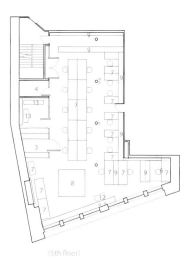

(5th floor)

(4th floor)

2007

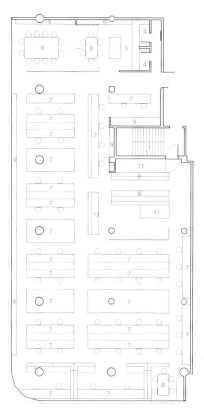

(West 26th Street)